Scientist Extraordinary—T.H. Huxley

CYRIL BIBBY, M.A., M.SC., PH.D., F.L.S., F.R.S.A., DIP.ED., is one of a large Liverpool family and went to Sudley Road Council School and the Collegiate School in that city. Securing an open major scholarship to Queens' College, Cambridge, he read for the Natural Sciences Tripos, concentrating at first on mathematics and physics and being fortunate enough to spend some time in the Cavendish Laboratory under Searle and Rutherford. Hopes of a research grant after graduating at Cambridge being killed by the stringent economies of the nineteen-thirties, he went as sixth form physics and chemistry master to a Liverpool grammar school. Within a year he had married Frances Hirst, a Girton mathematician, whom he had met as a fellow student and with whom he continued to collaborate in various anti-war, anti-fascist and socialist activities. Meanwhile, his interest had moved decisively from the physical to the biological sciences and he conducted spare-time research in pollen analysis and quaternary prehistory, the results being recognised by a master's degree of Liverpool University. His next teaching post was as senior biology master at a Derbyshire grammar school, from which early in the war he went to London to take charge of a nation-wide programme of sex education and health education generally. After the war he moved into the professional preparation of teachers and, having developed a deep interest in the nineteenth century, did research in this field for which the University of London awarded a doctorate. He has also done research in race relations, visited many universities (in Europe, America and Africa) and acted as consultant to UNESCO and WHO. At present he is Principal of Kingston upon Hull College of Education.

Thomas Henry Huxley 1883

Scientist Extraordinary

The Life and Scientific Work of
THOMAS HENRY HUXLEY
1825 – 1895

by

CYRIL BIBBY

PERGAMON PRESS

OXFORD · NEW YORK · TORONTO
SYDNEY · BRAUNSCHWEIG

Pergamon Press Ltd., Headington Hill Hall, Oxford

Pergamon Press Inc., Maxwell House, Fairview Park, Elmsford, New York 10523

Pergamon of Canada Ltd., 207 Queen's Quay West, Toronto 1

Pergamon Press (Aust.) Pty. Ltd., 19a Boundary Street, Rushcutters Bay, N.S.W. 2011, Australia

Vieweg & Sohn GmbH, Burgplatz 1, Braunschweig

First edition 1972

Library of Congress Catalog Card No. 78–147937

Printed in Hungary

08 016514 1

To all who try to
learn something about everything
and everything about something

Contents

List of illustrations

Preface

THE nineteenth century glitters with the names of great scientists. It opened with Laplace's celestial mechanics and Cuvier's early volumes on comparative anatomy, followed almost immediately by Young's wave theory of light. Within a decade, Davy had isolated sodium and potassium by means of electrolysis, Dalton had put forward his chemical laws and Lamarck had published his *Philosophie Zoologique.* During the second decade there came Avogadro's hypothesis, Herschel's nebular theory of the stars, William Smith's work on the fossil-dating of rocks, and Oersted's discovery of the magnetic effects of electric currents. By the quarter of the century, Fraunhofer had observed the spectra of fixed stars, Faraday had liquefied gases and Purkinje had laid a sound basis for sensory physiology.

It was at this point in the history of science that T. H. Huxley was born in rented rooms above a butcher's shop in Ealing. While he was still an infant, Ohm's Law was announced, von Baer published his great treatise on zoology and Niepce took his first photographs. As Huxley played about the pleasant Ealing meadows, there appeared the pioneer *Principles of Geology* by Lyell, Quetelet's *Anthropometrie* and the seminal *Handbuch der Physiologie des Menschen* by Müller. By this time Huxley was ten and his brief two years of schooling were already behind him. It could scarcely have been imagined that one day his name would be better known than most of these.

The assessment of a scientist's historical importance is a difficult task. Some few stand out as giants of undiminished stature; many more, famous in their lifetimes, sink after a century into comparative obscurity. Murchison and Owen laboured mightily on fossils during the middle years of the century, but who today—apart from specialists in their field—knows even their names? Liebig, so important in the basic investigation of biochemistry, is best remembered for a particular type of condenser that he used. Tyndall, one of Huxley's closest friends and in their own day a name to conjure with, is now seen to have been by comparison but a minor figure in the development of science. There are others, like Pasteur and Darwin, at the peak of their powers while Huxley was still in his thirties, whose fame will never fade. And, by one of those quirks of fortune so dependent on the public's love of sensation, it is mainly as the defender of Darwin's *Origin of Species* that most people—including many scientists—still think of T. H. Huxley.

If, as a matter of fact, Huxley had done no more than establish the right of a 'dangerous' scientific theory to a fair hearing against the denunciations of orthodoxy, he would still deserve an honoured place in the history of science. But in his own lifetime be became a legend for his brilliance and for his subtlety as an interpreter of the world of living things. And today, after half a century during which he has been considerably underestimated, we are beginning once more to realise that he is one who will always stand among the giants.

We can now see in what ways his thinking on evolution supplemented Darwin's. We can recognise how his wide-ranging work in comparative anatomy and taxonomy forms a vital part of the central corpus of those branches of science. We can understand that some of his views on anthropology and ethnology were so long neglected simply because those sciences had not yet caught up with him. And, with the hindsight of a century, we can be startled by the astonishing modernity of some of his off-the-cuff comments about the deepest nature of the physical world.

Most of all, we can see what a magnificent *man* he was. It is this that has made the writing of his biography so immensely rewarding and which, I hope, will make its reading equally enjoyable.

Principal's Lodge,   CYRIL BIBBY
Kingston upon Hull College of Education

Acknowledgements

GRATEFUL acknowledgement is made to the many institutions which allowed access to their libraries and archives, and to the individual librarians and archivists who have been so helpful. In particular I would mention the Imperial College of Science and Technology, the British Museum, the Royal Institution, the Royal Society of Arts, the Linnean Society, the Royal Society, the former London County Council, Eton College, Dulwich Reference Library, Ealing Reference Library, Heston and Isleworth Reference Library, Charing Cross Hospital Medical School, the Henry E. Huntington Library, the American Philosophical Society, many Universities (Aberdeen Cambridge, Columbia, Edinburgh, Harvard, Johns Hopkins, Leeds, Liverpool, London, Manchester and Oxford) and, finally, Mrs. Leonard Huxley and Sir Julian Huxley.

The portraits of Huxley are reproduced from my general biography, *T. H. Huxley: Scientist, Humanist and Educator*, published by Watts in 1959 but now out of print. Full acknowledgement is made of the permissions and facilities granted in this connection by the Imperial College of Science and Technology, the National Portrait Gallery, the British Museum (Natural History), the Victoria and Albert Museum, the Royal Society, the Ealing Reference Library, and Sir Julian Huxley. The pencil sketches by Huxley are from his notebooks, while the scientific diagrams are from the periodicals in which they originally appeared.

C. B.

CHAPTER 1

Obscurity to eminence

WHEN Thomas Henry Huxley was born at Ealing, on 4 May 1825, no wealth or social status, no lineage of learning or powerful family connections, marked him out for eminence. Family tradition said that the Huxleys came, many generations back, from a farm called Huxley Hall, not far from Chester. One branch eventually moved south to Coventry, where a Thomas Huxley married Margaret James, who presented him with a large family. George Huxley, one of their several sons, married Rachel Withers in 1810 and had eight children, of whom the seventh is the subject of this biography.

At the time of Huxley's birth, his family lived above a butcher's shop in Ealing, then a sleepy little Middlesex village. His father was a not very successful teacher at Ealing School, which young Thomas Henry attended for two years from the age of eight. Tom was miserably unhappy. "My regular school training was of the briefest", he later wrote (*C.E.* I, 5), "perhaps fortunately, for though my way of life has made me acquainted with all sorts and conditions of men, from the highest to the lowest, I deliberately affirm that the society I fell into at school was the worst I have ever known ... the people who were set over us cared about as much for our intellectual and moral welfare as if they were baby-farmers. We were left to the operation of the struggle for existence among ourselves, and bullying was the least of the ill practices current among us." This account is in some ways surprising, for Ealing claimed to be the finest private school in England, and its social standing was high. Perhaps Huxley attended during a particularly bad period, or perhaps life was especially difficult for the sensitive son of an evidently ineffective teacher. At any rate, George Huxley left the school in 1835, in circumstances which have never been made quite clear, and returned to his native Coventry, where he earned some sort of a living by running a local savings bank. With this move, Tom's brief schooldays came to an end at the early age of ten—which seems a somewhat inadequate preparation for one who was to become perhaps the most brilliant and certainly the most influential scientist of the century.

Nor does Huxley's home background appear to have been particularly favourable. In those days there was nothing very unusual about the death of two of the children in infancy, or about the fairly early death of Rachel, the admirable mother. But it seems (*T.H.H.* 5) that the father became "sunk in worse than childish imbecility of mind" and died eventually at the Barming asylum; that sister Ellen's husband became "a bloated mass of beer and opium"; that brother George suffered from "extreme mental anxiety"; that William became completely estranged through some obscure family quarrel; and that James was by the age of fifty-five "as near mad as a sane man can be". Only Eliza, the eldest sister, seems to have been quite normal—and even her husband decided for some unknown reason to change his name and emigrate to Tennessee.

Yet, when Thomas Henry Huxley died at Eastbourne, on 29 June 1895, the world lost a man of genius and England the most powerful scientist she has ever known. In part by sheer strength of intellect, in part by reason of a deeply philosophical cast of mind, he penetrated more deeply than most into the essentials of scientific method. Partly by moral courage, partly by personal charm, partly by invincible persistence and unflagging effort, he was able to break down a great barrier of traditional resistance to scientific advance. By means of an immensely effective combination of public propaganda, private lobbying and sheer dull plodding committee work, he usually managed throughout his life to steer scientific affairs in the direction he deemed to be right. He was not one of those who simply travelled forward on the crest of the scientific wave: he as much as anybody created the wave.

Huxley never had the opportunity of becoming a university student or of taking a degree in the ordinary way—but his honorary degrees included a D.C.L. from Oxford, L.L.D.s from Cambridge and Edinburgh and Dublin, a Ph.D. from Breslau and M.D.s from Bologna and Erlangen and Würzburg. He became Croonian Lecturer at the Royal Society, Fullerian Lecturer at the Royal Institution and Hunterian Professor at the Royal College of Surgeons. Over many years he was Examiner in Physiology and in Comparative Anatomy to the University of London; he turned down invitations to a Professorship at Edinburgh and to both a Chair and a Mastership at Oxford; he rejected a most flattering and lucrative offer from Harvard. At various stages of his career he was Governor of Eton, of University College in London, of Owens College in Manchester; he became Crown Senator of the University of London and Rector of Aberdeen; he was an Elector to the Cambridge Chairs of Anatomy, Physiology, and Zoology and Comparative Anatomy. It must all have been a fairly satisfying achievement for a non-graduate.

Much of Huxley's enormous influence upon the rapidly developing university world of the second half of the nineteenth century was exerted in private and has only been documented since his death. At Oxford, he secured the Linacre Chair of Physiology for George Rolleston, virtually placed Ray Lankester in his Biology Fellowship at Exeter College and later in the Linacre Chair, helped E. B. Poulton into the Hope Chair of Zoology and J. J. Sylvester into the Savilian Chair of Geometry. At Cambridge, he persuaded Trinity to found its Praelectorship in Physiology and saw that Michael Foster filled it, chose F. M. Balfour and Adam Sedgwick as Biology Fellows, and sent Sydney Vines to revive the reaching of Botany. F. O. Bower took Huxley's methods from South Kensington to Glasgow, Patrick Geddes took them to Edinburgh, H. M. Ward to Manchester and Newton Parker to Cardiff. Other disciples carried the master's message overseas. To New Zealand it was taken by T. J. Parker; to Singapore by Charles Gould; to Casale by Enrico Giglioni; to Naples and then Milan by Angelo Andres; to the great Mohammedan University of Aligarh by Ameer-Ali; to Baltimore by H. N. Martin; to Princeton and Columbia by Henry F. Osborn. "If I know anything of the world", Huxley once boasted (*H.P.* 31. 105), "I know a man when I see him". And his men spread his influence far and wide.

Among the rapidly developing scientific societies of the time, it was the same surprising story of public eminence and *éminence grise*. Huxley was a Fellow of the Royal Society, the Linnean Society, the Zoological Society and the Royal College of Surgeons. He became an Honorary Member or Fellow of the Odontological Society, the Physiological Society, the Royal Irish Academy, the Royal Medico-Chirurgical Society, the Dublin Botanical and Zoological Societies, the Cambridge and Glasgow Philosophical Societies, the Royal College of Surgeons of Ireland and the Royal Society of Edinburgh. At various times he was President of the Royal Society, the Geological Society, the Palaeontographical Society, the Ethnological Society and the British Association.

Probably never before or since has one man played so large a part in the professional organisation of British science.

As for scientific societies overseas, the fifty-odd which honoured him included the Royal Society of New South Wales, the Geological Society of Australasia, the Königliche Kaiserliche Geologische Reichanstalt, the Académie Royale de Médecine de Belgique, the Société Géologique de Belgique, the Société d' Anthropologie de Bruxelles, the Gabineta Portuguez de Leitura em Pernambuco, the Royal Society of Copenhagen, the Koninklijke Naturkundige Vereenigung in Nederlandisch-Indie, the Institut Egyptien, the Institut de France, the Caesarea Leopoldino-Carolina Academia Naturae Curiosorum, the Gesellschaft für Erdkunde of Berlin, the Regia Scientiae Academia Borussica, the Berliner Gesellschaft für Anthropologie, the Academia de' Lincei di Roma, the Società Italiana di Antropologia e di Etnologia, the New Zealand Institute, the Academia Real das Sciencias de Lisboa, the Imperialis Academia Scientiae Petropolitana, the Regia Scientiarum Academia Suecica, the American Academy of Arts and Sciences, the American Philosophical Society, and the New York Academy of Sciences. A full list would read almost like a roster of the leading scientific societies of the world.

Unfortunately, as the editors of his scientific memoirs have remarked (Foster and Lankester, I, v), "Huxley produced so great an effect on the world as an expositor of the ways and means of science in general and the claims of Darwin in particular, that some, dwelling on this, are apt to overlook the immense value of his original contributions". In a life always lived as fully outside the laboratory as within, he produced more than 150 research papers, dealing with subjects as varied as the morphology of the heteropoda and the hybridism of gentians, the taxonomy of crayfish and the phylogeny of crocodiles, the phenomena of gemmation and the dental characteristics of the Canidae, the physical anthropology of the Patagonians and the human remains from Neanderthal. A special issue of *Nature* (9 May 1925), commemorating the centenary of Huxley's birth, rightly remarked that "The range of his papers extended literally from Medusae to man, and at both these limits his observations and interpretations endure as permanent points of reference". So permanent and so basic, indeed, that Chalmers Mitchell is not the only one to have felt, on first reading a Huxley monograph, that it seemed (Poulton, 1925) "all so familiar, rather like *Hamlet* which, read for the first time, was found to be 'so full of quotations'". Today, when these monographs are rarely read, the modern biologist tends to take their theses as self-evident foundations of his science, and usually fails to realise that someone had first to form them.

How did it all happen? How did a lad, who left school at the age of ten after but two years' schooling, become not only a great biologist but also a great innovator of biological teaching, not only the acknowledged champion of scientific freedom but the equally acknowledged statesman of science, the most influential scientist of his century and conceivably of any century? It is indeed an intriguing question.

Much, of course, can be accounted for by his incredible capacity for work. "The great secret", he once explained (T. J. Parker, 1895) as if it were the simplest thing in the world, "is to preserve the power of working continuously sixteen hours a day if need be. If you cannot do that you may be caught out any time." But it was more than simple stamina: it was also the ability to hold any number of irons in the fire and keep them all hot simultaneously. "By the way," he wrote to Darwin (*L.L.* I, 246) one day in 1863,

you ask me what I am doing now, so I will enumerate . . .

A. Editing lectures on Vertebrate skull and bringing them out in the *Medical Times*.

B. Editing and re-writing lectures on Elementary Physiology, just delivered here and reported as I went along.

C. Thinking of my course of twenty-four lectures on the Mammalia at Coll. Surgeons in next spring, and making investigations bearing on same.

D. Thinking of and working at a *Manual of Comparative Anatomy* (may it be d—d), which I have had in hand these seven years.

E. Getting heaps of remains of new Labyrinthodonts from the Glasgow coal-fields, which have to be described.

F. Working on a memoir on *Glyptodon* based on a new and almost entire specimen at the College of Surgeons.

G. Preparing a new decade upon Fossil fishes for this place [School of Mines].

H. Knowing that I ought to have written long ago a description of a most interesting lot of Indian fossils sent to me by Oldham.

I. Being blown up by Hooker for doing nothing for the *Natural History Review*.

K. Being bothered by sundry editors just to write articles 'which you know you can knock off in a moment'.

L. Consciousness of having left unwritten letters which ought to have been written long ago, especia y to C. Darwin.

M. General worry and botheration. Ten or twelve people taking up my time all day about their own affairs.

N. O. P. Q. R. S. T. U. V. W. X. Y. Z.
Societies.
Clubs.
Dinners, evening parties, and all the apparatus for wasting time called 'Society'.
Colensoism and botheration about Moses . .
Finally pestered to death in public and private because I am supposed to be
what they call a 'Darwinian'.
If that is not enough, I could exhaust the Greek alphabet for heads in addition.

Reinforcing this remarkable industry there was Huxley's powerful possession by the great puritan virtues. "What I earnestly maintain", he wrote (*H. P.* 15, 106) in 1859 to his friend Dyster, "is that thoroughly good work in science cannot be done by any man deficient in high moral qualities—it is the morale which is essential to the right working of the intellect." And this implied several things, including honesty about one's own errors: "The most considerable difference I note among men", he once remarked (Huxley, L., 1925), "is not in their readiness to fall into error, but in their readiness to acknowledge these inevitable lapses." It also required resistance to that all-too-common corrosion of character by the sweet acid of public approbation, which has caused so many promising men to fizzle out in their forties. "The honours of men I value so far as they are evidences of power", Huxley wrote (*L. L.* I, 101), "but, with the cynical mistrust of their judgment and my own worthiness which always haunts me, I put very little faith in them."

But most of all there was Huxley's sheer ability, about whose uniqueness those who knew him best never had the slightest scintilla of doubt. He had, Justin M'Carthy (1899, II, 312) assures us, "an intelligence so luminous that it shed light all around him on any topic which came within his range". John Skelton (1895, 294) averred that he had "probably the most trenchant intellect of the time". Wallace experienced in his presence a feeling of awe and inferiority which neither Darwin nor Lyell produced; both Darwin and Hooker declared that in comparison with Huxley they felt quite infantile in intellect. And it was not a narrow or merely scholastic sort of intellect: it was many-dimensioned and as effective in practical affairs as in abstract reasoning. As a modern American writer (Irvine, 1955, 71) has perhaps too colourfully put it, "Huxley had more talents than two lifetimes could have developed. He could think, draw, speak, write, inspire, lead, negotiate, and wage multifarious war against earth and heaven with the cool professional ease of an acrobat supporting nine people on his shoulders at once."

CHAPTER 2

A foot on the ladder

TOM HUXLEY did not, apparently, much resemble his father, except (*C. E.* I, 4) for "an inborn faculty for drawing ... a hot temper, and that amount of tenacity of purpose which unfriendly observers sometimes call obstinacy". His mother, however, restless and talkative and untiring until the day of her death, he took after so completely that his description of her (*ibid.*) might almost serve as a sketch of himself: "a slender brunette, of an emotional and energetic temperament, and possessed of the most piercing black eyes ... she had an excellent mental capacity. Her most distinguishing characteristic, however, was rapidity of thought. If one ventured to suggest that she had not taken much time to arrive at any conclusion, she would say 'I cannot help it; things flash across me' ... if my time were to come over again, there is nothing I would less willingly part with than my inheritance of mother-wit."

Few famous figures have left such scanty records of their childhood, and nobody knows how young Huxley spent most of his five or six years after leaving Ealing. We know that he devoured his father's books during the daytime and, at the age of twelve, sat up in bed with a blanket about his shoulders reading Hutton's *Geology* by candlelight. We know that his quick wits made him welcome in serious conversations among educated adults of the neighbourhood. We know also that he was taken to observe a post mortem autopsy, following which he sank into a strange state of lethargy and became seriously ill. He himself ascribed this illness to dissection-poisoning, but it seems more likely to have been a case of severe emotional shock with psychosomatic sequelae. At any rate, he was sent to recuperate on a Warwickshire farm, where he was found one day (*L.L.* I, 8) "looking so thin and ill, and pretending to make hay with one hand, while in the other he held a German book". Much more is known of Huxley's activities from the age of fifteen to seventeen, for there survives a fascinating little notebook, sewn up from a few small sheets of paper, in which he made irregular jottings during the next couple of years.

The first entry in *Thoughts and Doings* (among *H.P.*), as he called his tiny journal, is a translation from a German edition of the philosopher Novalis: "Philosophy can bake no bread; but it can prove for us God, freedom, and immortality. Which now, is more practical, Philosophy or Economy?" He tried to make a galvanic battery, with an "experiment to get crystallised carbon. Got it deposited, but not crystallised." He "Began speculating on the causes of colours at sunset. Has any explanation of them ever been attempted?" On 22 November 1840 he "Had a long talk with my mother and father about the right to make Dissenters pay church rates—and whether there ought to be any Establishment. I maintain that there ought not. . . . The argument that the rate is so small is very fallacious. It is as much a sacrifice of principle to do a little wrong as to do a great one." And, another note on the same day: "Had a long argument with Mr. May on the nature of the soul and the difference between it and matter. I maintained that it could not be proved that matter is essentially—as to its base—different from soul. . . . We cannot find the absolute basis of matter: we only know it by its properties; neither know we the soul in any other way. . . . Why may not soul and matter be of the same substance . . . but with different qualities?" How ignorant Tom Huxley was of some simple facts; how mature and lively in his speculation!

It seems to have been by no special inclination that Huxley became first a medico and then a biologist. "My great desire", he tells us (*C.E.* I, 7), "was to be a mechanical engineer, but the fates were against this, and while very young I commenced the study of medicine under a medical brother-in-law. . . . I am not sure that I have not all along been a sort of mechanical engineer *in partibus infidelium.*" At any rate, in the January of 1841 he moved to Rotherhithe, apprenticed initially to a practitioner among the poor of dockland. In the East End, Huxley (*L.L.* I, 15) "saw strange things . . . people who came to me for medical aid and who were really suffering from nothing but slow starvation. I have not forgotten—and am not likely to forget so long as memory holds. . . . Alleys nine or ten feet wide, I suppose, with tall houses full of squalid drunken men and women. . . . All this almost within hearing of the traffic of the Strand, within easy reach of the wealth and plenty of the city." But nothing seemed to quench his fire for self-education, as continued entries in *Thoughts and Doings* bear witness:

June 20 [1841]

What have I done in the way of acquiring knowledge since January?
Projects begun—
1. German }
2. Italian } to be learnt
3. To read Müller's *Physiology*
4. To prepare for the matriculation examination at London University which requires knowledge of:—
   (a) Algebra—Geometry }
   (b) Natural Philosophy } did not begin to read for this till April
   (c) Chemistry
   (d) Greek–Latin
   (e) English History down to end of seventeenth century
   (f) Ancient History
      English Grammar
5. To make copious notes of all things I read ... I *must* adopt a fixed plan of studies ... and let me remember this—that it is better to read a little and thoroughly, than cram a crude undigested mass into my head, though it be great in quantity.

He made an electromagnet; read Guizot's *History of Civilisation in Europe;* studied the political constitution of France; noted quotations from Carlyle, Lessing, Goethe and Isaac Iselin. Then, on 30 January 1842, this entry:

I have for some time been pondering over a classification of knowledge. My scheme is to divide all knowledge in the first place into two grand divisions ...

Subjective   Objective

Metaphysics

Metaphys. proper Maths. Logic Theology Morality Hist. Physiology Physics

... I am in doubt under which head to put morality, for I cannot determine exactly in my own mind whether morality can exist independent of others, whether the idea of morality could ever have arisen in the mind of an isolated being or not. I am rather inclined to the opinion that it is objective.

Leaving Rotherhithe, and becoming apprenticed in North London to his brother-in-law, Dr. Scott [Salt], he began to attend botany lectures in his spare time at Sydenham College in Chelsea. One morning in May 1842, a public competition was announced to take place in August (*L.L.* I, 17): "I remember looking longingly at the notice, and some one said to me, 'Why don't you go in and try for it?' I laughed at the idea, for I was very young, and my knowledge somewhat of the vaguest." But, he wrote *(ibid.)*, "I worked really hard from eight or nine in the morning until twelve at night. ... A great part of the time I worked till sunrise", and after a mere two months he sat down to the examination along with the other candidates. On the day the results were due, it was rumoured that the winners would all be University College men, but Dame Rumour was wrong. The 1842 Silver Medal of the Pharmaceutical Society went to the self-taught, seventeen-year-old T. H. Huxley. Charing Cross Hospital gave him a Free Scholarship (*T.H.H.* 7) and he seems to have had no difficulty there in carrying off prizes in chemistry and anatomy and physiology. He received a Gold Medal in the First Medical Examination of the University of London. As a nineteen-year-old student he discovered the structure, still known as 'Huxley's Layer', at the base of the human hair, and had the satisfaction of seeing his first research paper published in the *Medical Gazette*. He had constructed his own ladder to success, and his feet were firmly on the bottom rung.

CHAPTER 3

Science at sea

EARLY in 1846, his First Medical examination behind him but a full qualification still some way ahead, aged twenty and his free scholarship at an end, Huxley decided to earn his daily bread in the Royal Navy —which in those days set no very high professional standard for the guardians of its seamen's health. On 13 March he became Assistant-Surgeon R. N. at seven shillings a day, and was almost immediately faced with a bill of £46 12*s*. 6d. for a complete rig of full dress, undress, sword, deal chest, brushes and soap.

Huxley's official chief at Haslar was the distinguished Arctic explorer, Sir John Richardson, who soon spotted his unusual potential; which explains why Huxley was not packed off, as so many young men were, to one of the death-trap stations of West Africa. He was posted instead to H.M.S. *Rattlesnake*, a 28-gun donkey-frigate being fitted out for South Sea exploration. "Our object", he wrote (*L.L.* I, 25) in great excitement to his sister Lizzie, "is to bring back a full account of ... Geography, Geology, and Natural History ... we shall form one grand collection of specimens and deposit it in the British Museum or some other public place. ... Depend upon it unless some sudden attack of laziness supervenes, such an opportunity shall not slip unused out of my hands." *Rattlesnake* was commanded by Captain Owen Stanley (brother of Dean Stanley), who fortunately encouraged the scientific zeal of his young part-qualified medico. He allowed him to take aboard as many books as he pleased, promised the use of the chart room, and gave him introductions to several eminent zoologists. From Edward Forbes, Huxley learned how to dredge up specimens from the sea; and the ship's official Naturalist, John MacGillivray, seemed not averse from the help of an unpaid assistant. "I must confess", Huxley told Lizzie (*L.L.* I, 27), " I do glory in the prospect of being able to give myself up to my own favourite pursuits without thereby neglecting the proper duties of life."

On 6 October he joined his ship and, whilst waiting for her to sail, went along to the British Association for the Advancement of Science, conveniently meeting that year at nearby Southampton. Forbes gave him a living specimen of the lancelet, *Amphioxus lanceolatus*, that strange translucent creature of the shallow seas, which lies on the border between invertebrate and vertebrate. Huxley went off with his specimen, examined its blood under the microscope, and discovered certain characteristics of the corpuscles not thitherto known. Thus, before sailing, he was able to complete his second research paper, which was read in his absence at the next year's meeting of the British Association.

This was the heroic age of scientific investigation afloat, with Britannia not merely ruling the waves but making the most determined effort to understand them. The Admiralty provided generous facilities for collecting specimens of the far-flung Empire's fauna and flora, together with all conveniences and comforts for its official 'gentlemen' naturalists. Things were, however, to be very different for Huxley, who messed not with the officers but with the middies, during the four years for which he sailed the southern seas. *Rattlesnake* left Spithead on 3 December 1846, in a disgraceful state of unfitness and leaking at the seams, and then touched again at Plymouth to take on gold specie for Cape Town and Mauritius. "Thank God!", Huxley confided to his diary (Huxley, J., 1935, 15) as they lay in the Sound, "fitting out is at last over. We have no more caprices to fear but those of the wind—a small matter after having been exposed to those of the Admiralty." The next day, the 11th, they finally left English waters.

"I really doubt", Huxley wrote (*L.L.* I, 26) to his sister, "whether Jonah was much worse accommodated, so far as room goes, than myself. My total length, as you are aware, is considerable, 5 feet 11 inches, possibly, but the height of the lower deck of the *Rattlesnake*, which will be my especial location, is at the outside 4 feet 10 inches. What I am to do with the superfluous foot I cannot divine." As they approached warmer climes, the discomfort increased with the temperature, until Huxley (1854) noted in his diary: "I wonder if it is possible for the mind of a man to conceive anything more degradingly offensive than the condition of us 150 men, shut up in this wooden box, being watered by hot water, as we are now. . . . The lower and main decks are completely unventilated: a sort of solution of man in steam fills them from end to end. . . . It's too hot to sleep, and my sole amusement consists in watching the cockroaches, which are in a state of intense excitement and happiness." By 23 January they had reached Rio de Janeiro, where they stayed ten days while repairs were made to deal with some of the leaks. Huxley helped with some dredging and a few entomological excursions ashore; but, he wrote (*L.L.* I, 32) to his mother, "On the whole ... I think we have been most successful in imbibing sherry cobbler, which you get here in great perfection".

MacGillivray, like most naturalists at that time, was mainly interested in collecting specimens that could be dried or stuffed or mounted for museum cataloguing. Huxley, on the other hand, concentrated on the delicate and often deliquescent creatures that came up in the dredges —which consisted of an adapted wire-mesh meat safe and a towing-net made from a wooden hoop and bunting. "It is a curious fact", he wrote (1854), "that if you want a boat for dredging, ten chances to one they are always actually or potentially otherwise disposed of; if you leave your towing-net trailing astern in search of new creatures, in some promising patch of discoloured water, it is, in all probability, found to have a wonderful effect in stopping the ship's way, and is hauled in as soon as your back is turned; or a careful dissection waiting to be drawn may find its way overboard as a 'mess'." (Nevertheless, he later defended his *Rattlesnake* shipmates (*L.L.* II, 264) by affirming that, "whether ... book-learned or not, they were emphatically men, trained to face realities and to have a wholesome contempt for mere talkers. Any one of them was worth a wilderness of phrase-crammed undergraduates.") He had little space, less light, and his microscope had to be lashed down against the ship's rolling. The microtome had not yet been invented, there were no facilities of any sort for embedding or serial sectioning, and the specimens were all of a type difficult to preserve and liable to disintegrate into watery slime. Despite these difficulties, Huxley managed to packet back home, from successive ports of call, a series of papers of peculiar brilliance. Day in and day out he dissected and drew, with hands and eyes that more than made up for deficiencies in working conditions. With no teacher to tell him what he should see, he simply recorded what in fact he saw, and what he saw was as novel as it was incontrovertible.

After examining the 'Portuguese man-of-war', *Physalia*, Huxley hoped (*L.L.* I, 33) to "achieve one of the great ends of Zoology and Anatomy, viz. the reduction of two or three widely separated and incon-

14SCIENTIST EXTRAORDINARY – T. H. HUXLEY

gruous groups into modifications of the single type, every step of the
reasoning being based upon anatomical facts." A few weeks later he
noted (Huxley, J., 1935, 32): "There is another month's work yet in it;
but notwithstanding its complexity I hope in time to get a very complete
account of its structure and even of the forms through which its different
organs pass. At the same time I think I can already perceive that it will
form a great link in the chain of the *Acalephae* . . . and even the *Medusae*.
I feel half ashamed to put such a thought on paper but I have a feeling
that by the more or less perfect manner in which this is worked out,
my capacities for these undertakings must stand or fall." The *Acalephae*
—a term no longer used—comprised the 'jelly fish', the 'comb-jellies',
the 'men-of-war', and those long 'trailing' transparent creatures known
as *Dyphidae* and *Physophoridae*. Huxley separated the *Acalephae* from
the star-fish and sea-urchins with which they were then lumped, and
instead put them with the polyps and Medusae, thus forming the group
now known as *Coelenterata*. It was an object lesson in the possibilities of
simple but exact observation without any expensive apparatus but with
a skilled hand and a seeing eye.

After a month at the Cape, *Rattlesnake* set sail in April for Mauritius,
which Huxley considered (*L.L.* I, 34) "a complete paradise, and if I had
nothing better to do, I should pick up some pretty French Eve (and there
are plenty) and turn Adam". But although he resisted the attractions
of Mauritius, Huxley lost his heart soon after setting foot in Sydney.
Made much of by the society-starved pioneers of that now great city,
the *Rattlesnake* crew found themselves inundated with invitations to
social events. At one of them, Huxley met Henrietta Anne Heathorn,
three months his junior, and soon they were head over heels in love.
"I really don't know whether she is pretty or not", he confided (*L.L.*
I, 39) to his sister, "I have never been able to decide the matter in my
own mind. Sometimes I think she is, and sometimes I wonder how the
idea ever came into my head." But, pretty or not, she was the girl for
him, and his courtship was a dashing one. He boldly came up and claimed
a dance—and, when her brother declared it impossible since they were
about to leave, engaged her for the first dance next time they met. This
was at a Government House ball, and the third time at a small party
in the parsonage. Nettie saw three naval men enter, Hal (he was always
'Hal', never 'Tom', to her) amongst them. "O thought I there is that
delightful doctor. What an evening of glamour it was. . . . He uttered

magic words—before we left he begged of me the red camelia I wore—
which after my darling died I found preserved amongst his papers—
labelled The First" (*H.P.* 62. 4). Their next meeting was at New Town,
where Nettie kept house for her half-sister, Oriana Fanning. "My heart
leaped", Huxley confided to his diary (Huxley, J., 1935, 83). "But I
thought to myself, Tom, you are a fool, what on earth is there in you,
and you have only seen one another four times. ... No word of love
was spoken but we understood one another. ... And this is what you
call prudence, Signor Tom, is it? Certainly. Waste of time is the highest
improvidence, and I lost none. ... Bless you, bless you, dearest, a thousand
times." Before long, the young couple were firmly engaged to marriage.

Whilst still in Mauritius, Huxley had written (*id.* 37), "Morals and
religion are one wild whirl to me—of them the less said the better.
In the region of the intellect alone can I find free and innocent play for
such faculties as I possess." His religious doubts caused considerable
distress to his fiancée, but he was more distressed by deep doubts about
how they could ever afford to marry. Perhaps it was this distress, combined
with worries about whether or not he was really succeeding in his unsuper-
vised researches, which caused his 1848-9 cruise to be so unproductive.
Leaving Sydney in April, *Rattlesnake* spent over four months within
the Great Barrier Reef, the finest coral formations in the world, yet
Huxley scarcely examined a specimen. Then they were off the Howick
Islands, with admirable opportunities for work on the faunae of rocks
and mangrove swamps, but Huxley lay in his cabin reading *The Inferno*
in Italian. "I have been getting very apathetic of late", he noted (*id.* 143),
"and I think I never was so mortally sick of anything as of this wearisome
monotonous cruise." Fortunately, his spirit revived before *Rattlesnake*'s
final 1849 cruise to New Guinea and the Louisiade Archipelago, and
his diary of that summer is enlivened by vivid notes and sketches of the
natives and their houses, of their canoes and ornaments, and of their
customs and their language. There was then no real science of anthropology—he later helped to create it—and no techniques or methodology
or even vocabulary for proper ethnological studies. But his interest was
thoroughly aroused, to persist and grow stronger as the years went by.

"When Huxley was young", Chalmers Mitchell (1900, 6) has pointed
out, "the great reputation of Cuvier overshadowed English anatomy,
and English anatomists did little more than seek in nature what Cuvier
had taught them to find." Linnaeus had earlier divided animals into

the six great classes of quadrupeds, birds, amphibians, fish, insects and worms—this last class, the *Vermes*, being but a huge 'rag bag' for most of the *invertebrata*. In 1817 Cuvier, the so-called "Dictator of Science", formulated a scheme of his own, which put Linnaeus's first four classes into the *Vertebrata*, placed insects among the *Articulata*, recognised the *Mollusca* as a distinct group, but still threw most other animals together as *Radiata*. This was the state of systematic zoology, with sea anemones and star-fish lumped along with parasitic worms and infusoria, when Huxley set sail on *Rattlesnake*. Compared with this, his eventual division of the animal kingdom into *Protozoa, Infusoria, Coelenterata, Annuloida, Annulosa, Molluscoida, Mollusca* and *Vertebrata* seems the essence of modernity.

The Radiata, according to Cuvier, had in common a general tendency to be more or less disposed round a centre like the petals and sepals of a flower, with ill-defined nervous and muscular systems, no vascular system, and an almost plant-like homogeneity of tissue structure; while the lower members of the group were considered virtually devoid of special organs. But Huxley's endless dissections disclosed a vast range of distinction in minute anatomy, and he saw that Cuvier's classification would not do. Within six months he had posted to the Linnean Society a paper on Physalia, quickly followed by another on the Dyphidae and the Physophoridae, and for the first time there was some really critical thinking on that great group now known as the *Hydrozoa*. A year later he posted his striking memoir, "On the Anatomy and the Affinities of the Family of the Medusae", which eventually reached the Royal Society and appeared in its *Philosophical Transactions*. Very early in this paper, Huxley (1849) identified its revolutionary core: "I would wish to lay particular stress upon the composition of this [the stomach] and other organs of the Medusae out of *two distinct membranes*, as I believe that it is one of the essential peculiarities of their structure, and that a knowledge of the fact is of great importance in investigating their homologies." Then, towards its end, he commented almost casually, "It is curious to remark that throughout, the outer and inner membranes appear to bear the same physiological relation to one another as do the serous and mucous layers of the germ".

In these early researches, Huxley (*L.L.* I, 58) told Sir John Richardson after *Rattlesnake*'s return to England, "I paid comparatively little attention to the collection of new species, caring rather to come to some clear and definite idea as to the structure of those which had indeed been long known, but very little understood. Unfortunately for science, but fortunately for me, this method appears to have been somewhat novel with observers of these animals, and consequently new and remarkable facts were to be had for the picking up." But the "picking up" was in this case of prime importance, for it enabled him to make his illuminating suggestion, basic to all later embryological thinking, that the two foundation membranes of the medusae correspond with the two embryonic layers of higher animals. And this suggestion led directly to the division of all animals into the three great groups of protozoa, coelenterata and the three-layered remainder (Lankaster's *Holoblastica, Diploblastica* and *Triploblastica*), thus providing the essential basis for Haeckel's 'Gastraea' Theory and for Kowalewsky's great discovery of the affinity of the ascidians and the vertebrates.

The other group whose fundamental revision Huxley started whilst at sea was that of the Mollusca. The term at that time embraced not only the true mollusca, but also a wide variety of non-segmented and non-radiate soft-bodied animals, such as the 'sea-squirts' and the 'sea-mats' and the 'lamp-shells', which were simply thrown in with the molluscs because nobody knew what else to do with them. Neither did Huxley; but he could see that something needed doing. As early as 16 April 1847, before *Rattlesnake* had reached Mauritius, he was noting (Huxley, J., 1935, 35), "I have a grand project floating through my head, of working up a regular monograph of the Mollusca, anatomy, physiology and histology, based on examination of at least one species of every genus". The project never materialised in quite this grand form, for in the event he concentrated on types with a clearly defined head, eventually described in his paper "On the Morphology of the Cephalous Mollusca". At that time, comparative anatomy was dominated by the idea of the 'archetype', promoted especially by Goethe and Oken in the metaphysical sense of a platonic ideal, often thought of as an idea in the mind of a Creator. There was one ideal of the vertebrate, one of the molluscan, one of the articulate, and one of the radiate type, and all creatures were to be considered as expressions of one archetype or another. For Huxley, however, the archetype was not a metaphysical ideal but an empirical tool, an idealised common structural plan to be induced from the facts of morphological variety and used as a basis for taxonomic understanding. Examining snails, slugs, cuttlefish, octopuses and squids, he induced an archetypical cephalous molluscan (which was bilaterally symmetrical, had on its ventral surface a flat muscular foot, carried on its dorsal surface a simple domed shell, possessed a mantle-cavity between foot and shell, and was served by several separate nervous ganglia). Huxley's grandson, Julian, has remarked how closely this morphological archetype resembles the evolutionary ancestor of the molluscs deduced by zoologists eighty years later, adding (*id.* 65), "Never was his engineer's instinct of grasping the essence of a construction better exemplified than in this work".

Somewhat less fundamental, but still of significance, was Huxley's work on the *Tunicata*. These we now know to be degenerate relations of the vertebrates, having an early tadpole-like stage which possesses a primordial backbone and central nervous system. In 1850 nobody suspected that the fleshy sea-squirts, living an apparently almost vegetable life, were the adults of such active juveniles. But Huxley, examining the actively swimming *Appendicularia*, realised that they too were tunicates, and he suggested that their peculiar tail was a larval feature persisting into adult life. He also confirmed the relationship of the sea-squirts to *Pyrosoma*, a colonial creature sometimes 10 feet or more in length, with an intensity of luminescence far beyond that of any other phosphorescent organism. Similarly, he showed that the gelatinous *Salpidae* were variants of the tunicate plan, and confirmed the long-disbelieved claim of Chamisso, that they existed in both solitary and catenary forms. More important, he demonstrated that the single salps reproduced asexually, whilst those in chains reproduced sexually, thus disclosing an alternation of generations which became one of the bases of his 1852 Royal Institution lecture, "Upon Animal Individuality".

It is interesting to note how clearly these early researches by Huxley foreshadowed the general nature of most of his later work. Occasionally, as when he worked on *Penicillium*, there were carefully conducted experiments, but Huxley was never a great experimenter. He was, however, an extremely skilled dissector, with outstanding rapidity and accuracy of execution, and he had that capacity for recognising the relevant which is the mark both of the great scientist and of the great artist. He was much aided by his enormous industry and by his marked ability as a draughtsman. But, above all, his scientific work was distinguished by its essentially synthetic and critical nature, its wide-ranging reassessment of both pre-existing and newly acquired knowledge, its basically philosophical consideration of large questions. He therefore fits less readily than Darwin or Mendel into the stereotype of the scientist as a deviser of ingenious experiment, but this does not mean that his very different type of contribution to science was any the less valuable.

Rattlesnake's planned return voyage via Singapore and the Cape was ruled out by the death of Captain Stanley, and in the May of 1850 she sailed direct for England. On 5 October she reached Plymouth, then proceeded to Chatham, and was finally paid off on 9 November. Quite unaware of the immense impact which had been made upon England's scientists by the series of substantial papers arriving at intervals from an unknown assistant-surgeon, Huxley could scarcely have imagined what a welcome awaited him.

CHAPTER 4

Research on special leave

THE matured Huxley who stepped ashore from *Rattlesnake* in the November of 1850 was a very different man from the raw assistant-surgeon who had gone aboard four years earlier. "Could the history of the soul be written for that time", he noted (Huxley, J., 1935, 266) in his diary, "it would be fuller of change and struggle than that of the outward man, but who shall write it? I, the only possible historian, am too much implicated." He had learned, for example (*C.E.* I, 3), that "It was good for me to live under sharp discipline; to be down on the realities of existence by living on bare necessaries; to find out how extremely well worth living life seemed to be when one woke up from a night's rest on a soft plank, with the sky for canopy and cocoa and weevily biscuit the sole prospect for breakfast." He had fallen deeply in love and disciplined himself to a long wait before its fulfilment. And, perhaps most important of all, he now knew for certain that he had unusual powers of observation and original thought.

It was not long before the leading biologists of the day were confirming the importance of his work, and Forbes sent him a letter (*L.L.* I, 59) which must have been very gratifying: "I can say without exaggeration that more important or more complete zoological researches have never been conducted during any voyage of discovery in the southern hemisphere. The course you have taken of directing your attention mainly to impreservable creatures, and to those orders of the animal kingdom respecting which we have least information, and the care and skill with which you have conducted elaborate dissections and microscopic examinations of the curious creatures you were so fortunate as to meet with, necessarily gives a peculiar and unique character to your researches, since thereby they fill up gaps in our knowledge of the animal kingdom. This is the more important, since such researches have been almost always neglected during voyages of discovery." Soon Huxley was seeing

Sir Joseph Dalton Hooker, who later wrote (*L.L.* I, 216) that "the researches Mr. Huxley laid before me were chiefly those on the Salpae, a much misunderstood group of marine Hydrozoa. ... his observations on their life-history, habits and affinities were on almost all points a revelation to me, and I could not fail to recognise in their author all the qualities possessed by a naturalist of commanding ability, industry, and power of exposition". Within a fortnight of landing at Chatham, Huxley had been invited to dine with Sir Charles Lyell, Sir Roderick Murchison and Sir Henry de la Beche. Within a month, the powerful Sir Richard Owen had persuaded the Admiralty to give Huxley six months' nominal appointment to *Fisguard* so that he could continue his researches free from normal naval duties. It is doubtful if there has ever been another so striking case of an unknown youngster, by reason of researches carried out unaided far from home, landing with one leap at the very forefront of his science.

Huxley may perhaps be forgiven the unmistakable note of self-satisfaction with which he wrote (*L.L.* I, 62) to tell Lizzie, "I have taken a better position than I could have expected among these grandees, and I find them all immensely civil and ready to help me on". Yet, in this same letter, there was an even more unmistakable note of determination to be his own master: "I am under no one's *patronage*, nor do I ever mean to be ... if it should be necessary for me to find public expression to my thoughts on any matter, I have clearly made up my mind to do so, without allowing myself to be influenced by hope of gain or weight of authority ... I will leave my mark somewhere, and it shall be clear and distinct $\boxed{\text{T.H.H. his mark}}$ and free from the abominable blur of cant, humbug, and self-seeking which surrounds everything in this present world." Living at first for a while in St. John's Wood with his brother George, and then moving for greater privacy into lodgings in the same neighbourhood, Huxley worked with enormous energy at the specimens and notes amassed whilst away at sea. But, he sadly wrote (*L.L.* I, 66) to his fiancée in March 1851, "To attempt to live by any scientific pursuit is a farce. Nothing but what is absolutely practical will go down in England. A man of science may earn great distinction, but not bread. He will get invitations to all sorts of dinners and conversaziones, but not enough income to pay his cab fare." The fact was, of course, that the phenomenon of the professional scientist had scarcely yet arrived on the historical scene. This was the year of the Great Exhibition, mounted in Hyde Park by the most advanced nation in the world to herald the modern age of science and technology; but England still employed more people in domestic service than in any occupation except agriculture, and still mainly relied for its science upon those few fortunate enough to have some other source of income. Huxley, indeed, must have been one of the very first Englishmen to make biology serve as a 'career' in our contemporary connotation of that term.

Just a few months after his return to England, and a few weeks before his twenty-sixth birthday, Huxley heard that he was to be elected Fellow of the Royal Society. Even more astonishing, he was within an ace of being awarded the Royal Medal: in the event it went to a man old enough to be his father, but it came to him a year later. Huxley had originally intended working for the Second M.B. examination on his return to England: now, with the letters F.R.S. after his name, he seems to have put aside this intention as somewhat supererogatory. He was no longer just a self-taught tyro: he was the young eagle of British biology. And, when he was commanded early in 1851 to report to the Director-General of the Royal Naval Medical Service, the outcome was very satisfying. "Sir William [Burnett] was very civil", Huxley wrote (*L.L.* I, 71) to Nettie, "and told me that the Commander of the *Fisguard* had applied to the Admiralty to know what was to be done with me, as my leave had expired. 'Now', said he, 'go to Forrest' (his secretary), 'write a letter to me, stating what you want, and I will get it done for you'. So away I went and applied for an indefinite amount of leave, on condition of reporting the progress of my work every six months, and as I suppose I shall get it, I feel quite easy on that head." In the spring of 1852 the President of the British Association asked the Treasury to grant £300 for the publication of Huxley's researches, the President of the Royal Society repeated the request, Lord Rosse spoke to the Under-Secretary of the Treasury, and finally Huxley himself approached the First Lord of the Admiralty. Not even all these pressures could squeeze cash out of the government for the projected publications, but the paid leave of absence was extended to June 1853, and then for yet another six months.

During his three years of biological research on special leave at the navy's expense, Huxley poured out papers at an astonishing rate. In June 1851, after the first six months, he reported (*L.L.* I, 75) to the Admiralty the completion of seven memoirs:

1. On the Auditory Organs of the Crustacea. Published in the *Annals of Natural History*.
2. On the Anatomy of the genus Tethea. Published in the *Annals of Natural History*.
3. Report upon the Development of the Echinoderms. To appear in the *Annals* for July.
4. On the Anatomy and Physiology of the *Salpae*, with four plates. Read at the Royal Society, and to be published in the next part of the *Philosophical Transactions*.
5. On two Genera of Ascidians, Doliolum and Appendicularia, with one plate. Read at the Royal Society, and to be published in the next part of the *Philosophical Transactions*.
6. On some peculiarities in the Circulation of the Mollusca. Sent to M. Milne-Edwards, at his request, to be published in the *Annales des Sciences*.
7. On the Generative Organs of the *Physophoridae* and *Diphydae*. Sent to Prof. Müller of Berlin for publication in his *Archiv*.

Six months later there were four more papers to report—one on the hydrostatic acalephae, another on the genus Sagitta, one on the anatomy and physiology of the rotifera, and one on Thalassicola. In 1852 the British Association received a further paper on the structure of the ascidians, while the Royal Society printed his important study of the cephalous mollusca. The following year saw the publication of papers on the cellulose in the tunic of ascidians, on the development of teeth, and on the then much-debated cell theory. Before he was twenty-nine, Huxley had seen twenty-three of his investigations reach print, and during this same period he was working on fifteen others. It is scarcely too much to say that this torrent of publications, continuing through the next few years, transformed invertebrate zoology.

In these papers, Huxley demonstrated that various aberrant ascidians were in fact modifications of the general sea-squirt type; he laid a rational foundation for the classification of the medusae (the jelly fish and their allies); he gave an account of the phenomenon of budding, alternating with sexual reproduction, in these animals; he made a great advance on all earlier efforts to recognise a common plan in the many modifications of the great group of cephalous molluscs. And, as MacBride (1925, 735) has remarked, "all our later knowledge of invertebrate development and anatomy is built on this foundation so well and truly laid by Huxley ... [and although] Huxley was not an embryologist ... his deep feeling for fundamental similarities of structure led him to make some astonishingly correct embryological guesses, which might almost be termed embryological prophecies". Even more important, Huxley began to clarify the meaning of the terms 'variety' and 'species', distinguishing the morphological and physiological senses of the latter; while his schemes of classification, based not on *a priori* assumptions but on inductive generalisations, had a profound influence on taxonomic method. But all this work has become so deeply embedded in the central corpus of the science that its luminous and revolutionary nature can be appreciated only by those who have turned back and browsed among biological publications prior to 1850.

Yet, whilst contributing handsomely to the future of biology, Huxley could not quite see how his own future was to be provided for. And, while full of the wonder of science, he was becoming increasingly disillusioned about scientists. Within less than a fortnight of being paid off at Chatham, he had realised that a career in science would need fighting for, and the prospect did not appeal to him. "I have a woman's element in me", he told his sister Lizzie (*L.L.* I, 61). "I hate the incessant struggle and toil to cut one another's throat among us men." The feeling was genuine enough, and to the end of his days he retained an inner tenderness, but between struggle and defeat he chose struggle. In the November of 1851 he wrote to tell his friend MacLeay in Sydney a few of the hard facts behind the smooth façade of English science. "The fighting and scratching to keep your place in the crowd exclude all other thoughts", he confided (*L.L.* I, 91 and 93). "When I last wrote I was but at the edge of the crush at the pit-door of this great fools' theatre—now I have worked my way into it and through it, and am, I hope, not far from the checktakers. I have learnt a good deal in my passage. ... It is astonishing with what an intense feeling of hatred Owen is regarded by the majority of his contemporaries ... The truth is, he is the superior of most, and does not conceal that he knows it, and it must be confessed that he does some very ill-natured tricks now and then." At one time Huxley had so despaired of earning a living at science that he even contemplated emigrating to Australia and becoming a brewer. But now he told MacLeay *(ibid.)*,

> I have finally decided that my vocation is science, and I have made up my mind to the comparative poverty which is its necessary adjunct ... I say this without the slightest idea that there is anything to be enthusiastic about in either science or its professors. A year behind the scenes is quite enough to disabuse one of all rose-pink illusions. But it is equally clear to me that for a man of my temperament,

at any rate, the sole secret of getting through this life with anything like content-
ment is to have full scope for the development of one's faculties. Science alone
seems to me to afford this scope—Law, Divinity, Physic, and Politics being in a
state of chaotic vibration between utter humbug and utter scepticism.

In the March of 1852, the increasingly jealous Owen tried to prevent
publication of one of his erstwhile protégé's papers. "He won't be able
to say a word against it", Huxley told Nettie (*L.L.* I, 97), "but he will
pooh-pooh it to a dead certainty. . . . Let him beware. On my own subjects
I am his master, and am quite ready to fight half a dozen dragons." This
incident may perhaps partially explain something of the ferocity with
which Huxley savaged Owen after the publication of Darwin's *Origin of
Species*. Meanwhile he was still trying desperately to improve his financial
position, partly to help his sister with her growing family in Louisiana,
but mainly to make it possible to marry. Nothing came of a mooted
Chair of Natural History at Sydney; a hoped-for appointment at Toronto
was side-slipped to a close relative of a Canadian politician; applications
at Aberdeen and Cork and King's College in London met with no more
success. He did, however, get one great opportunity: a public lecture at
the Royal Institution.

It was on a difficult subject ['Animal Individuality', he told Lizzie (*L.L.* I, 99)]
requiring a good deal of thought; and as it was my first appearance and before
the best audience in London, you may imagine how anxious and nervous I was
. . . I entered the theatre with a very pale face, and a heart beating like a sledge-
hammer nineteen to the dozen. For the first five minutes I did not know very
clearly what I was about, but by degrees I got possession of myself and of my
subject, and did not care for anybody. I have had 'golden opinions from all sorts
of men' about it, so I suppose I may tell you I have succeeded. . . . There is one
comfort, I shall never be nervous again about any audience; but at one's first
attempt, to stand in the place of Faraday and such big-wigs may excuse a little
weakness.

That summer Huxley was elected at the age of twenty-seven to the
Council of the Royal Society, and everyone gave him in effect the advice
received by Dante, *A te sequi la tua stella*. He now knew that his star
was science, and that it was bound before long to rise fast. "My course
in life is taken", he wrote the following summer (*L.L.* I, 84) to Nettie.
"I will *not* leave London—I *will* make myself a name and a position
as well as an income by some kind of pursuit connected with science,
which is the thing for which nature has fitted me if she ever fitted any

one for anything." So, when at last his special leave came to an end, he fought stubbornly for its further extension. The Admiralty was equally stubborn, considering—and, it may be thought, not unreasonably—that three years' pay without any naval duties was quite sufficient for a young man who had served only four years afloat. In January 1854 it would budge no further. Huxley succeeded in delaying things for another two months, but on 1st March he was instructed to explain immediately his failure to obey a thrice-repeated order to board *Illustrious* at Portsmouth. He blandly explained that it was quite impossible to do so until the Admiralty had made up its mind about a grant towards the publication of his researches, and that was the last straw. A few days later he was struck off the Navy List, and his only regular income came to an abrupt end.

CHAPTER 5

Settled at Jermyn Street

WITHIN two months of being struck off the Navy List, a piece of good fortune came Huxley's way. Forbes, who gave two courses of lectures at the School of Mines in Jermyn Street, was appointed Professor of Natural History at Edinburgh, and Huxley was invited to take over one of his School courses at £100 per annum. Then he was offered the other course, and soon after was also given some temporary coastal work by the Geological Survey. Before very long he had in addition some part-time teaching at St. Thomas's Hospital, together with a few lectures at Marlborough House for the Science and Art Department. His expulsion from the navy was no longer financially catastrophic.

In the autumn of 1854 Huxley was pressed to follow Forbes to Edinburgh, to deputise for the ailing Professor of Physiology with a view to ultimately succeeding him. "It was", as he recognised (*L.L.* I, 114) in a letter to his fiancée, "a tempting offer made in a flattering manner ... but. ... Had I accepted, I should have been at the mercy of the actual Professor—and that is a position I don't like standing in, even with the best of men." Then, in November, Forbes suddenly died, and a permanent professorship was beckoning. "There is", Huxley explained (*H.P.* 2. 4) to Hooker, "a mortal difference between £200 and £1000 a year", and he was greatly tempted. But, as he told Dyster (*H.P.* 15. 46), "I dread leaving London and its freedom—its Bedouin sort of life—for Edinburgh and no whistling on Sundays." In April Edinburgh was still tempting, but by this time Huxley had a post worth £200 as Naturalist to the Survey and, with a firm income of £400 per annum, felt that he could afford to stay in London and even to contemplate marriage.

Henrietta Heathorn arrived in England in the May of 1855, and the long parting was at last over. "God help me!", Huxley told Hooker (*H.P.* 2. 10), "I discover that I am as bad as any young fool who knows no better, and if the necessity for giving six lectures a week did not sternly interfere, I should be hanging about her ladyship's apron-strings all day." Nettie's health had been nearly ruined by incompetent colonial doctoring, consisting exclusively of calomel and blood-letting, and a London specialist told Huxley that she had only six months to live. "Well", he replied (*L.L.* I, 127), "six months or not, she is going to be my wife." Early in July he told Hooker (*H.P.* 2. 14) of his plans: "I terminate my Baccalaureate and take my degree of M.A.trimony (isn't that atrocious?) on Saturday, July 21. After the unhappy criminals have been turned off, there will be refreshments provided for the sheriffs, chaplains and spectators. Will you come?" On their honeymoon at Tenby, Nettie was so ill that Huxley had to carry her to and from the beach each day, but she was fascinated by his biological work. "One sunny morning", she later recalled (*H.P.* 31. 82), "Dr. Dyster looked in and found us on the back verandah, my husband, coat off and shirt sleeves tucked up dissecting a big fish whilst I wrote down its description. 'I have seen many newly married couples' remarked our friend 'but never before have I met with a young husband cutting up a fish & getting his wife to describe it'." It was the beginning of an intensely happy marriage, during which Nettie's health recovered to outlive her vigorous husband.

On their return from Tenby, the newly-weds moved to Waverley Place in Marylebone, and Huxley was soon up to his eyes in work. Murchison, who had replaced de la Beche as Director of the School of Mines, recognised from the start the peculiar power of his most junior colleague. Before he had been in the place a year, Huxley was elected with one of the senior professors to audit the School's accounts; he was soon one of the few authorised to sign cheques on behalf of the School; he and Professor Smyth were deputed to take charge of the recataloguing of the collections. By 1858 Huxley was telling Dyster (*H.P.* 15, 102) "to speak nautically, I have been there long enough to 'know the ropes'—and I shall take pleasure in working the place into what I think it ought to be". A year later, he was arranging for the Chair of Physics to be offered to his scientific ally Tyndall. He may perhaps be forgiven the slight vein of vaunting in a letter (*L.L.* I, 158) to sister Lizzie:

> You want to know what I am and where I am—well, here's a list of titles. T.H.H., Professor of Natural History, Government School of Mines, Jermyn Street; Naturalist to the Geological Survey; Curator to the Palaeontological Collections (*non-official* maid-of-all-work in Natural Science to the Government); Examiner in Physiology and Comparative Anatomy to the University of London;

Fullerian Professor of Physiology to the Royal Institution (but that's just over); F.R.S., F.G.S., etc. Member of a lot of Societies and Clubs, all of which cost him a mint of money.

Fortunately, Huxley's many duties did not destroy the playfulness which kept bubbling up in his conversation and correspondence. When one friend asked his advice about the suitability of a certain biology book for a class of young ladies, Huxley's reply (*H.P.* 15. 42) was, "Adolph Grube grubs not much about the genitalia—& you need have no fear of any phallic phantoms as the annelida enantia & tubicula are improvided with any such improprieties". When another tried to inveigle him into doing some part-time teaching at a women's college, he replied (Huntington MS.) by asking, "what on earth should I do among all the virgins, young and old, in Bedford Square?... depend upon it I should be turned out in a week (though I don't drink) for some forgetful excursus into the theory of Parthenogenesis or worse". And his self-confidence was now such as to allow playfulness even in his description (*H.P.* 2. 23) of Sir Richard Owen: "What a capital title that is they give him of the *British Cuvier*. He stands in exactly the same relationship to the French as British Brandy to cognac."

There are many testimonies from students to the effectiveness of his teaching through the years. "As a class lecturer", said one (*L.L.* II, 414), "Huxley was *facile princeps*, and only those who were privileged to sit under him can form a conception of his delivery. Clear, deliberate, never hesitant nor unduly emphatic, never repetitional, always logical, his every word told." "Sparing of gesture, sparing of emphasis, careless of mere rhetorical or oratorical art, he had nevertheless the secret of the highest art of all ... he had simplicity", reported another (*H.P.* 2. 147). "His lectures were like his writings, luminously clear ...", wrote a third (T. J. Parker, 1896), "full of a high seriousness, but with no suspicion of pedantry; lightened by an occasional epigram or flashes of caustic humour, but with none of the small jocularity in which it is such a temptation to a lecturer to indulge." Yet another (Mivart, 1897) remembered "that rich fund of humour, ever ready to well forth when occasion permitted, sometimes accompanied with an extra gleam in his bright dark eyes, sometimes expressed with a dryness and gravity of look which gave it a double zest". A fifth (Armstrong, 1933) recalled how he "sat in face of his blackboard and watched him embroider it most exquisitely with chalks of varied hue; the while he talked like a book; with absolute precision, in chosen words". But Huxley still felt the need to improve his own knowledge and, on the last day of 1856, he pencilled what he thought would be a final entry into his adolescent journal (*Thoughts and Doings*):

> 1856–7–8 must still be 'Lehrjahre' to complete training in principles of Histology, Morphology, Physiology, Zoology and Geology by *Monographic Work* in each Department. 1860 will then see me well grounded and ready for any special pursuits in either of these branches. It is impossible to map out beforehand how this must be done. I must seize opportunities as they come, at the risk of the reputation of desultoriness. In 1860 I may fairly look forward to fifteen or twenty years 'Meisterjahre', and with the comprehensive views my training will have given me, I think it will be possible in that time to give a new and healthier direction to all Biological Science.

It was an ambitious plan, but it was to be largely fulfilled.

Ever since the latter half of the seventeenth century, when Robert Hooke examined a thin slice of cork under the microscope and gave the name 'cell' to the individual unit of structure, attention had been concentrated more on the easily visible cell walls than on their less obvious living contents. This was natural enough in view of the limited techniques then available; but it meant that, even after the importance of the protoplasm had been appreciated, there was a tendency to exaggerate the autonomy of each cell. In 1805 the 'cell theory' was promulgated by Oken in the form, "All organic beings originate from and consist of 'vesicles' or cells". During the 1830s Schleiden had claimed that the higher plants were but aggregates of fully individualised independent cellular units. And Schwann had asserted that animal cells correspond in every respect to those of plants. Some of the German workers in particular continued to produce admirable research results in the field of general cell theory, but these were commonly confused by somewhat woolly philosophical speculation. In 1858 Huxley sought, in his striking "Review of the Cell Theory", to distinguish fact from fancy. It was, Michael Foster declared (*L.L.* I, 140) in 1895, "a paper which more than one young physiologist at the time read with delight, and which even today may be studied with profit, he ... drove the sword of rational inquiry through the heart of conceptions, metaphysical and transcendental, but dominant". Huxley's main contention was that cells are not so much the cause as the result of organisation, just as the line of shells and seaweeds on the shore are the result and not the cause of tidal forces. This was counter to the then prevailing view, which tended to treat the cell as a virtually self-contained unit of life, and which was still ascendent eight years later when Huxley produced his acute apophthegm (*L.L.* I, 277), "the facts concerning form are questions of force, every form is force visible". By the end of the century, Strasburger had begun to correct the balance by his demonstration of intercellular protoplasmic bridges, and succeeding embryological work has emphasised the importance of forces more widely diffused than the individual cell's own boundaries. Huxley may possibly have gone too far in his opposition to the idea of cellular independence, but in essence his view was not very different from that so much more recently stated by Gray (1931, 3), "The real unit of life must be of a protoplasmic nature ... cellular structure is not in itself of primary significance".

Despite his deep interest in histology, physiology and general zoology, most of Huxley's thirty-odd new publications between 1855 and 1859 arose directly out of palaeontological material examined in the course of his daily duties at Jermyn Street. One of these, a descriptive memoir "On *Cephalaspis* and *Pteraspis*", demonstrated that these Devonian fossils were the head-shields of primitive fish and not, as previously believed, the shells of cuttlefish. Typically, he accompanied this work by a thorough study of related living forms, including details of their skulls and vertebral columns, and by a histological study of their exoskeletons. His examination of *Stagonolepis* showed that it was not a fish but a crocodile, and led directly to a determination of the geological age of the important Elgin sandstones. Other work in palaeontology during this period dealt with ganoid (with 'enamelled' scales) Devonian fish, with coal-measure crustaceans, with a new species of *Plesiosaurus* from Glastonbury, with amphibian and reptilian remains from South Africa and Australia, with a pterosaurian from the Stonesfield slate and a fossil cetacean from New Zealand, and with the dermal armour of *Crocodilus hastingiae*. He also made studies of several extinct labyrinthodonts, a type of fossil amphibia with highly convoluted tooth structures. For one who had originally disclaimed any real interest in fossils, it was an impressive achievement, suitably marked by his election in 1859 as Secretary of the Geological Society.

Betweenwhiles, Huxley occupied himself with work on the structure and function of the nervous systems of various marine invertebrates, together with studies of the Malpighian bodies of the spleen, the enamel and dentine of the teeth, the agamic reproduction of greenfly, and miscellaneous minor matters. Some observations on submerged forests, started during the Tenby honeymoon, were followed up by a paper on geologically recent changes of land–sea levels in the Bristol Channel. A holiday with Tyndall in Switzerland served to disclose a most egregious blunder by Forbes concerning the structure of the Brenon glacier, and led to a joint paper "On the Structure and Motion of Glaciers" for the Royal Society. And, during these years, a rapidly developing interest in science education led Huxley both to lecture on the subject and to organise a weekly scientific column in the *Saturday Review*.

In 1856, a few minutes before midnight on Christmas Eve, Mrs. Huxley bore her first baby, Noel, "a fair-haired, blue-eyed, stout little Trojan" (*L.L.* I, 158). In 1858 their second child, Jessie Oriana, appeared; and in 1859 the singularly gifted Marian. But his wife's health was still wretched and Huxley himself was frequently plagued by toothache and general debility, so in the evenings they would lie down facing each other on their two sofas, seeking strength for the tasks of tomorrow. One of these tasks involved putting a considerable dent into the massive reputation of Sir Richard Owen.

This reputation was solidly based on several decades of highly productive work, including monumental studies of vertebrate skeletons, and nothing can detract from Owen's immense achievement in descriptive palaeontology. Moreover, his introduction into comparative anatomy of the terms 'analogue' and 'homologue', the former referring to distinct organs performing the same function in different creatures, while the latter referred to different forms of the same organ, was of basic importance. He was, however, a follower of Oken and his highly speculative philosophy, and in particular was committed to his theory of the vertebrate skull. According to this theory, the skull was simply a much expanded anterior portion of the vertebral column, with four vertebrae forming respectively the ear region, the jaw region, the eye region and the nose region. Huxley, on the other hand, was highly suspicious of the grounding of homologies merely on anatomical resemblance. Following up the work of Rathke and other embryologists, he showed that the cartilaginous skulls of fish can be matched, part by part, with the bony skulls of higher animals—and, moreover, that the bones of the skull are derived from structures which precede the vertebrae in development. By this marriage between comparative anatomy and embryology, made public in his 1858 Croonian Lecture, "On the Theory of the Vertebrate Skull", he dealt a death blow to established cranial theory. "The spinal column and the skull start from the same primitive condition, whence they immediately begin to diverge", he pointed out (1858b). "It may be true to say that there is a primitive identity of structure between the spinal or vertebral column and the skull; but it is no more true that the adult skull is a modified vertebral column than it would be to affirm that the vertebral column is a modified skull." And, laying down a principle which became central in all later work of this sort, "study of the gradations presented by a series of living things may have the utmost value in suggesting homologies, but the study of development alone can demonstrate them". When Michael Foster (1896) wrote that "This lecture marked an epoch in England in vertebrate morphology", he was thinking of its scientific content. It also marked a more important epoch by weakening the hitherto overwhelming authority of Owen, so shortly to be the leader of the scientific opposition to Darwin's theory of evolution.

CHAPTER 6

Darwin's bulldog

IN 1831, when Darwin set out on his seminal voyage in *Beagle*, Huxley was still a mere toddler of six. By 1842, when Huxley began his elementary medical studies at Charing Cross, Darwin was already writing the first abstract of his theory of evolution. By the time Huxley joined the navy in 1846, Darwin had collected such masses of supporting data as would have brought any less cautious (or, perhaps, less timorous) man to the point of publication. These dates delineate the great difference in seniority of the two men, commonly obscured by the popular linking of their names.

It is, indeed, somewhat surprising that the support of one so junior should have been so anxiously sought by a scientist of such high standing. Yet, from the time that he first began writing out the actual text of his *Origin of Species*, Darwin had fixed upon Lyell, Hooker and Huxley as the three who should be its judges. Lyell had much earlier recognised, in the biological sections of his *Principles of Geology*, the essential facts of differential survival (even using the phrase "struggle for existence"), and only a certain submission to traditional preconceptions prevented him from immediately accepting Darwin's theory. Hooker had initial doubts, but the weight of evidence soon convinced him. Yet, only a few weeks before the publication of his great work, Darwin was still uncertain what Huxley's judgement would be. "Hooker is a complete convert", he told Wallace (Mitchell, 1900, 101), "If I can convert Huxley I shall be content".

Darwin, with characteristic humility, admitted (Barlow, 1958, 140), "I have no great quickness of apprehension or wit which is so remarkable in some clever men, for instance Huxley"; and he would probably have accepted Irvine's recent judgement (1955, 71) that "Huxley ... enjoyed all the luxuries of genius. Darwin possessed only the bare essentials." There is, indeed, something very tender and touching in the relationship between these two eminent Victorians: the younger man taking on the protective part of elder brother; the older exclaiming at the intellectual and gladiatorial achievements of the younger. Half a century earlier, poor Lamarck (who, unlike Darwin with his highly successful stock exchange investments, died in lonely poverty) had written (Eiseley, 1959), "It is not enough to discover and prove a useful truth ... it is necessary also to be able to propagate it and get it recognised." It is unlikely that Darwin remembered this passage, for he had a powerful faculty of forgetting what he had read of earlier evolutionists, but he must have dimly perceived that he needed someone to do his fighting for him. At any rate, he was grateful to have Huxley as his "general agent"; Huxley was proud to be described as "Darwin's bulldog"; and, so far as the general public was concerned, that was their chief connection.

The furore which followed the publication of *The Origin* was so great that many in later generations have tended to assume that the theory of evolution was Darwin's own idea. This is very far from the truth. True, in 1859 many still accepted Archbishop Ussher's dating of the creation at Sunday, 23 October 4004 B.C., and even those who believed in a greater antiquity for the earth were generally in no doubt that each species had been separately created. The strata of the rocks and their fossil content were explained in terms of a series of cataclysms such as Noah's flood, while the marvellous adaptations of plants and animals to their environments were presented as impressive evidence of divine design. But, below the public surface of scientific and theological orthodoxy, there had never ceased to flow many private rivulets of doubt. Even in the Middle Ages a few bold spirits had risked speculation, and the Renaissance greatly stimulated it. Fracastoro and Leonardo in the sixteenth century, Steno and others in the seventeenth, suggested that the earth's past could be explained in terms of natural forces still at present operative. The great voyages of discovery presented Europe with knowledge, vague and imprecise at first, of strange new creatures and strange new facts about their distribution. Sir Thomas Browne (1685) puzzled that "America abounded with Beasts of prey and noxious Animals, yet contained not in it that necessary creature a Horse"; his near-contemporary John Ray pondered upon the meaning of fern-leaf fossil imprints (Gunther, 1928, 260) which "seem to shock the Scripture-History". The telescope increasingly revealed the immensity of the heavens and encouraged speculation about cosmic evolution through great stretches of time; the microscope disclosed tiny organisms scarcely imaginable as inhabitants of Noah's ark, and illuminated the complex formative processes of embryonic growth. There began to develop an uneasy suspicion that the universe was a place of continuous change and development. With the eighteenth century, the underground rivulets became important streams, bursting noisily now and then above the surface. Especially in France, it became a common literary device to cast dangerous thoughts into the form of imaginary conversations; while Maupertius, in his 1746 *Vénus Physique*, wrote quite openly about the production of new races by artificial selection. Then, in 1809, Lamarck produced his great *Philosophie Zoologique*.

England also had its eighteenth-century innovators, including Erasmus Darwin (the grandfather of Charles), whose 1794 *Zoonomia* was unambiguously evolutionist. The following year there came James Hutton's *Theory of the Earth*, making a major conceptual break-through: "We find no vestige of a beginning—no prospect of an end", he wrote (1795, I, 208); and "This decaying nature of the solid earth is the very perfection of its constitution as a living world." Moreover, although England, badly frightened by the French Revolution, soon tried to sweep dangerous ideas under the carpet, she by no means fully succeeded. In 1813 the Royal Society received a paper in which William Wells (1818 *sic*), referring to artificial selection by animal breeders, went on to remark, "What is here done by art seems to be done with equal efficacy, though more slowly, by nature, in the formation of varieties of mankind". Six years later, William Lawrence traced out the mechanism of natural selection more generally and more precisely. Then in the very year in which *Beagle* set sail, an appendix to Patrick Matthew's book, *On Naval Timber and Arboriculture* (1831), presented in a nutshell the main essence of Darwin's theory: "Those individuals who possess not the requisite strength, swiftness, hardihood, or cunning, fall prematurely without reproduction ... their places being occupied by the more perfect of their own kind who are pressing on the means of subsistence." Some of these writers, like Wells and Lawrence, were essentially concerned with the question of whether *Homo sapiens* was one species or several, but the wider implications of their views should have been apparent. Then, in 1844, Robert Chambers published anonymously his *Vestiges of the Natural History of Creation*, which went through four printings in its first seven months (and a later edition of which Huxley reviewed adversely with what he still later confessed to have been needless savagery).

Why, in view of all this, Darwin so persistently denied any appreciable debt to his predecessors is an interesting problem. More important, however, is the question, why did *Origin of Species* let loose great storms of controversy which reverberated ceaselessly for a decade and did not die away in Tennessee until a century later? And why did Darwin need an heroic protagonist like Huxley to gain him a fair hearing? And why were Huxley's victories so immensely popular with all to whom his name was not anathema? The answers to these questions are complex. In part, it was because the various interlocking Establishments —political, clerical and scientific—were becoming very nervous about the rumbles of unrest arising in all directions. In 1842 there had been widespread Chartist riots; in 1845 Newman's secession to Rome; in 1848 *The Communist Manifesto;* in 1852 the Australian revolt at Eureka Stockade; in 1853 Maurice's scandalous *Theological Essays;* in 1857 the Indian Mutiny. It seemed high time for those in authority to make a firm stand. And, in particular, there was the fear that Darwin's theory would subvert the argument from design, which had been the strong rock of natural theology. So, from fear or stubbornness or vanity in some cases and from a concern for intellectual rigour in others, often from an uneasy awareness that there was no satisfactory explanation of how evolution could actually have been affected, in a few cases from an admirable general resolve not to admit excessive speculation without sufficient supporting evidence, most scientists greeted *Origin of Species* with reserve if not suspicion. Even among those who were willing to concede the possibility that species had evolved, there was commonly a profound reluctance to accept that the mechanism of evolution could be in the 'blind chance' of natural selection.

So far as Huxley was concerned, his own researches had disclosed some of the weaknesses of the archetype theory and his temperament made him willing not merely to accept but positively to welcome a new view of things. He had himself, expecially in his work on the cephalous mollusca, shown that a wide range of morphological modifications could be derived (using that word logically rather than chronologically) from one original form. In his work on the medusae and their allies, he had traced a gradual progression from simple to complex types; and, more important, he had clearly demonstrated the significant relationships between the embryonic stages of widely differing animal groups. Moreover, in his important address "On the Persistent Types of Animal

Life", he had argued that such cases of lack of progression through geological time did not invalidate the idea of evolution. But, prior to 1859, he had nowhere met sufficiently weighty evidence that evolution had in fact occurred or a sufficiently convincing suggestion of what its mechanism might have been.

So, he explained (*L.L.* I, 169), "I took refuge in that thätige Skepsis which Goethe has so well defined; and, reversing the apostolic precept to be all things to all men, I usually defended the tenability of the received doctrines when I had to do with the transmutationists, and stood up for the possibility of transmutation among the orthodox". He claimed to have read Lamarck attentively, but it seems possible that he had not so much read Lamarck as read other people's inadequate and misleading accounts of the great Frenchman's views. What Huxley was looking for (*L.L.* I, 170) was "a hypothesis respecting the origin of known organic forms, which assumed the operation of no causes but such as could be proved to be actually at work ... clear and definite conceptions which could be brought face to face with facts and have their validity tested". His advance copy of *The Origin* provided him with what he wanted, and when he had read it his immediate reflection *(ibid.)* was, "How exceedingly stupid not to have thought of that". He still believed that there were gaps in the evidence, but (*L.L.* I, 171) "The only rational course for those who had no other object than the attainment of truth was to accept 'Darwinism' as a working hypothesis and see what could be made of it. Either it would prove its capacity to elucidate the facts of organic life, or it would break down under the strain".

When, the very day before publication, Huxley wrote (*L.L.* I, 175) to tell *The Origin*'s author, "I think you have demonstrated a true cause for the production of species", Darwin heaved a huge sigh of relief. "Like a good Catholic who has received extreme unction", he replied (Darwin, F., 1887, II, 232), "I can now sing *Nunc Dimittis*". Perhaps he had been most relieved of all by Huxley's message (*L.L.* I, 176), "I trust you will not allow yourself to be in any way disgusted or annoyed by the considerable abuse and misrepresentation which, unless I greatly mistake, is in store for you. ... And as to the curs which will bark and yelp, you must recollect that some of your friends, at any rate, are endowed with an amount of combativeness which (though you have often and justly rebuked it) may stand you in good stead. I am sharpening up my claws and beak in readiness."

As it turned out, his first engagement required not so much the bull-dog's teeth or the eagle's beak as the serpent's guile. *The Times* sent Darwin's book to one of its regular anonymous staff reviewers, to whom Huxley made the generous offer of helping in the labour of writing while claiming none of the credit. As he explained (*H.P.* 2. 57) to Hooker (the only one let into the secret), "I was thoroughly in the humour and full of the subject. Of course as a scientific review the thing is worth nothing, but I earnestly hope that it may have made some of the educated mob, who derive their ideas from the Times, reflect. And whatever they do, they *shall* respect Darwin & be d—d to them." Dear innocent Darwin read the review with delight and immediately wrote (*H.P.* 5. 92) to tell Huxley all about it:

> It included an eulogium of me which quite touched me, although I am not vain enough to think it all deserved. The author is a literary man and a German scholar. He has read my book attentively; but, what is remarkable, it seems that he is a profound naturalist ... he writes and thinks with quite uncommon force and clearness; and, what is even still rarer, his writing is seasoned with most pleasant wit. ... Who can it be? Certainly I should have said that there was only one man in England who could have written this essay, and that you were the man; but I suppose that I am wrong ... for how could you influence Jupiter Olympus and make him give you three and a half columns to pure science?

Huxley's next step was to inoculate the influential Royal Institution audience against the calumnies which he felt sure were soon to come. "I hardly know of a great physical truth", he declared in a Friday Evening Discourse (Huxley, T. H., 1860) early in the following February, "whose universal reception has not been preceded by an epoch in which most estimable persons have maintained that the phenomena investigated were directly dependent on the Divine Will, and that the attempt to investigate them was not only futile, but blasphemous. And there is wonderful tenacity of life about this sort of opposition to physical science. Crushed and maimed in every battle, it yet seems never to be slain; and after a hundred defeats it is at this day as rampant, though happily not so mischievous, as in the time of Galileo." In April *The Westminster Review* appeared, with Huxley's enthusiastic account of Darwin's book —which, he remarked (*C.E.* II, 22):

> Everybody has read ... or, at least, has given an opinion upon its merits and demerits; pietists, whether lay or ecclesiastic, decry it with the mild railing which sounds so charitable; bigots denounce it with ignorant invective; old ladies of

both sexes consider it a decidedly dangerous book, and even savants, who have no better mud to throw, quote antiquated writers to show that its author is no better than an ape himself; while every philosophical thinker hails it as a veritable Whitworth gun in the armoury of liberalism.

And, after a comprehensive exposition of the history of thought in this field—with such occasional asides as (*C.E.*, II, 52); "Extinguished theologians lie about the cradle of every science as the strangled snakes beside that of Hercules"—he assessed the book as the most important since von Baer's *Uber Entwicklungsgeschichte der Tiere*. The really decisive clash, however, took place that summer, when Wilberforce and Huxley faced each other on the platform of the British Association at Oxford.

The famous battle was not of Huxley's choosing. When Daubeny, the University's Professor of Botany, presented a paper to Section D, "On the Final Causes of the Sexuality of Plants, with Particular Reference to Mr. Darwin's Work on *Origin of Species*", Huxley declined an invitation to take part in the discussion, for he felt that the audience was one which would allow sentiment to interfere unduly with reason. And, even when Owen made mis-statements about the comparative anatomy of man and gorilla, he contented himself with a direct contradiction and a promise to produce his evidence later. But soon the University grapevine was saying that the Bishop would settle the heretics' hash on the last day of the month, and Huxley was urged by his friends not to leave Oxford until after that date. Attracted by the prospect of episcopal pyrotechnics, an audience of some 700 arrived at the Museum on 30th June and the meeting was transferred to a larger hall. Wilberforce and Huxley sat not far from each other on the platform. Massed in the middle of the room were the clergy, in one corner sat a small knot of pro-Darwin undergraduates, and down the length of one side the ladies waited and fluttered their handkerchiefs. The programmed paper by Dr. Draper of New York, "On the Intellectual Development of Europe Considered with Reference to the Views of Mr. Darwin", was duly and dully delivered. Two or three members discussed the paper for a few minutes, but the crowd soon tired of grapeshot and called out for the heavy artillery. Bland and jovial, aware of his brilliance and comfortable in the knowledge that the audience was with him, 'Soapy Sam' spoke (*L.L.* I, 183) "for a full half an hour with inimitable spirit, emptiness and unfairness". And he made the fatal error of an offensive personal inquiry about Huxley's own simian ancestry. "The Lord hath delivered him into mine hands", the still young biologist muttered to his neighbour Sir Benjamin Brodie (*L.L.* I, 184), and proceeded to enlist against his adversary the Victorians' high regard for purity, truthfulness and good taste.

He was careful not to rise until the meeting called for him—then he let himself go. His quiet gravity contrasting with the Bishop's smiling insolence, his triumph was complete. The many accounts of the episode differ in detail, but nothing conflicts with that which Huxley himself sent (*H.P.* 15. 115) to his friend Dyster in South Wales:

> Samuel thought it was a fine opportunity for chaffing a savan *[sic]*—However he performed the operation vulgarly & I determined to punish him—partly on that account and partly because he talked pretentious nonsense. So when I got up I spoke pretty much to the effect—that I had listened with great attention to the Lord Bishops speech but had been unable to discover either a new fact or a new argument in it—except indeed the question raised as to my personal predilections in the matter, of ancestry—That it would not have occurred to me to bring forward such a topic as that for discussion myself, but that I was quite ready to meet the Right Revd. prelate even on that ground—If then, said I the question is put to me would I rather have a miserable ape for a grandfather or a man highly endowed by nature and possessed of great means of influence & yet who employs those faculties & that influence for the mere purpose of introducing ridicule into a grave scientific discussion—I unhesitatingly affirm my preference for the ape. Whereupon there was inextinguishable laughter among the people —and they listened to the rest of my argument with the greatest attention. ... I think Samuel will think twice before he tries a fall with men of science again. ... I believe I was the most popular man in Oxford for full four & twenty hours afterwards.

Not everyone was pleased: when the Bishop of Worcester told his wife what had happened, she is said (Montague, 1959, 3) to have replied, "Descended from the apes! My dear, let us hope that it is not true, but if it is, let us pray that it will not become generally known." But Science had served notice on Theology that she would no longer be subservient, and one lady present fainted at the declaration of independence. In his quiet country retreat, far from the fray, Darwin received the news (*H.P.* 5. 123) with nervous chuckles of delight: "how durst you attack a live bishop in that fashion? I am quite ashamed of you! Have you no respect for fine lawn sleeves? By jove, you seem to have done it well!"

The validity of a theory is nowise determined by its consonance or conflict with popular opinion, or by the degree of readiness of experts to move in its direction, or by its convenience as ideological camouflage for vested interests, or by the personal characteristics of its proponents or opponents. All these, however, may markedly influence the speed with which a new theory gains ground, and this was conspicuously the case with Darwin's theory. The worst of the abuse was spent within a decade, and after another decade what opposition remained was thoroughly respectful. 'Darwin's bulldog' had done more than any man to compel that respect.

CHAPTER 7

Beyond Darwin

BECAUSE he fought so valiantly on Darwin's behalf, it is often imagined that Huxley shared all his views, but this was not at all the case. "I by no means suppose that the transmutation hypothesis is proven or anything like it", he told Lyell (*L.L.* I, 174) in the summer of 1859, "But I view it as a powerful instrument of research. Follow it out, and it will lead us somewhere; while the other notion is like all the modifications of 'final causation', a barren virgin." Even after the autumn publication of *The Origin*, Huxley remained vividly aware that there is a greater problem than why species vary—namely, why they remain so much themselves. He was fascinated by the contemplation of what might be the forces maintaining the unity of the individual, of the species, of the larger group; and he sometimes wondered, not that the changes of life through the ages have been so great, but that in some respects they have been so small. It was this sort of reservation on Huxley's part, arising partly from logical clarity and partly from philosophical depth, which caused Darwin to feel on occasion that his 'bulldog' was a less than whole-hearted supporter. And that was why, in his 1860 *Westminster Review* article (*C.E.* II, 78), after boldly asserting that Darwin's theory was "as superior to any preceding or contemporary hypothesis ... as was the hypothesis of Copernicus to the speculations of Ptolemy", Huxley went on to remind his readers, "But the planetary orbits turned out to be not quite circular after all, and, grand as was the service Copernicus rendered to science, Kepler and Newton had to come after him."

Unusually for his time, Huxley fully appreciated (*C.E.* II, 26) that "the word 'species' ... has a double sense and denotes two very different orders of relations ... two senses, or aspects, of 'species'—the one as morphological, the other as physiological". And, he explained (*H.P.* 19. 212) to Charles Kingsley, "[Darwin] *has* shewn that selective breeding is a *vera causa* for morphological species; but he has not yet shewn it a *vera causa* for physiological species". He believed that a skilful experimenter probably could, in time, produce the required proof, but as yet it had not been done.

It was apparent to Huxley that a great weakness in Darwin's presentation was its lack of any satisfactory theory of heredity, to explain the production and transmission of those so-called 'chance' or 'spontaneous' variations upon which natural selection acted. Moreover, he strongly suspected that Darwin was wrong in concentrating upon continuous variation to the almost complete exclusion of genetic 'jumps' or 'saltations'.

> Suppose that external conditions acting on a Species A, give rise to a new Species B... , [he wrote to Lyell (Amer. Phil. Soc. MS.) a few months before *The Origin* appeared].
> I know of no evidence to shew that the interval between the two species must *necessarily* be bridged over by a series of forms, each of which shall occupy, as it were, a fraction of the distance between A and B. ... In an organic compound having a precise & definite composition—you may effect all sorts of transmutations by substituting an atom of one element for an atom of another element—You may in this way produce a vast series of modifications—but each modification is definite in its composition & there are no transitional or intermediate stages between one definite compound & another. I have a sort of notion that similar laws of definite combination rule over the modifications of organic bodies.

And, as soon as he had read his advance copy of Darwin's book, he wrote (*L.L.* I, 176) to warn its author on this point: "you have loaded yourself with an unnecessary difficulty in adopting *Natura non facit saltum* so unreservedly".

In 1862 Huxley knew no more than most others about the fundamental genetical researches so soon to be published by the obscure Moravian monk Mendel in an equally obscure journal, but he understood exactly what was needed. "The great desideratum for the species question at present", he told Hooker (*H.P.* 2. 108), "seems to me to be the determination of the law of variation. Because no law has yet been made out, Darwin is obliged to speak of variation as if it were spontaneous or a matter of chance ... Why does not somebody go to work experimentally and get at the law ... for some one species of plant?" Huxley's own experimental work on heredity was negligible, but he seems to have had several glimpses, not only of some of the truths which Mendel was discovering, but also of much later genetic theory.

In 1869, for example, he made some suggestions (*C.E.* II, 115) in strikingly modern tone:

> It is a probable hypothesis, that what the world is to organisms in general, each organism is to the molecules of which it is composed. Multitudes of these, having diverse tendencies, are competing with one another for opportunity to exist and multiply ... hereditary transmission is the result of the victory of particular molecules contained in the impregnated germ. Adaptation to conditions is the result of the favouring of the multiplication of those molecules whose organising tendencies are most in harmony with such conditions ... the existence of an internal metamorphic tendency must be as distinctly recognised as that of an internal conservative tendency.

Then, nine years later, in an article for the ninth edition of *The Encyclopaedia Britannica*, he made a further suggestion (*C.E.* II, 203) which came close to the modern concept of allelomorphic genes: "it is conceivable, and indeed probable, that every part of the adult contains molecules, derived both from the male and from the female parent; and that, regarded as a mass of molecules, the entire organism may be compared to a web of which the warp is derived from the female and the woof from the male. ... The primitive male and female molecules may ... mould the assimilated nutriment, each according to its own type, into innumerable new molecules ... according to fixed laws." Passages like these, with such striking remarks (Thomson, 1925, 717) as that the protoplasm rather resembled "a sort of active crystal with the capacity of giving rise to a great number of pseudomorphs", make one regret that Huxley never worked systematically in the field of genetics.

Although he tentatively anticipated de Vries's 'mutationist' emphasis, Weismann's 'germinal selection' and Roux's 'Kampf der Teile in Organismus', Huxley's views attracted little attention at the time. It is perhaps not surprising that he was extremely dubious about Darwin's somewhat nebulous 'pangenesis' theory of heredity, with its suggestion that each tissue and organ gave off minute 'gemmules' which were spread about the body in the blood-stream and later recombined in the generative cells. When Darwin submitted the draft in 1865, Huxley tried to dissuade him from publishing this naïve suggestion—which, he pointed out, was in any event largely a restatement of earlier speculations by Buffon. But he preferred not to take the responsibility of virtually prohibiting publication, lest (*L.L.* I, 268) "Somebody rummaging about your papers half a century hence will find Pangenesis and say, 'See this wonderful anticipation of our modern theories, and that stupid ass Huxley prevented his publishing them'". Interestingly enough, geneticists today are not quite so certain that Darwin was absolutely wrong as they were only a decade ago. It might yet turn out that his strongly Lamarckian streak, in its search for a mechanism by which acquired characters could be inherited, had led him to an hypothesis curiously prophetic of modern views on the role of plasmagenes. However that may be, Huxley felt that the first requirement in this field was more experiment and, upon receiving Bateson's book *On Variation* in 1894, he wrote (*L.L.* II, 372) to say, "how glad I am to see . . . that we are getting back from the region of speculation into that of fact again". A year later he was dead, and five years after that the rediscovery of Mendel's papers put the experimental study of genetics for the first time on a firm basis. Still, even before effective experiment has been done, there is a place for disciplined speculation; and, on the centenary of Huxley's birth, Bateson (1925, 715) remarked, "Geneticists certainly are not likely to forget him".

Although Huxley considered that in some respects Darwin had assumed too much, he also thought him too timid in the application of his theory to *Homo sapiens*. In *The Origin,* Darwin had contented himself with the mild observation, "Light will be thrown on the origin of man and his history"—to which, greatly daring, he added in a later edition the preliminary intensifier, "Much". He had himself no real doubt that humans had also evolved; but, as he explained to Wallace (Darwin, F., 1887, II, 109) prior to publication, "I think I shall avoid the whole subject, as so surrounded with prejudices, though I fully admit that it is the highest and most interesting problem for the naturalist". Such a submission to prejudice was not in Huxley's nature. Owen had asserted that the brain of the gorilla differed more from that of man than it did from the brains of the lowest quadrumana, and this Huxley flatly denied. Nor was Bishop Wilberforce left long in ignorance of the undermining of his scientific adviser (Imperial College MS.):

> Professor Huxley presents his compliments to the Lord Bishop of Oxford —Believing that his Lordship has as great an interest in the ascertainment of the truth as himself, Professor Huxley ventures to draw the attention of the Bishop to a paper in the accompanying number of the *Natural History Review* "On the Zoological relations of Man with the Lower Animals". The Bishop of Oxford will find therein full justification for the diametrical contradiction with which he heard Prof. Huxley meet certain anatomical statements put forth at the first meeting of Section D, during the late session of the British Association at Oxford.

Owen had declared unambiguously that the structure known to anatomists as the *hippocampus minor* (a small eminence on one of the convoluted cerebral surfaces) occurred only in the human brain, and unambiguously he was wrong. "The fact is", Huxley commented (*H.P.* 2. 98), "he made a prodigious blunder in commencing the attack, and now his only chance is to be silent and let people forget the exposure."

But (Keith, 1925, 720) "Owen was blinded by the glamour of his own fame. ... He could not conceive that any one would be so foolhardy as to attempt to scale the battlements which the church had thrown round man's origin and divinity. Yet it was this foolhardy attempt which Huxley was to lead." Throughout 1860 he had been hard at work, examining every simian and primate specimen that he could lay hands on, with particular attention to their brains, hands and feet. He established that there was in fact a marked discontinuity in brain structure, but that it occurred between the lemurs and the higher monkeys and apes, and not between apes and humans. In the following spring, he gave a series of lectures to working men, on "The Relations of Man to the Rest of the Animal Kingdom", and the fat was really in the fire. *The Athenaeum* then reported a lecture in which Owen denied the existence of a hippocampus minor in the gorilla. A week later there was a somewhat sarcastic letter of correction from Huxley; the following week a brief rejoinder by Owen; the next week a decisive rebuttal by Huxley with the pungent concluding sentence (*Athenaeum*, 13 April 1861), "Life is too short to occupy oneself with the slaying of the slain more than once". Before the month was out, almost every literate person in the land was familiar with the word "hippocampus", until then an esoteric technical term known only to anatomists.

Owen had lost the opportunity to give way gracefully and, in consequence, his fall was the more resounding. There were innumerable cartoons and squibs, of which one, over the signature of "Gorilla" and addressed from "The Zoological Gardens", included this account (*Punch*, 18 May 1861) of the controversy:

> Then HUXLEY and OWEN,
> With rivalry glowing,
> With pen and ink rush to the scratch;
> Tis Brain *versus* Brain,
> Till one of them's slain;
> By Jove! it will be a good match!...

Next HUXLEY replies
That OWEN he lies
And garbles his Latin quotation;
That his facts are not new,
His mistakes not a few,
Detrimental to his reputation.

To twice slay the slain,
By dint of the Brain
(Thus HUXLEY concludes his review),
Is but labour in vain
Unproductive of gain,
And so I shall bid you "Adieu!"

For the lower orders, less likely to smile quietly at *Punch* than to chortle
over the vigorous burlesque pamphlets of the time, there was (Anon.,
1863) *A report of a SAD CASE Recently tried before the Lord Mayor,
OWEN versus HUXLEY. In which will be found fully given the Merits of
the great Recent BONE CASE*, with page after page of this sort of stuff:

> *Policeman X*—"Well, your Worship, Huxley called Owen a lying Orthognathous
> Brachycephalic Bimanous Pithecus; and Owen told him he was nothing but a
> thorough Archencephalic Primate."
> *Lord Mayor*—"Are you sure you heard this awful language?"

Even the infants of England heard obscure echoes of the case when *The
Water Babies* was read to them at bedtime. If an actual water baby had
ever been found, Kingsley (1863, 172) suggested, "they would have put
it into spirits, or into the Illustrated News, or perhaps cut it into two
halves, poor dear little thing, and sent one to Professor Owen, and one
to Professor Huxley, to see what they could each say about it". (Although
it is doubtful if many juvenile readers recognised the hippocampus
minor in its new jocular guise of a "hippopotamus major".)

Following his lectures to London working men in the spring of 1861,
Huxley was invited to give two addresses on "The Relation of Man to the
Lower Animals" at the Philosophical Institute of Edinburgh. "Fancy
unco' guid Edinburgh requiring illumination on the subject!", he joked
to his wife (*L.L.* I, 192). "They know my views, so if they do not like
what I shall have to tell them, it is their own fault." Rather to his surprise,
Huxley's audience received him well, but outside the lecture hall it was
different. The Presbyterian *Witness* (11 January 1862) came out with a

furious attack on this "blasphemous contradiction to biblical narrative and doctrine ... the vilest and beastliest paradox ever vented in ancient or modern times amongst Pagans or Christians", and in fine sarcasm it suggested that the meeting should have resolved itself into a Gorilla Emancipation Society. When Huxley gathered together the substance of his writings and lectures on this topic, and worked them into *Evidences as to Man's Place in Nature*, Lyell took fright. "I hope you send none of these *dangerous* sheets to press without Mrs. Huxley's imprimatur", he wrote (*H.P.* 6. 70) upon seeing the proofs. But Huxley was not the man to be held back by such a warning and, despite (or perhaps aided by) virulent press attacks, the book was an immediate and immense success. Thirty-one years later, Huxley looked back (*C.E.* VII, xi) and drew the moral:

> I doubt not that there are truths as plainly obvious and as generally denied as those contained in "Man's Place in Nature", now awaiting enunciation. If there is a young man of the present generation, who has taken as much trouble as I did to assure himself that they are truths, let him come out with them, without troubling his head about the barking of the dogs of St. Ernulphus. 'Veritas praevalebit' —some day; and, even if she does not prevail in his time, he himself will be all the better and the wiser for having tried to help her.

By the mid-1860s, both the uniformitarian geologists and the evolutionary biologists were facing a serious challenge from the mathematical physicists. With enormous confidence—indeed, one may perhaps say, with some intellectual arrogance—Thomson (later Lord Kelvin) proceeded to cut down the age of the solar system which had so recently come to appear almost unbounded. Calculations of the rate of dissipation of the sun's radiant energy limited its possible past duration and future continuance. Calculations of the slowing of the earth's rotation by the frictional effect of the tides imposed severe limitations upon the age of the earth. Calculations of the cooling of the world's crust greatly constricted the period during which it had been cool enough for the development of life. Losing nerve before the weight of the physicists' attack, both geologists and biologists began to retreat. Darwin himself (Eiseley, 1959, 235) found Thomson "an odious spectre" and started to play once more with the Lamarckian idea of inheritance of habit. Huxley, however, was not convinced that the case of the physicists was so immaculate as either they or the scientific world in general tended to conceive it.

In his 1869 Presidential Address to the Geological Society, on "Geological Reform", he counter-attacked on three fronts. He challenged Thomson's basic preconceptions about the physical nature of the phenomena on which his mathematical operations had been performed. He challenged the view that a shortened time-span for the earth necessarily disallowed the theory of natural selection. And he challenged the general tendency to assume that an argument is automatically strengthened by its employment of an impressive mathematical apparatus. On the first score, he argued that there was no real certainty about the current theory of the sun's heat (as being merely an initial quantity undergoing continual dissipation) and also suggested that there might be a continuous new source of heat in unknown chemical activities within the earth. On the second score, he pointed out (*C.E.* VIII, 329) that "The only reason we have for believing in the slow rate of the change in living forms is the fact that they persist through a series of deposits which, geology informs us, have taken a long while to make. If the geological clock is wrong, all the naturalist will have to do is to modify his notions of the rapidity of change accordingly." On the third score—and this is a point which needs making more often today—he declared (*id.* 232),

> I do not presume to throw the slightest doubt upon the accuracy of any of the calculations made by such distinguished mathematicians. . . . But I desire to point out that this seems to be one of the many cases in which the admitted accuracy of mathematical processes is allowed to throw a wholly inadmissible appearance of authority over the results obtained by them. Mathematics may be compared to a mill of exquisite workmanship, which grinds you stuff of any degree of fineness; but, nevertheless, what you get out depends upon what you put in; and as the grandest mill in the world will not extract wheat-flour from peascods, so pages of formulae will not get a definite result out of loose data.

At that time, of course, Huxley had no more knowledge than anybody else about atomic transformation or radioactivity or nuclear energy. What he did have was a vivid awareness that the universe is vastly more complex and subtle in its nature than the science of his time had yet conceived. He refused to be intellectually intimidated by physicochemical any more than by biological or theological received opinion, and he had a fertile imagination of what conceivably might be. In the second decade of the century, Prout had postulated that the chemical elements were constituted of common sub-atomic units, but few gave any credence to this view. By the mid-1850s most chemists simply ridiculed suggestions along these lines. Even when, in the 1860s and later, it became necessary to recognise that Mendeléev's periodic table had indeed established some real pattern among atomic weights, people thought in terms of an existing condition rather than of a continuing process. It is thus of considerable interest that, at least as early as 1887, Huxley had perceived (*C.E.* I, 77 and 79) that

> In the living world, facts of this kind are now understood to mean evolution from a common prototype. It is difficult to imagine that in the not-living world they are devoid of significance. Is it not possible, nay, probable, that they may mean the evolution of our 'elements' from a primary undifferentiated form of matter? ... The idea that atoms are absolutely ingenerable and immutable 'manufactured articles' stands on the same sort of foundation as the idea that biological species are 'manufactured articles' stood thirty years ago. ... It seems safe to prophesy that the hypothesis of the evolution of the elements from a primitive matter will, in future, play no less a part in the history of science than the atomic hypothesis.

In the same essay, after outlining the then current view of matter and energy, he pointed out (*id.* 103) that "it is possible to raise the question whether this universe of simplest matter and definitely operating energy ... may not itself be a product of evolution from a universe of such matter, in which the manifestations of energy were not definite—in which, for example, our laws of motion held good for some units and not for others, or for the same units at one time and not at another". Perhaps even more surprising, from a nineteenth-century biologist, was this comment (*id.* 94): "It seems safe to look forward to the time when the conception of attractive and repulsive forces, having served its purpose as a useful piece of scientific scaffolding, will be replaced by the deduction of the phenomena known as attraction and repulsion, from the general laws of motion."

Yet we should not be too surprised by these bold speculations. They were the natural outcome of Huxley's general refusal to remain intellectually cramped by contemporary conceptions of the nature of things. As early as 1863 he had written (*L.L.* I, 242),

> I know nothing of Necessity, abominate the word Law (except as meaning that we know nothing to the contrary), and am quite ready to admit that there may be some place, 'other side of nowhere', *par example*, where $2+2 = 5$, and all bodies naturally repel one another instead of gravitating together. I don't know whether Matter is anything distinct from Force. I don't know that atoms are anything but pure myths. ... In other words, I believe in Hamilton, Mansel and Herbert Spencer so long as they are destructive, and I laugh at their beards as soon as they try to spin their own cobwebs.

It was this sort of wide-ranging scientific acuity and philosophical bent which so immensely impressed Huxley's contemporaries, and which makes a similar impact today on anyone who will take the trouble to read his writings. We can understand why his biologist friends were continually urging him to devote all his energies to science, and not 'squander' them on scientific education and organisation. But he made his decision with eyes wide open: the times continually called for him to flex his muscles in the great world of affairs as well as at his laboratory bench, and we should be grateful that he did so.

CHAPTER 8

A decade of daily life

It is impossible to make any proper assessment of Huxley without understanding how his daily life was lived. It will be instructive to take one decade, neither his busiest nor the least busy, and look at the vast range of activities in which he was engaged. In 1859 he was still the brilliant nova in the scientific firmament, coruscating to the terror or delight of his observers, but as yet without much financial security or any established place in society. By 1869 he was recognised everywhere as a scientist of the solidest standing, he was very much the family man with seven sturdy children, his income was approaching £2000 per annum, and he was in demand on all sides for influential committees and commissions.

Huxley's teaching and regular palaeontological research at the School of Mines always had first claim on his time, but early in 1859 he also began a systematic study of the dog family. Then he learned that a London publisher was taking over the sadly ailing *Natural History Review*, which looked like dying in Dublin—and that, as he told Hooker (*H.P.* 2. 67), "if I chose to join as one of the editors, the effectual control would be pretty much in my own hands". This seemed an ideal opportunity to realise his long-cherished dream of a not-too-specialised scientific quarterly, and doubtless he was attracted by the prospect *(ibid.)* that "The tone of the Review will be mildly episcopophagous". So, despite the advice of friends not to take on this extra burden, he went ahead. He was also feeling rather cock-a-hoop at this time over the successful outcome of a petition, which he had promoted two years earlier, asking the University of London to establish degrees in science. In 1860 England's first B.Sc. was instituted, very much along the lines which he had recommended.

In this same year Huxley felt obliged, as Secretary of the Geological Society, to oppose the admission of women to its meetings. This action, superficially so alien to his generally liberal outlook, has been rather widely quoted against him, but there is no reason to doubt the explanation (*L.L.* I, 212) which he gave to Lyell:

> the Geological Society is not, to my mind, a place of education for students, but a place for discussion for adepts. ... I am far from wishing to place any obstacle in the way of the intellectual advancement of women. On the contrary, I don't see how we are to make any permanent advancement while one half of the race is sunk, as nine-tenths of women are, in mere ignorant parsonese superstition. ... I have fully made up my mind ... to give my daughters the same training in physical science as their brother will get. ... They, at any rate, shall not be got up as man-traps for the matrimonial market. If other people would do the like the next generation would see women fit to be the companions of men in all their pursuits.

In the autumn of 1860, while his summer triumph over the Bishop of Oxford was still reverberating around the land, Huxley suffered what was perhaps the most traumatic loss of his life. On 20 September, getting out his long-disused adolescent notebook *(Thoughts and Doings)*, he made this final entry: "And the same child, our Noel, our first-born, after being for nearly four years our delight and our joy, was carried off by scarlet fever in forty-eight hours.... On Saturday night the fifteenth, I carried him here into my study, and laid his cold still body here where I write.... Amen, so let it be." Charles Kingsley sent consolations of conspicuous charity, but by this time Huxley knew that he no longer had any religious belief to bring him comfort, and even in extreme despair he would not delude himself. "My convictions, positive and negative", he replied (*L.L.* I, 219), "on all matters of which you speak, are of long and slow growth and are firmly rooted. ... I have searched over the grounds of my belief, and if wife and child and name and fame were all to be lost to me one after the other as the penalty, still I will not lie." Fortunately, some solace came in December, when Leonard (Julian's father) was born, and so called to contain the dead Noel's name in his own. Also fortunately, Huxley had not too much time for introspection, being kept pretty fully occupied by lectures at South Kensington to teachers, lectures at Jermyn Street to working men, checking the proofs of Herbert Spencer's *First Principles*, and speaking on behalf of the Literary Fund as a scientist who believed (*L.L.* I, 215) that "Science and Literature are not two things, but two sides of one thing".

After spending the last week of 1860 climbing in Wales with Tyndall, Huxley began an equally busy 1861. His wife, still badly ailing, took the children for a quiet holiday with the Darwins at Down, followed by three months' convalescence at Folkestone. In order that she should not return to a home of sad memories, Huxley sold their house whilst she was away and moved to 26 Abbey Place (now Abercorn Place). He was researching at this time on the embryology of the chick's skull, but his major scientific memoir was the "Preliminary Essay upon the Systematic Arrangement of the Fishes of the Devonian Epoch". He was now deeply involved in producing the first four quarterly numbers of his *Natural History Review*, but also found time to help with the examinations of the Science and Art Department, to aid Elizabeth Garrett (Anderson) when all medical schools were closed against her on account of her sex, and to study philosophy through the small hours of the night. No wonder that his friends were worried about his over-work and that Hooker (*L.L.* I, 229) urged him, "Do take the counsel of a quiet looker on and withdraw to your books and studies in pure Natural History; let modes of thought alone. You may make a very good naturalist, or a very good meta-physician (of that I know nothing, don't despise me), but you have neither time nor place for both."

At the very beginning of 1862 there came Huxley's scandalous Edinburgh lectures on "The Relation of Man to the Lower Animals"—delivered, as he told Dyster (*H.P.* 15. 106), in the belief that "After all, it is as respectable to be modified monkey as to be modified dirt". To his audience he put the same point more positively (*L.L.* I, 193): "thoughtful men, once escaped from the blinding influence of traditional prejudices, will find in the lowly stock whence man has sprung the best evidence of the splendour of his capacities; and will discern, in his long progress through the past, a reasonable ground of faith in his attainment of a nobler future". He was scarcely back in London before finding himself immersed in a novel investigation bearing closely on human origins. The Neanderthal skull had been attributed (Eiseley, 1959, 273) to "one of the wild races of north-western Europe spoken of by Latin writers"; J. W. Dawson (*di.* 274) thought that "It may have belonged to one of those wild men, half-crazed, half-idiotic, cruel and strong, who are always more or less to be found living on the outskirts of barbarous tribes"; and even the great Virchow misinterpreted it as a pathological specimen. Lyell, like everybody else, was confused by the conflicting testimony and, before completing his *Antiquity of Man*, asked Huxley to provide authoritative anatomical data and diagrams. Huxley's task was not an easy one for, as Irvine (1955, 23) has put it, "He was trying to be an anthropologist before anthropology had really been invented". The only thing to do was to invent it, and Huxley proceeded to devise a series of quantitative indices for, and the first real *rationale* of, craniology. His methods, described in *Man's Place in Nature*, were still being used over sixty years later, when Keith (1925, 721) compared the book, in the completeness and convincingness of its proofs, with Harvey's *De Motu Cordis*.

In February, Huxley found himself called on, at short notice, to deliver the Geological Society's Anniversary Address in the absence of the President through illness. "I am going to criticise Palaeontological doctrines in general", he told Hooker (*L.L.* I, 204), "in a way that will flutter their nerves considerable. ... I mean to turn round and ask, 'Now, Messieurs les Palaeontologues, what the devil *do* you really know?'" According to Lyell (*L.L.* I, 205),

> Huxley delivered a brilliant critical discourse on what palaeontology has and has not done ... a masterly sketch comparing the past and present in almost every class in zoology, and sometimes of botany ... which he said he had done because it was useful to look into the cellars and see how much gold there was there, and whether the quantity of bullion justified such an enormous circulation of paper. I never remember an address listened to with such applause, though there were many private protests against some of his bold opinions.

Unfortunately, one of Huxley's main points, that the assumption of contemporaneity between rocks of similar fossil content and stratigraphic situation is unwarranted (and often misleading), is not always heeded even today. In May, Huxley was admitted M.R.C.S.—presumably a formality necessary before he could be appointed Examiner and Hunterian Professor to the Royal College of Surgeons. He was still examining at London University, working to widen the range of university Exhibitions awarded in the sciences, bringing out successive numbers of *The Natural History Review*, publishing palaeontological papers especially on labyrinthodonts and fossil crustaceans, and collaborating with Ernst Haeckel on radiolarian ocean deposits. Betweenwhiles, he served on his first Royal Commission (on the Scottish fisheries), lectured to his London working men and to miscellaneous audiences in Scotland and Ireland, studied Swiss glaciers with Tyndall and Lubbock, and formed in Cambridge an unfortunately short-lived "Society for the Propagation of Common Honesty in All Parts of the World". Otherwise, apart from seeing to his wife when their third daughter Rachel was born, he seems to have been no busier in 1862 than usual.

In the following year, when his brother George died leaving his finances in a sorry state, Huxley had to sell his Royal Medal for its value as gold in order to help the widow. Throughout 1863 the Fisheries Commission took up an increasing amount of time, but he managed to carry on a good deal of palaeontological and a certain amount of ethnological research, and also to see his first book, *Man's Place in Nature*, through the press. In London, he added a series of ten lectures for the general public to his annual series for working men, while in the provinces he gave a series of lectures at Hull Royal Institution and others at Leeds and elsewhere. He found himself caught up in the controversy about Colenso, the unorthodox Bishop of Natal, and engaged in lengthy correspondence with Kingsley on philosophy and religion. "If you tell me that an Ape differs from a Man because the latter has a soul and the ape has not", he wrote (*L.L.* I, 243), "I can only say that it may be so; but I should uncommonly like to know how you know either that the ape has not one or that the man has." But life was not all work and argument, and Huxley must have felt the peculiar pleasure of tickled vanity when, after dinner one night, he was able to note (*L.L.* I, 248), "I have come to the conclusion that our friend Bob [Sir Robert Lowe] is a most admirable, well-judging statesman, for he says I am the only man fit to be at the head of the British Museum [presumably Natural History], and that if he had his way he would put me there."

By 1864 Huxley had an income of £950 plus royalties, so that, despite continuing help to less affluent relatives, he could face with comparative equanimity the arrival of their sixth child, Nettie. But he could still not entirely conceal his annoyance at the ceremony of baptism which, he said (Lubbock MS.), his wife looked upon as "a kind of spiritual vaccination without which the youngsters might catch Sin in worse forms as they grow up". This year saw the publication of his second and third books (the *Elements of Comparative Anatomy* and the *Atlas of Comparative Osteology*), another study of the Neanderthal remains, four substantial papers on animal fossils, and his "Criticisms on 'The Origin of Species'". This last was a compendious rebuttal of criticisms of Darwin's theory made by Kölliker (for whom Huxley had a high regard) and Flourens (for whom —rather unfairly—he had very little). He was perhaps unduly unkind in describing the latter (*C.E.* II, 98) as "displaying a painful weakness of logic and shallowness of information [whilst assuming] a tone of authority which always touches upon the ludicrous, and sometimes passes the limits of good breeding"; but that was punishment for Flourens's demeaning of *The Origin*'s author as a person. "Hang the two scalps in your wigwam!", Huxley wrote (Darwin, F., 1887, III. 28) to Darwin at Down. "If I do not pour out my admiration... I shall explode!", came the contented chortle in reply (*H.P.* 2. 129). Apart from such activities as these, Huxley gave a series of lectures to working men on "The Various Races of Mankind", was appointed to his second Royal Commission, and persuaded a group of eminent scientists to join him in conducting science examinations for teachers from the ordinary elementary schools. "The English nation", he explained (*H.P.* 2. 129), "will not take science from above, so it must get it from below. We the doctors, who know what is good for it, if we cannot get it to take pills, must administer our remedies *par derrière.*"

But perhaps the most important thing that Huxley did in 1864 was to help organise the *X* Club, barely remembered today but for nearly thirty years a powerful *sub rosa* influence on English science. Its nine members (Busk, Frankland, Hirst, Hooker, Huxley, Lubbock, Herbert Spencer, Spottiswoode and Tyndall) mustered between them a Secretary, Foreign Secretary, Treasurer and three successive Presidents of the Royal Society, six Presidents of the British Association, and several officers of the Geological and Linnean and Ethnological Societies. No tenth member was ever elected, all suggestions being negatived by tacit agreement that any new name must contain all the consonants not included in the names of the original nine. So, for some 240 meetings, the *X* stood in triple symbolism for the originally envisaged ten, the missing tenth, and the permanently undecided name of the club. They always dined immediately before meetings of the Royal Society, and Huxley was one day highly amused to overhear (*L.L.* I, 259) a conversation between two distinguished members of the Athenaeum: "I say, A.", asked B., "do you know anything about the *X* Club?"; to which A. replied, "Oh, yes, B., I have heard of it. What do they do?" "Well", said B. in summary judgment, "they govern scientific affairs, and really, on the whole, they don't do it badly."

During 1864–5, as Keith (1925, 722) has perhaps somewhat overstated it, Huxley "encircled the earth as a hovering anthropological hawk", and the outcome was his "Methods and Results of Ethnology". Only ten years earlier, the Asiatic Society of Bengal had received an account of primitive tribes barely distinguishing them from orang-outangs, while as recently as 1862 a speaker at the British Association had compared the

Negro with a foetal and the Mongol with a new-born European. Huxley cut clean through the common confusion between biological nature on the one hand and cultural characteristics on the other, and in particular pointed out the dangers of relying on philology as a guide to ethnic origins. And, in a passage of conspicuous modernity (*C.E.* VII, 209), he emphasised, "I speak of 'persistent modifications' or 'stocks' rather than of 'varieties', or 'races', or 'species', because each of these last well-known terms implies, on the part of its employer, a preconceived opinion touching one of those problems, the solution of which is the ultimate object of the science; and in regard to which, therefore, ethnologists are especially bound to keep their minds open." This was the year which saw the defeat of the South in the American Civil War, during which Huxley's warm concern for his young nephew, fighting in the Confederate Army, was outbalanced by his conviction that slavery was immoral. Now that the North had won, he wrote for *The Reader* an article on "Emancipation —Black and White", in which he emphasised the fact that the female half of the species had still not been emancipated.

Huxley believed that women were unlikely ever to surpass (or perhaps even to equal) men in either physique or intellect, but he was in no doubt about what the proper position of women in society should be. "With few insignificant exceptions", he wrote (*C.E.* III, 71),

> girls have been educated either to be drudges, or toys, beneath men; or a sort of angels above him. ... The possibility that the ideal of woman-kind lies neither in the fair saint, nor in the fair sinner ... that women are meant neither to be men's guides nor their playthings, but their comrades, their fellows, and their equals, so far as Nature puts no bar on that equality, does not seem to have entered into the minds of those who have had the conduct of the education of girls.

And, for those who asked what was the first step towards a better state of things, he had a simple answer (*id.* 72):

> We reply, emancipate girls. Recognise the fact that they share the senses, perceptions, feelings, reasoning powers, emotions, of boys, and that the mind of the average girl is less different from that of the average boy, than the mind of one boy is from that of another; so that whatever argument justifies a given education for boys, justifies its application to girls as well. So far from imposing artificial restrictions upon the acquirement of knowledge by women, throw every facility in their way. ... Let us have 'sweet girl graduates' by all means. They will be none the less sweet for a little wisdom; and the 'golden hair' will not curl less gracefully outside the head by reason of there being brains within.

In the November of 1865, Huxley gave Lyell a progress-report on the results of his palaeontological investigations in Ireland. "Being attracted vulture-wise by the scent of a quantity of carboniferous corpses ..." he wrote (*L.L.* I, 264), "I turned out ten genera of vertebrate animals of which five are certainly new ... I reckon there are now about thirty genera of labyrinthodonts known from all parts of the world and all deposits. Of these eleven have been established by myself in the course of the last half-dozen years." During the following year he produced papers on vertebrate remains from Kilkenny and on dinosaurs from South Africa, while his work on primitive fish clearly defined the fossil *Coelacanthidae*. The coelacanths had changed very little throughout the immense period of time from the Lower Carboniferous to the Upper Cretaceous, and formed one of the most remarkable of what Huxley called "persistent types". Had he been still alive a century later, he would have been one of the very few not almost incredulous when a living specimen was brought up by fishermen off the coast of Africa. During 1866 Huxley also described some prehistoric human skulls and skeletons discovered in Caithness, and took the opportunity to dispel a few traditional myths about the so-called Celtic and Saxon 'races'. He also delivered a series of ethnological lectures at the Royal Institution, and then tried (*L.L.* I, 276) to provoke Kingsley to a salutary exercise from the same rostrum: "I wonder if you are going to take the line of showing up the superstitions of men of science. Their name is legion, and the exploit would be a telling one."

Later that year, he was distressed to find himself in public opposition to both Kingsley and Tyndall over 'the Jamaica affair', in which a negro called Gordon had been executed under martial law for his alleged leadership of an insurrection. Huxley joined a committee which sought to have Governor Eyre tried for murder, insisting that the personal merits of Eyre and Gordon were quite irrelevant—for, he argued in the *Pall Mall Gazette* (31st October 1866), "unless I am misinformed, English law does not permit good persons, as such, to strangle bad persons, as such". And he set himself squarely (*L.L.* I, 282) against "The hero-worshippers who believe that the world is to be governed by its great men, who are to lead its little ones, justly if they can; but if not, unjustly drive or kick them the right way."

Other matters requiring attention during 1866 were the arrival of Ethel, his eighth child (Henry had come a year earlier); a visit to Cambridge to check on progress in the provision of facilities for scientific study; and yet another Commission, this time on the proposed Royal College of Science for Ireland. His educational interests were now deepening and, as President of Section D at the British Association meetings in Nottingham, he deplored the increasing narrowness of scientific specialisation and urged the importance of an adequate general scientific education in the schools. Towards the end of the year his brilliant little *Lessons in Elementary Physiology* appeared, with a profound influence on the development of biological education in the schools. But the most remarkable educational event of 1866 was undoubtedly the opening at Isleworth of the International College which, with Huxley and Tyndall among its governors, provided a fascinating and successful experiment in the common schooling of a wide range of nationalities (including French, Germans, Spaniards, Portuguese, Indians, Americans, Brazilians, Chilians, Nicaraguans and a negro from Bermuda).

Early in 1867 Huxley was busy with some fossil ichthyosaurs from Spitzbergen; but his main research was turning to the anatomy of birds, thitherto classified largely on the lines of their feeding habits, footwebbing, beaks and the like. He produced a new system of classification based mainly on palate and other bone structures, but never found time for more than partial publication. Ethnology was also interesting him more and more, and he gave two addresses at Birmingham, "On the Character, Distribution, and Origin of the Principal Modifications of Mankind". By this time his studies had quite convinced him that there were no grounds for believing that Europeans were biologically superior to Africans or that primitive peoples were constitutionally incapable of cultural advancement, and he went straight to the sexual centre of racial prejudice by arguing that miscegenation was harmful only where social conditions made it so.

Miscellaneous activities were as numerous in this year as in most others. In January he concluded a scientific lecture to a large audience in Chancery Lane by drawing attention to the appalling privations of the East End's unemployed, and proceeded to make a substantial collection in a human cranium lying conveniently to hand. In February he began a series of meetings with progressive schoolmasters to work out ways of getting science into the 'public' schools which catered for the children of the wealthy. In April he went to Brittany with Lubbock and Hooker to examine prehistoric remains. During the summer, he was urging on both Dohrn and Haeckel the merits of marriage and family life, in terms which charmingly reflected his own domestic happiness. By October, his schoolmaster allies were becoming despondent in their efforts at curricular reform, so he sent encouraging but typically acute advice to Farrar (1897, 152): "Do not despair ... you may depend on it victory is on your side—We or our sons shall live to see all the stupidity *in favour* of science & I am not sure that that will not be harder to bear than the present state of things." November saw him at the College of Preceptors, adding his weight to efforts at raising the professional status of teachers; in December he went to Sion College, the City's ancient centre of theological study, in a brave attempt to give the clergy some understanding of the antiquity of the earth and of man's place in it.

The following year found Huxley, if possible, busier than ever. There were five scientific memoirs, among them his one serious scientific bloomer—the establishment of the new species *Bathybius haeckelii*, which eleven years later turned out to be not a unicellular marine organism but a precipitate resulting from the action of preservatives upon ocean dredgings. He gave up his Fullerien Professorship at the Royal Institution, but other commitments accumulated. These included the Commission on Science and Art Instruction in Ireland, lectures at the Birmingham and Midland Institute, an exquisite address "On a Piece of Chalk" to the working men of Norwich, the annual meetings of the British Association, and the Royal Society of Arts conference on technical education. This year was also the beginning of Huxley's twelve years as honorary Principal of the South London Working Men's College, at whose opening he delivered his much-quoted address, "A Liberal Education and Where to Find It". The passages commonly quoted from this address do not, strangely enough, include such subversive remarks (*Q.J. Educ.*, February 1868) as, "Compare your average artisan and your average country squire, and I don't believe you will find a pin to choose between the two in point of ignorance, class feeling, or prejudice. ... Why should we be worse off under one regime than under the other?" But it is worth while to reprint once again his striking definition (*C.E.* III, 86) of his subject:

> That man, I think, has had a liberal education who has been so trained in youth that his body is the ready servant of his will, and does with ease and pleasure all the work that, as a mechanism, it is capable of; whose intellect is a clear, cold, logic engine, with all its parts of equal strength, and in smooth working order; ready, like a steam engine, to be turned to any kind of work, and spin the gossamers

as well as forge the anchors of the mind; whose mind is stored with a knowledge of the great and fundamental truths of Nature and of the laws of her operations; one who, no stunted ascetic, is full of life and fire, but whose passions are trained to come to heel by a vigorous will, the servant of a tender conscience; who has learned to love all beauty, whether of Nature or of art, to hate all vileness, and to respect others as himself. Such an one and no other, I conceive, has a liberal education; for he is, as completely as man can be, in harmony with Nature.

But the most publicised event of 1868 was Huxley's Sunday evening 'lay sermon' at Edinburgh, which proceeded from an exposition of the still fairly novel idea of the common protoplasmic basis of all life to its ruthlessly logical conclusion (*C.E.* I, 154): "It must be true, in the same sense and to the same extent, that the thoughts to which I am now giving utterance, and your thoughts regarding them, are the expression of molecular changes in that matter of life which is the source of our other vital phenomena." An outraged press greeted the lecture as gross and brutal materialism and, when it was published in the following year, it carried *The Fortnightly* into seven printings. We have the word of John Morley (1917, I, 90) for it that "No article that has appeared in any periodical for a generation back (unless it be Deutsch's article on the Talmud in the *Quarterly* of 1867) excited so profound a sensation as Huxley's memorable paper 'On the Physical Basis of Life' (1869). The stir was like the stir that in a political epoch was made by Swift's *Conduct of the Allies*, or Burke's *French Revolution*."

Much the same mixture of scientific research, regular teaching, public lectures and meetings of commissions and committees, combined with any number of other activities, continued through 1869. Huxley's five palaeontological papers were mainly upon the dinosaurs, which he saw as occupying a key position in the evolution of birds from reptiles. In developmental anatomy he published work on the skulls of mammals; in ethnology he had papers upon the peoples of India and North America; in general taxonomy there was his *Introduction to the Classification of Animals*. Once or twice during the year he crossed swords with the Positivists; lecturing engagements took him to Bradford, Leeds, Liverpool and Newcastle; and he gave his last full series of lectures at the Royal College of Surgeons. As President of the Ethnological Society, Huxley tried (without success) to persuade the government to build up a systematic series of uniformly posed photographs from every ethnic group in the British Empire. As President of the Geological Society, he delivered his striking address on "Geological Reform", in which he took up the challenge to evolutionary biology thrown down by Thomson and his fellow physicists. As a leading member of the newly founded Metaphysical Society, he would soon be preparing his scandalously ironic paper, "Has the Frog a Soul, and of What Nature is That Soul, Supposing it to Exist?" And, as perhaps its prime mover, he had the satisfaction in 1869 of introducing the first number of *Nature*.

Despite all these claims on his time, Huxley could not bring himself to deny a request by William Rogers, the liberal Rector of Bishopsgate, popularly known as 'Hang-theology Rogers', to demonstrate how science could be successfully taught to elementary schoolchildren. So, having stipulated (*L.L.* I, 309) that "we shall have a clear understanding on the part of boys and teachers that the discourses are to be *Lessons* and not talkee-talkee lectures", from April to June he took each week a large class of children with a considerable number of adult observers. Not surprisingly the thing snowballed, and in November he found himself teaching the elements of science to a class of women at South Kensington, under the happily invented heading "Physiography" (later to spread round the world as the title of his immensely successful elementary textbook of general science).

And so, year by year, the busy days went by. For recreation, there was an occasional opera or concert; at first there were furious games of fives with Herbert Spencer and then, as the children grew older, there were informal games of cricket and family walks through St. John's Wood. For reading, and for re-reading, there were Shakespeare and Milton and Goethe and Dante; there was Keats and somewhat later there was Meredith. There were regular meetings at the Graphic Society and, in later years, there were the Rabelais Club and the Literary Society and the Royal Academy. Before the children went to bed there might be half an hour amusing them by rapid sketchings or by sea stories or by carving absurd animals out of orange peel. Huxley was too busy to see as much of his children as he might have wished, but at least they were not kept upstairs with a governess: they met and talked and played with visitors of all degrees of eminence. "What I like about the family is the way they all seem to care so much for each other", wrote the future second Lady Monkswell (*T.H.H.* 233); and "the happy family" was a phrase used by Huxley's friends without any need of further identification.

CHAPTER 9

The organisation of knowledge

"PROFESSOR HUXLEY, the inventor of Protoplasm . . .", declared *Vanity Fair* (28 January 1871), "roam[s] over the deserts of the metropolis to the terror of the ecclesiastical police and the intense disgust of the respectable portion of society . . . but, with all his hardness and anti-transcendentalism, his geniality of temperament and his happy talent for illustration are hardly less remarkable than the logical clearness of his discourse. . . . Take him for all in all, there is no popular teacher who has contributed more to the awakening of the intellect, and whose career in the future may be more confidently associated in idea with all that is manly, and progressive in social science, and comprehensive, to say the least, in physical research." This was long before television had produced that modern phenomenon of the 'personality' whose every trivial word and action makes news; but, in that period of a varied and vigorous press, Huxley was the most news-worthy of men.

Throughout the decade of the 1870s he served as the immensely active Secretary of the Royal Society and at various times was President of the Geological Society, the Ethnological Society and the British Association. He was the most effective—indeed, the dominating—member of the first London School Board. He became Vice-President of the Working Men's Club and Institute Union, a Governor of Owens College and of Eton, and reforming Rector of Aberdeen University. For two summers he was professor *locum tenens* at Edinburgh; during a third he visited various universities in the U.S.A.; and in six years he served on four Royal Commissions. During two years of the decade, his health quite broken by overwork, he did virtually no laboratory research; yet from the other eight there came some thirty papers in the scientific periodicals. And, among the ten books which appeared from his pen in this period, there were his *Crayfish: an Introduction to the Study of Zoology*, his *Manual of the Anatomy of Vertebrated Animals*, his *Manual of the Anatomy of*

Invertebrated Animals and (jointly with H. N. Martin) his *Course of Practical Instruction in Elementary Biology.*

A striking feature of Huxley's scientific work was the manner in which, although conscientiously slogging away at whatever materials came in the course of his daily college duties, he always tried to organise the results into what his generation called a 'philosophic' framework. It was this conviction of the importance of general views which led him, on occasion, to rebuke other scientists who seemed too much tempted by the prospect of immediate even if isolated results. In the summer of 1865, for example, when Ernst Haeckel wanted Huxley to get him a place on a British governmental expedition, he received (*L.L.* I, 267) the very firm advice, "I would counsel you to stop at home, and as Goethe says, find your America here. ... It is the organisation of knowledge rather than its increase which is wanted just now." And Huxley practised what he preached. "Huxley's work", says D. M. S. Watson (1925), "stands in the greatest contrast to that of Owen, and indeed to that of all who had preceded him. In no single case did he describe a fossil simply because it was new. Every fact which he recorded was used for some definite purpose, for the elucidation of a point of morphology, or for its bearing on evolution." His detail of description was often inferior to that of Owen, and sometimes to that of other men such as Heinrich Pander and Alexander Kowalewsky, but nearly always his papers had some extra dimension of significance.

One has only to read Huxley's three great Addresses to the Geological Society to understand how this was achieved. Perfect clarity of communication avoided all ambiguity; clear-cut distinction between fact and opinion prevented the clouding of issues; wide-ranging knowledge permitted the perception of important relationships; and a lively imagination produced uninhibited and occasionally audacious hypotheses. In his 1862 Address, for example, he declined point-blank to assume that animal life necessarily began with the earliest forms which had been identified up to that date: he believed it likely (*C.E.* VIII, 304) that "the Palaeozoic, Mesozoic, and Cainozoic faunae and florae, taken together, bear somewhat the same proportion to the whole series of living beings which have occupied this globe, as the existing fauna and flora do to them". In the 1869 Address, at a time when most geologists were almost exclusively concerned with the post-Cambrian deposits and their contents, Huxley urged (*C.E.* VIII, 316) that geology should be conceived as "the history of the earth, in precisely the same sense as biology is the history of living beings", and advocated the study not merely of stratigraphic geology (the earth's "anatomy"), but also of the earth's developmental processes (its "telluric physiology") and of their fundamental causes ("geological aetiology"). In the Address of 1870, he argued against any assumption that evolution necessarily took place at similar rates in all groups or under all conditions, and suggested (*C.E.* VIII, 365) that "every class must be vastly older than the first [then known] record of its appearance upon the surface of the globe". He was, indeed, inclined to accept as genuinely fossil the *Eozoon* formations discovered by Dawson in Ontario—a view in which, after a long period of scepticism, he is followed today by those workers who regard them as the remains of immensely ancient organisms such as blue-green algae.

Earlier workers on fossil fish, including the great Louis Agassiz himself, had mainly produced detailed description of individual specimens: Huxley from the start began to investigate the relationships between different types, a procedure which ever since has been virtually taken for granted. As early as 1858, he had shown by careful comparative study that the very incomplete fossil remains known as *Cephalaspis* and *Pteraspis* were not the shells of cuttlefish but the head-shields of very primitive fish. And, although it was not then known that these creatures were agnaths ('jawless ones'), he made (1871, 129) the interesting comment, "Should jaws be absent, the *Cephalaspidae* would approach the *Marsipobranchii* [the group to which the blood-sucking lamprey belongs] more nearly than any of the other amphirhine fishes do".

Some workers today regard the possession of jaws as necessary to the category 'fish', and do not include the agnaths in this group. For them, the earliest true fish are the 'lobe-fins', which first occurred in the Lower Devonian rocks and had a jointed series of fin-bones believed to have evolved later into the limb-bones of the quadrupeds. Among them were the Crossopterygii ('fringe fins'), including the sub-group of *Coelacanthidae*, which has fins which were almost proto-feet and also possessed simple internal nostrils and air bladders in addition to gills. Huxley, like others, saw the obvious resemblances between the ancient coelacanths and the modern *Dipnoi* (the 'mud fish' of South America and Australia); but he was never one to let surface similarities obscure deeper differences. "It is a remarkable circumstance", he noted (*id.* 148), "that, while the Dipnoi present in so many respects, a transition between the piscine and the amphibian types of structure, the spinal column and the limbs should be not only piscine, but more nearly related to those of the most ancient Crossopterygian Ganoids than to those of any other fishes." Thus, whilst visualising evolution from fish to amphibia via something like the dipnoids, he made an important reservation which we now know to have been well justified.

At the lower end of the vertebrate scale, below even the near-fish agnaths, lies that curious little creature *Amphioxus*, the lancelet. Its blood, in which he demonstrated a mixture of vertebrate and invertebrate characters, had been the subject of the young Huxley's second research publication, prepared whilst waiting to set sail in *Rattlesnake*. In 1874 he returned to the species and was soon informing Haeckel (Uschmann and John, 1960, 23) of the outcome: "I have found the skull and brain of Amphioxus. ... Does this take your breath away? ... Well, in due time you shall be convinced. ... Amphioxus is nearer than could have been hoped to the condition of the primitive vertebrate." The so-called "skull" was no more than the very beginning of skeletal development in the cranial region, and the "brain" was so primitive and simple as scarcely to deserve that name, but it was precisely such extreme simplicity that Huxley had been seeking. His preliminary note to the Royal Society was unfortunately never followed by a fuller communication, nor its errors of detail corrected, but the key position of the lancelet in the evolution of the vertebrates (with its resemblances on the one hand to the '*Appendicularia*' larva of the ascidian sea-squirt and on the other hand to the '*Petromyzon*' larva of the lamprey) was quite firmly established.

At the other end of the evolutionary scale of the fishes lie the amphibia, and during the 1870s Huxley simply soaked himself in this group. "I am benevolent to all the world", he mused in one letter (*L.L.* I, 416) to W. K. Parker, "being possessed of a dozen live axolotls and four or five big dead mesobranchs. Moreover I am going to get endless Frogs and Toads by judicious exchange with Gunther. We will work up the Amphibia as they have not been since they were crea—— I mean evolved." But, although he once subscribed himself, "Ever yours amphibially", this was another job that unfortunately he never found time to finish.

Superficially, the amphibians seem to resemble the reptiles more than they do the fish, and the reptiles to resemble the amphibians more than they do the birds. By 1864, however, Huxley had dug down to a deep level of comparison and had established a basic tripartite division of the

Pencil sketch by Huxley of a scene in Mauritius, 1847, used as an illustration in *Diary of the Voyage of H.M.S. Rattlesnake*.

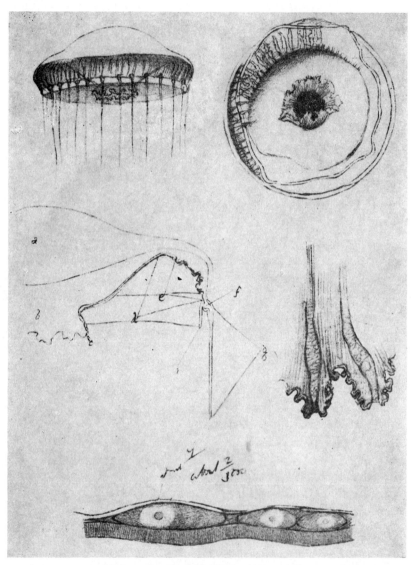

Pencil sketches by Huxley of a pelagic jelly-fish, 1848, used as an illustration in *Diary of the Voyage of H.M.S. Rattlesnake.*

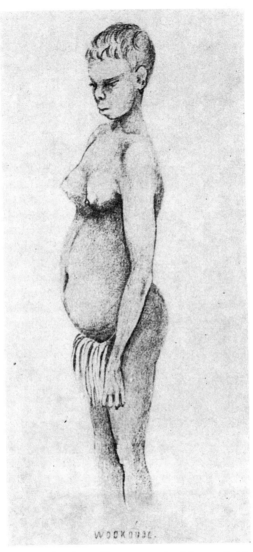

Pencil sketch by Huxley of an Australian woman aborigine, probably 1848, used as an illustration in *Diary of the Voyage of H.M.S. Rattlesnake*.

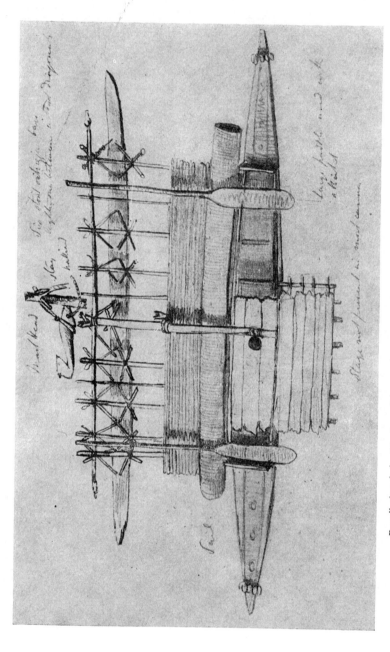

Pencil sketch by Huxley of an outrigger canoe in Louisiade Archipelago, 1849–50, used as an illustration in *Diary of the Voyage of H.M.S. Rattlesnake.*

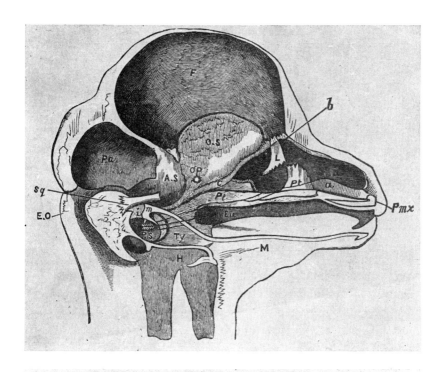

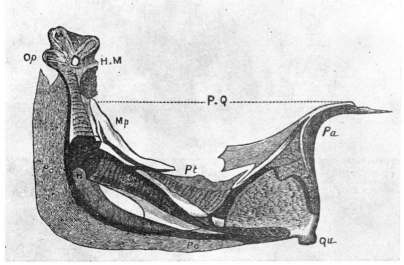

Diagrams illustrating the failure of the 'theory of the vertebrate skull', from Huxley's
paper in *Proc. Roy. Soc.* 1858.

the *norma verticalis* to the eye (fig. 5), its bulging sides completely hide the zygomatic arches. It is, therefore, in Mr. Busk's nomenclature, *cryptozygous*.

The *squama occipitis* has a well marked convexity, separated in

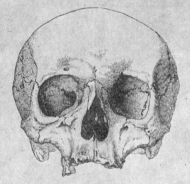

Fig. 3.   The skull *A*.   *Norma facialis.*   Fig. 3*a*.   The palate of the skull *A*.

the middle line by a depression (fig. 1) from the parietal region.   A slighter depression occurs on the middle of the coronal suture; but, neither in this region, nor elsewhere, can I discover any indications of artificial distortion, unless a certain amount of asymmetry of the

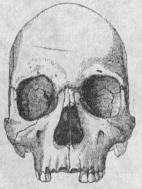

Fig. 4.   The skull *B*.   *Norma facialis.*   Fig. 4*a*.   The palate of the skull *B*.

occiput (fig. 5), produced by the flattening of the right side (probably from nursing) can be regarded as such.   The coronal suture is open, throughout its whole extent, on both the inner and the outer faces of the skull; as are the lambdoidal, occipito-mastoid, alisphenoidal,

Diagrams illustrating two widely contrasted forms of the human cranium, from Huxley's paper in *J. Anat. & Physiol.* 1867.

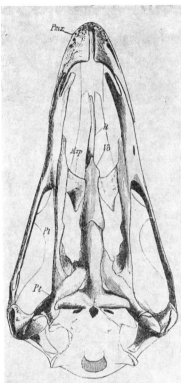

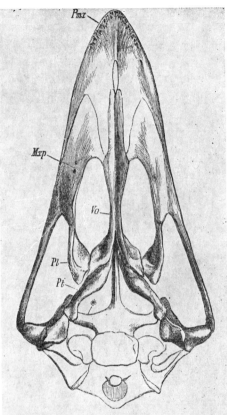

Fig. 1.—Under view of the skull of *Struthio camelus*. From a specimen in the Museum of the Royal College of Surgeons.

Pmx. The præmaxillæ. *R*. The sphenoidal rostrum. *Vo*. The vomer. *Pl*. The palatine bone. *Mxp*. The maxillo-palatine plate of the maxillary. *Pt*. The pterygoid.

Fig. 3.—Under view of the skull of *Dromæus novæ-hollandiæ*. (From a specimen in the Museum of the Royal College of Surgeons.)

Diagrams illustrating the classification of birds by cranial osteology, from Huxley's paper in *Proc. Zool. Soc.*, 1867.

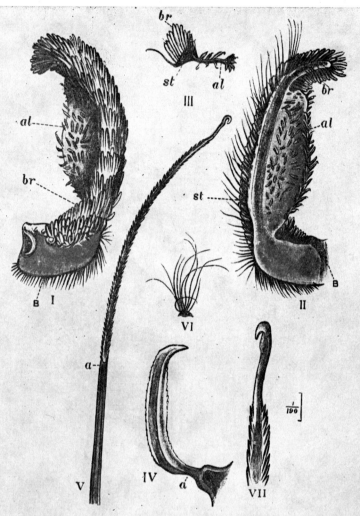

FIG. 6.—*Chæraps* (?).

I. The outer face of the podobranchia of the antepenultimate thoracic limb of the left side (× 3). II. The inner face of the same podobranchia: B, basal portion; *st*, stem; *al*, ala; *br*, branchial filaments. III. A transverse section of the middle of the podobranchia (× 3). IV. A sickle-shaped hook of a branchial filament $\frac{1}{180}$ of an inch in length. V. One of the coxopoditic setæ more highly magnified: *a*, the circumferential inflexion of the wall of the seta. The central canal does not stop at this point, but is continued to the end of the seta. VI. A bundle of coxopoditic setæ (× 3). VII. The extremity of one of the long setæ of the posterior edge of the stem. The vertical line represents $\frac{1}{190}$ of an inch magnified to the same extent.

Diagrams illustrating the fine morphology of a crayfish, from Huxley's paper in *Proc. Zool. Soc.*, 1878.

vertebrates. The fish and amphibia he put together in the *Ichthyopsida*, the reptiles and birds into the *Sauropsida*, with the *Mammalia* providing the third great group. Later zoologists have, of course, introduced many modifications, but in its time this grouping was a major advance. In 1870, in his address "Palaeontology and the Doctrine of Evolution", Huxley told the Geological Society (*C.E.* VIII, 382), "for my part, I entertain no sort of doubt that the Reptiles, Birds, and Mammals of the Trias are direct descendants of Reptiles, Birds and Mammals which existed in the latter part of the Palaeozoic epoch, but not in any present area of the dry land which has yet been explored by the geologist". He admitted that this might seem a bold assumption; and even today it will appear too bold to many scientists. When Huxley spoke, it was arguable—indeed, it is still arguable—whether any triassic (let alone earlier) fossils could properly be called "bird" or "mammal". It is noteworthy, however, that in fairly recent years J. Z. Young (1958, 487) has concluded that "Already in the early triassic period the small pseudosuchias [a type of bipedal lizard] ... showed the essential characteristics of the bird group". Even more recently, Gaylord Simpson (1960, I, 169) has emphasised that "Late mammal-like reptiles and earliest mammals now known intergrade so perfectly that anatomical definition depends arbitrarily on a single point", and he has produced a quantitative analysis showing that certain types had by triassic times achieved a 65% mammalian character. One wonders whether, after all, Huxley's bold belief may not yet be proved correct.

In 1875 Huxley produced a pregnant paper on *Stagonolepis Robertsoni*, an early reptile from the triassic rocks of Elgin (where, incidentally, he also cleared up considerable confusion by showing that the local sandstones consisted of two quite distinct series, differing in age by perhaps 100 million years). The bones were very incomplete and badly preserved, and he had to invent a new technique—the removal of the bones and the fabrication of casts from the resulting cavities—which has since been widely used. He pointed out the crocodilian nature of the armour and, simultaneously with Owen, showed that what Agassiz had identified as fish scales were in fact bony scutes. Widening out to a general examination of fossil crocodiles, he traced their gradual acquisition of the secondary bony palate which enables them to drown their prey under water, and divided the group into three evolutionary divisions. This must have been one of the very earliest attempts to produce such a classificatory scheme on a definitely evolutionary basis, but he disclaimed any assumption that evolution had necessarily taken place through the particular forms with which his own generation happened to be acquainted. It is also noteworthy that, so long ago as 1878, he was perfectly well aware that the concept embodied in the slogan "ontogeny repeats phylogeny" is a gross and often misleading oversimplification. The proper way to present the position, he suggested (*C.E.* II, 219), is "that the reptile embryo, at one stage of its development, is an organism which, if it had an independent existence, must be classified among fishes; and all the organs of the reptile pass, in the course of their development, through conditions which are closely analogous to those which are permanent in some fishes".

A reptile group of great interest to Huxley was that of the *Dinosauria*, so named by Owen to mean "terrifying lizards". They were not lizards and by no means all were terrifying; some in fact were quite small, while most were sluggish and probably quite inoffensive herbivores. There were, however, forms like *Brontosaurus*, weighing up to 40 tons and measuring up to 70 feet, and *Tyrannosaurus*, walking upright on its massive hind limbs and rearing its fierce-toothed mouth 20 feet above the ground. Huxley's studies of the Mesozoic reptiles were less extensive and less detailed than those by some of his contemporaries, but they were characteristically accompanied by careful work on related living forms and were marked by impressive generalising ability. He was one of the first to recognise the bird-like structure of the hind limbs and hips of dinosaurs such as *Iguanodon*, and he specially drew attention to the structural similarity between the leg bones of the bipedal dinosaurs and those of the half-hatched chick. At a time when many believed that the flying—or, more probably, gliding—pterosaurs were the nearest reptilian relations of the birds, Huxley saw through the superficial resemblances of habit to the deeper differences of skeletal organisation. "Thus", he told a New York audience (*C.E.* IV, 113) in 1876,

> though the pterodactyle is a reptile which has become modified in such a manner as to enable it to fly, and therefore, as might be expected, presents some points of resemblance to other animals which fly; it has, so to speak, gone off the line which leads directly from reptiles to birds, and has become disqualified for the changes which lead to the characteristic organisation of the latter class. Therefore ... the pterodactyles ... are not even approximately linear, in the sense of exemplifying those modifications of structure through which the passage from reptile to bird took place.

In the course of a comprehensive study of the skeletal structure of living and fossil birds, Huxley raised bird classification from a state somewhat resembling stamp collecting to that of a science. He recognised three great groups: the *Sauraurae*, initially consisting only of Archaeopteryx; the *Ratites*, consisting of extinct and extant non-flyers such as the ostrich and emu and cassowary; and the *Carinates*, which included the vast majority of species. Today there is some doubt whether his "Ratites" constitute a homogeneous grouping, but he had nevertheless made a major contribution to taxonomic method. According to Mitchell (1895), "His classification of birds, based in the main upon osteological characters, is the foundation of all modern classifications".

As part of this systematic study, Huxley published in 1868 a paper on the classification and distribution of the fowls and related forms (the *Alecteromorphae* and *Heteromorphae*), and proposed a simple but fundamental change in the accepted zoogeographical system. Philip Sclater had ten years earlier established six distributional regions, which he believed to represent six separate centres of creation, four in the eastern hemisphere and two in the western. The first four regions (Palaearctic, Ethiopian, Indian and Australian) he associated as "Palaeogea" and the latter two (Nearctic and Neotropical) as "Neogea". Huxley—apart, of course, from abandoning all theological preconceptions about centres of creation—proposed that the basic division should be on a latitudinal rather than a longitudinal basis, north against south rather than east against west. The Palaearctic, Nearctic, Ethiopian and Indian regions he grouped together as "Arctogea", and the Neotropical and Australian regions as "Notogea". The "Neotropical" region (South America extending about as far north as Mexico) he preferred to call "Austro-Columbian", pointing out that a very large part of it was far from tropical; the "Australian" region he preferred to call "Australasian", since it included Tasmania and some other large islands; and he distinguished New Zealand and its satellite islands as a separate "Novozelanian" province. In the main, Huxley's scheme was ignored or rejected by other workers in this field, but of more recent years things have begun to take a different turn. In 1954 K. P. Schmidt produced what has been widely accepted as the basic 'new' scheme of faunal regions, and it does not differ fundamentally from Huxley's. In 1957, after perhaps the most thorough zoogeographical studies since the days of Wallace, P. J. Darlington adopted Huxley's Arctogea (relabelled "Megagea") more or less as it stood, with only minor modifications of its four sub-provinces. In 1960 Fisher and Peterson once again mapped New Zealand as a distinct sub-region with its own distinctive sub-fauna. Leon Croizat (1960, 132) has even gone so far as to express the view that "Huxley was by far ahead of his contemporaries; and [his paper] makes me regret that Huxley did not eventually take the place of Wallace as the authority on dispersal." Croizat's eccentricities have made him suspect to many biologists, but in this judgement he may possibly be right.

In the case of mammals, as with birds, Huxley published comparatively few research papers, but those he did produce were of high quality. His 1861 paper on *Macrauchenia*, a three-toed camel-like fossil from Bolivia, was a model of exposition; as was his 1864 paper on the *Glyptodon* group, armadillo-like insectivores of which Argentina has yielded a considerable variety of fossil species. In 1870 he reviewed the horse-like fossils (especially the three-toed *Anchitherium* from the lower Miocene, and the somewhat more recent *Hipparion*) and asked (*C.E.* VIII, 359), "Is it not probable then, that, just as in the Miocene epoch, we find an ancestral form less modified than *Equus*, so, if we go back to the Eocene epoch, we shall find some quadruped related to the *Anchitherium*, as *Hipparion* is related to *Equus?*" Six years later, on a visit to the U.S.A., he examined Marsh's great collection of fossils at Yale and immediately saw the significance of its equine and near-equine specimens. Before setting sail home from New York, he used Marsh's detailed data to present, in a series of public lectures, a general scheme for the horse's ancestry. Today, with many more fossils to guide us, we can make a better estimate of the precise path of equine evolution, but this general scheme was not far wrong. He predicted (*C.E.* IV, 132) that, "when the still lower Eocene deposits, and those which belong to the Cretaceous epoch, have yielded up their remains of ancestral equine animals, we shall find, first, a form with four complete toes and a rudiment of the innermost or first digit in front, with, probably, a rudiment of the fifth digit in the hind foot; while in the still older forms, the series of digits will be more and more complete, until we come to the five-toed animals". The first of his prophecies was soon fulfilled in Eohippus *(Hyracotherium)*, a dog-sized fossil from the Eocene, discovered while his lectures were still going through the press.

The only other mammalian group on which Huxley did substantial work was the *Canidae*, the dog family. During 1879–80 he was absolutely immersed in this work, dissecting foxes and discovering some interesting glandular structures opening into the urethra, begging jackal skulls from friends in India and Ceylon, and in general bubbling over with the results of his investigations. "I wish it were not such a long story that I could tell you all about the dogs", he wrote (*L.L.* II, 10) to Darwin. "They will make out such a case for 'Darwinismus' as never was. From the South American dogs at the bottom (*C. vetulus, cancrivorus,* etc.) to the wolves at the top, there is a regular gradual progression." His work, he went on, had led him to the conclusion that *Canis familiaris* was a species of dual origin: "as to the domestic dogs, I think I can prove that the small dogs are modified jackals, and the big dogs ditto wolves. I have been getting capital material from India, and working the whole affair out on the basis of measurements of skulls and teeth." Whether he was right or wrong in this conclusion is not yet finally settled, and most people still believe that all the many varieties of the domesticated species of dog have been produced by artificial selection from a common progenitor. Multiple origins have, however, been demonstrated for some cultivated plants such as wheat and potato and maize, and the same might conceivably be true of some domesticated animals.

His work on the dog family produced in Huxley the conviction that taxonomy could no longer confine itself to concepts such as "species" and "variety"; and, accompanying his descriptions of the cranial bones and teeth of the *Canidae* by twenty tables of quantitative data in an entirely modern manner, he wrote (1880b), "The suggestion that it may be as well to give up the attempt to define species, and to content oneself with recording the varieties of pelage and stature which accompany a definable type of skeletal and dental structure in the geographical district in which the latter is indigenous, may be regarded as revolutionary; but I am inclined to think that sooner or later we shall have to adopt it." Comments like this make one regret the more that Huxley never brought the bulk of his work on the *Canidae* to the point of publication, and we can only hope that one day his many notebooks on the subject will be properly assessed.

It was also in 1880 that Huxley presented to the Zoological Society a wide-ranging paper on vertebrate, and especially mammalian, evolution and classification. Eleven years earlier, he had written (*L.L.* II, 312) to Darwin, "What a wonderful assemblage of beasts there seems to have been in South America! I suspect that if we could find them all they would make the classification of the Mammalia into a horrid mess!" The intervening decade had produced a great increase in anatomical knowledge about both living and extinct forms from all over the world, and Huxley tried to organise the accumulated data. For the mammals, as he had earlier done for the birds, he provided a tripartite terminology which long served as a basis for subsequent classifications. His *Prototheria* embraced those primitive mammals (such as the still surviving spiny ant-eater and duck-billed platypus) which retain some reptilian characteristics and lay eggs, from which the young hatch out and take milk secreted by the mother's non-nippled lactatory glands. His *Metatheria*, today confined to Australia and South America, were marsupials (such as the kangaroos) which have a double vagina, produce no placenta, and feed their young from pumping nipples inside the mother's marsupium or pouch. His *Eutheria* (to which the overwhelming majority of mammals belong) were those with a fully developed placental uterus and whose young suck milk from the mother's nippled breasts. He also, incidentally, suggested a hypothetical fourth division, the *Hypotheria*, for those fossil species which he felt sure would be discovered some day on the border-line between the very earliest mammals and those animals—somewhere between reptile and amphibian—from which the mammals had evolved.

Thus, despite his avowed distaste for "species work", Huxley has the rare distinction of having provided persistent bases for the classification of three important vertebrate groups in his earlier years and for several groups of vertebrate as he grew older. What he really disliked, of course, was unimaginative, merely descriptive, work: in the organisation of knowledge, whether discovered by himself or by others, he simply revelled. There was, as he himself recognised, very little of the naturalist about him, and he was never an experimenter of any distinction. Nevertheless, by reason of his wide-ranging comprehension and his capacity for synthesising logic, he made contributions to scientific understanding which not many other biologists can match and very few can surpass.

CHAPTER 10

Scientific education

"THAT which I mean by 'Science'", Huxley told Kingsley (*H.P.* 19. 198) in 1860, "is not mere physical [natural] science but all the results of exact methods of thought whatever be the subject matter to which they are applied ... people fancy that mathematics or physics or biology are exclusively 'Science'—and value the clothes of science more than the goddess herself." For him, the goddess was a spirit rather than a body, an essence rather than a substance. And it was this that made him more optimistic than most men about the potential richness of a thoroughly scientific culture—and yet quite clear that mere instruction in science would not automatically produce scientifically educated citizens. Moreover, for Huxley the phrase "scientific education" had a double meaning: it was not only education in science, but also education in a scientific manner. "Teaching in England", he told the 1868 Select Committee on Scientific Instruction (*T.H.H.* 138), "is pretty much a matter of chance, and the mass of the people are ignorant of the fact that there is such a thing as a scientific method of teaching."

Science teaching, he emphasised in his 1854 address "On the Educational Value of the Natural History Sciences", should not imply any special *mystique* of science: on the contrary (*C.E.* III, 45),

> Science is, I believe, nothing but *trained and organised common sense*, differing from the latter only as a veteran may differ from a raw recruit: and its methods differ from those of common sense only so far as the guardsman's cut and thrust differ from the manner in which a savage wields his club ... the vast results obtained by Science are won by no mystical faculties, by no mental processes, other than those which are practised by every one of us, in the humblest and meanest affairs of life. ... The man of science, in fact, simply uses with scrupulous exactness the methods which we all, habitually and at every moment, use carelessly.

Nor did he accept the view, still met far too often in discussions on this matter, that biology differs from the physico-chemical sciences in being

75

'inexact'. The real differences, he believed, were the greater complexity of biology's subject matter and the less complete development of its deductive generalisations. He also emphasised at that early date the importance of teaching children sociology; and pointed out the special educational significance of biology, as lying midway between the physico-chemical and the social sciences.

Huxley did not underestimate the direct utility of scientific knowledge. As he remarked (*C.E.* III, 90) to his South London Working Men's College in 1868, "If any one is concerned in knowing the ordinary laws of mechanics one would think it is the hand-labourer, whose daily toil lies among levers and pulleys. ... And if any one is interested in the laws of health, it is the poor workman... half whose children are massacred by disorders which might be prevented." And, speaking the following year (*C.E.* III, 114) to the prosperous professional and business men of the Liverpool Philomathic Society, he insisted that "There are hardly any of our trades, except the merely huckstering ones, in which some knowledge of science may not be directly profitable". Moreover, not only was science needed in such professions as engineering and medicine, but even the clergy (*id.* 110) should "acquire, as part of their preliminary education, some such tincture of physical [natural] science as will put them in a position to understand the difficulties in the way of accepting their theories". But, for Huxley (Johonnor, 1883, 149), the word "utility" had a high meaning: "in an Englishman's mouth, it generally means that by which we get pudding, or praise, or both. I have no doubt that is one meaning of the word utility, but it by no means includes all I mean by utility. I think that knowledge of every kind is useful in proportion as it tends to give people right ideas... and to remove wrong ideas."

Unlike some of his contemporaries such as Herbert Spencer, Huxley was vividly aware of the uselessness of much science teaching as it was too often carried on. Talking to teachers and their trainers in 1861, he told them (*C.E.* VIII, 219) that

the great benefit which a scientific education bestows, whether as training or as knowledge, is dependent upon the extent to which the mind of the student is brought into immediate contact with facts—upon the degree to which he learns the habit of appealing directly to Nature, and of acquiring through his senses concrete images of those properties of things, which are, and always will be, but approximatively expressed in human language ... the great business of the scientific teacher is, to imprint the fundamental, irrefragable facts of his science, not only by words upon the mind, but by sensible impressions upon the eye, and ear, and touch of the student.

Yet, whilst insisting upon the importance of practical work by the pupil, Huxley never fell for the extreme heuristic fallacy that children can find out everything for themselves, and he recognised that it is often necessary to take things on trust from the teacher. But the teacher, at least, must have a real and genuine knowledge of his subject (*id.* 227): "Addressing myself to you, as teachers, I would say, mere book learning in physical [natural] science is a sham and a delusion—what you teach, unless you wish to be imposters, that you must first know." For, as he commented in a later footnote (*id.* 228) to this lecture, "the scientific virus, like vaccine lymph, if passed through too long a succession of organisms, will lose all its effect in protecting the young against the intellectual epidemics to which they are exposed".

"They used to have a very odd way of teaching the classical languages when I was a boy", Huxley recalled (*C.E.* III, 290) in 1876. "The first task set you was to learn the rules of the Latin grammar in the Latin language. . . . But it would be no less absurd, if we were to set about teaching Biology by putting into the hands of boys a series of definitions of the classes and orders of the animal kingdom, and making them repeat them by heart. That is so very favourite a method of teaching, that I sometimes fancy the spirit of the old classical system has entered into the new scientific system, in which case I would much rather that any pretence at scientific teaching were abolished altogether." Some seven years later, speaking at the Liverpool Institute, he laid down (*C.E.* III, 167) four conditions for successful science teaching: "If this kind of instruction is to be of any good at all, if it is not to be less than no good, if it is to take the place of that which is already of some good, then there are several points which must be attended to. And the first of these is the proper selection of topics, the second is practical teaching, the third is practical teachers, and the fourth is sufficiency of time. If these four points are not carefully attended to by anybody who undertakes the teaching of physical science in schools, my advice to him is, to let it alone."

Although, almost from the start, Huxley seems to have had very definite ideas about how science should be taught, it took him some years to secure conditions in which his ideas could be put into practice. The small School of Mines to which he went in 1854 had utterly inadequate facilities and no real vision of what its future might be. With a staggering self-confidence, which only its eventual justification redeemed from braggadocio, he set about converting it to a great national centre of science education. Very quickly becoming indispensable to the smooth and efficient daily working of the School, he displayed an intriguing mixture of devotion to duty and independence of authority. As supporters gradually joined him on the professorial staff, and carefully selected students stayed on as demonstrators or junior lecturers, his position became ever stronger. When Lord Granville was appointed in 1861 to head a Commission of Inquiry into the working of the School, he received from Huxley a long private letter, in seven pages of foolscap, indicating the direction that future developments should take. Seven years later, when the Select Committee on Scientific Instruction was set up with Sir Bernhard Samuelson as chairman, Huxley urged the appointment of professors of botany and mathematics, the provision of much more laboratory accommodation, and the incorporation of the Royal College of Chemistry. In another two years' time, Huxley was himself serving on the Duke of Devonshire's Royal Commission on Scientific Instruction, which adopted what *The Times* (6 April 1871) called "PROFESSOR HUXLEY's plan for founding an imposing National College of Science" at South Kensington. Most substantial scholars, starting out in a fairly insignificant institution, would promote their own careers by moving on to other posts in places of higher repute. Very few would dare attempt what Huxley did: he simply stayed in the same school for the rest of his working life, and worked the place up into something worthy of him.

It was obvious to Huxley that everything depended on the production of good science teachers, and it was for schoolmasters that he first devised that scheme of study which spread all over the world as 'the type system'. And, since succeeding generations of pedants have largely perverted it into little more than a dreary series of dissections, it is well to recall how it was conceived and operated by its inventor. Before Huxley, botanical teaching had almost always been associated with medicine; zoology had been taught mainly by lecture and somewhat distant demonstration; and there had been virtually no teaching of biology as a unified science. There were, of course, a few exceptions: some botanists distributed flowers to their students for individual examination, Rolleston did the same at Oxford with a few animal specimens, the elder Balfour gave occasional microscopic demonstrations at Edinburgh, and Hofmeister went even further at Tübingen. But not until 1871, when the new buildings at South

Kensington at last provided the necessary facilities, was there any really systematic practical teaching of biology. Huxley went ahead immediately with a six-week summer course for teachers—"with a view", as he told Dohrn (*L.L.* I, 362), "of converting them into scientific missionaries to convert the Christian Heathen of these islands to the true faith". Three not-quite-completed rooms were rigged up as temporary laboratories; at 10 a.m. each morning he gave a lecture; and then, with the aid of three demonstrators, the schoolmaster-students spent the rest of each day in practical work. The revolution portended by this procedure may perhaps be gauged by the startled reaction of one physiology teacher of long experience who, seeing a drop of blood under the microscope for the first time in his life, called out (Parker, 1896), "Dear me! It's just like the picture in Huxley's *Physiology.*"

Soon the new laboratories were completed and preparations for another vacation course put in hand. Despite a serious breakdown through overwork, Huxley repeated the course in 1872 and impressed on his class (Mitchell, 1900, 181) that "The purpose of this course is not to make skilled dissectors, but to give every student a clear and definite conception, by means of sense images, of the characteristic structure of each of the leading modifications.... And it then becomes possible for him to read with profit; because every time he meets with the name of a structure, he has a definite image in his mind of what the name means in the particular creature he is reading about, and then the reading is not mere reading." His types not only included both animals and plants; but, at a time when most botanists confined themselves almost entirely to the angiosperms, his students also became familiar with algae, fungi, ferns and gymnosperms. By the beginning of 1873 his health was getting even more hazardous and, he told Tyndall (*L.L.* I, 389), "I find that if I am to exist at all it must be on strictly ascetic principles, so there is hope of my dying in the odour of sanctity yet". He brought in men like Thiselton-Dyer and Sydney Vines and F. O. Bower to give a helping hand, and the modern comprehensive approach to biology teaching was well under way.

The new methods were, of course, soon in regular use for full-time South Kensington students, and there are many reminiscences of the impact they made. Their effect, wrote Bower (1925, 712), "was at a single stroke to convert each student into a potential investigator.... Every laboratory class became at once a potential board of examination of the demonstrating staff."

Never, of course, had I heard such lectures; [Patrick Geddes (1925, 741) recalled] or indeed since. Nothing could be clearer than his demonstrations of his well-chosen specimens, always sufficient for his exposition and argument, yet never in redundance ... here was the very first of laboratories, as also of lectures, truly and broadly biological. ... Though necessarily mainly anatomical and histological, it was consistently and lucidly physiological too. Taxonomy was not stressed, but clearly indicated; and the larger physiology of Nature—ecology—early opened to us in its colours and perspectives. His introduction to embryology, as at once so protean yet so deeply orderly, was never to be forgotten; and his presentments of the palaeontological record ... transmitted to us his clear and concrete views of their gradual evolution.

Reading accounts like these, we can respond to the note of sadness sounded by Vines (1925, 714) half a century later: "it seems to me that the original glory has departed: the great leading idea of the unity of life has been lost sight of, and the course tends to degenerate into the uninspired study of the details of structure of certain typical animals and plants".

For ten days in the April of 1870, Huxley went with Hooker to the Eifel country, walking and geologising and sketching, but soon he was back in the thick of things again. In June, he heard that he was being proposed for an honorary degree at Oxford and that the suggestion had aroused bitter opposition. "There seems to have been a tremendous shindy in the Hebdomadal Board...", he wrote to Darwin (*L.L.* I, 331), "and I am told that Pusey came to London to ascertain from a trustworthy friend who were the blackest heretics out of the list proposed, and that he was glad to assent to your being doctored, when he got back, in order to keep out seven devils worse than that first!" There were others besides the clergy who had still not forgiven Huxley for his vigorous attacks on received opinion, and in 1870 there was also an organised attempt to block his election as President of the British Association. Sir Stafford Northcote, the President of the Council, took the unprecedented step of publicly dissociating himself from the proposal to honour Huxley, but in the event Northcote's nominee withdrew and Huxley was thereby elected unopposed.

During the early 1870s there was much discussion about the origin of life on earth; and both Helmholtz and Thomson (Kelvin), rather than believe that it might have evolved from non-living matter, preferred to postulate its arrival by meteorite. There was, moreover, still a good deal of scepticism about Pasteur's work, which had largely discredited the idea of spontaneous generation. Huxley, however, had repeated some of Pasteur's key experiments, and presented his results in a paper "On the Relations of Penicillium, Torula, and Bacterium". For his Presidential Address to the British Association, he took the topic of "Biogenesis and Abiogenesis" and, while admitting the superficial incredibility of the idea that the air must be thick with invisible germs, urged his audience to accept it as an undoubted fact. He unambiguously declared his belief in the original evolution of living protoplasm from non-living chemical substances, and even went on (*C.E.* VIII, 256) to say, "With organic chemistry, molecular physics, and physiology yet in their infancy, and every day making prodigious strides, I think it would be the height of presumption for any man to say that the conditions under which matter assumes the properties we call 'vital' may not, some day, be artificially brought together". This latter remark was listened to without a single token of applause, the audience being apparently appalled by the cool, unflinching audacity of the speaker.

In the following year, when it was widely expected that he would become President of the Royal Society, Huxley surprised everyone by accepting the more arduous but less honoured post of Secretary. But, although this meant innumerable dull committee meetings and all the labour of reading and editing any number of scientific papers, it also meant the occupation of a strategic position at the very centre of scientific affairs. Huxley was by now an extremely successful author, and his 1871 diary noted literary and miscellaneous earnings of over £1000 and a gross income of about £2000. In 1876, when the income tax was threepence in the pound, and each pound a golden sovereign, he took in a total of some £3000 (worth at least £20,000 before tax today) and at his death there was over £14,000 to dispose of. These financial facts seem to demolish fairly effectively the myth, propagated by some of his most devoted disciples such as Edward Clodd (1916, 45), that "Throughout his life he had to struggle with moderate means, and, through ill-health, to retire a relatively poor man".

The lean years were now over, but the fat ones were to be just as busy. "I have been pounding Mivart and the Quarterly Reviewer as you will see in Contemporary for November—", he informed Michael Foster (*H.P.* 4. 31) in the October of 1871. "Also discussing functions of Government vide Fortnightly for November; also discussing Ritualism see Quarterly for January; also an article on Lord Russell & Lord Somers see

Edinburgh for ditto: with a paper on the distinctive character of the eloquence of the Revd. Morley Punshon in the Nonconformist for December." The 'quality' periodicals, however, were not his only channels for permeating English society with the scientific attitude to life. "I have not", he once wrote (*C.E.* VIII, v), "been one of those fortunate persons who keep their fame as scientific hierophants unsullied by attempts—at least of the successful sort—to be understanded of the people"; and he seized every opportunity of satisfying the people's thirst for knowledge. Up and down the land there were flourishing literary and philosophical societies for the upper and professional classes, mechanics institutes for the skilled craftsmen and tradesmen, and working men's clubs for the artisans. Huxley (*C.E.* VII, ix) found that "the necessity for making things plain to uninstructed people was one of the very best means of clearing up the obscure corners in one's own mind", and he drew audiences as large as those for impersonations by the great Maccabe or an evening of illusions by Maskelyne and Cook.

Most of all, he enjoyed his lectures to the workers; and it was following one of these that Frederic Harrison (1911, I, 283) wrote to a friend: "The intimate alliance foretold by Comte between philosophers and the Proletariat has commenced. Last night I was at Professor Huxley's lecture. ... It will take many sermons to undo last night's work." Over a thousand gathered for his lecture "On Coral and Coral Reefs" at Hulme Town Hall; Manchester's vast Free Trade Hall was filled for his lecture on "Yeast"; everywhere his meetings were crowded. And by 1877 he felt optimistic enough to say (*C.E.* III, 421): "Scientific knowledge is spreading by what the alchemists called a 'distillatio per ascensum'; and nothing can now prevent it from continuing to distil upwards and permeate English society, until, in the remote future, there shall be no member of the legislature who does not know as much of science as an elementary schoolboy."

It was for the sake of the workers' children that Huxley stood for election to the first London School Board. Throughout the 1860s, pressure had been mounting for the establishment of a national system of elementary education, but always the conflicts between the religious denominations had prevented effective action. In 1868 Huxley had made his own position plain (*C.E.* III, 77):

> The politicians tell us, 'You must educate the masses because they are going to be masters'. The clergy join in the cry for education, for they affirm that the

people are drifting away from church and chapel into the broadest infidelity. The manufacturers and the capitalists swell the chorus lustily. They declare that ignorance makes bad workmen; that England will soon be unable to turn out cotton goods, or steam engines, cheaper than other people; and then, Ichabod! Ichabod! the glory will be departed from us. And a few voices are lifted up in favour of the doctrine that the masses should be educated because they are men and women with unlimited capacities of being, doing and suffering, and that it is as true now, as ever it was, that the people perish for lack of knowledge.

So, when it became clear in 1870 that Gladstone's government was going to put an Education Act on the Statute Book, and when that Act provided for the immediate establishment of a School Board for London, he determined to play his full part in providing decent schooling for the street arabs of the great metropolis. The elections to the Board were soon in full swing and, according to *The Times*, were the one home subject able to divert people's attention from the war in France. The religious sects poured into the campaign all the energies thitherto devoted to parliamentary manoeuvring, and put up as candidates the most powerful people they could find. The undenominationalists and the secularists and the feminists did likewise, for the cumulative vote system made it possible for vigorous and well-organised minorities to secure some representation. There was, nevertheless, a good deal of surprise when Huxley decided to stand; and even more when he ran in harness with W. R. Cremer, a radical carpenter who had been one of Garibaldi's reception committee on his visit to England.

Huxley had neither the time nor the organisational backing for an election campaign such as most of the other candidates waged, nor does he seem to have gathered much money for electoral expenses. "Two most disreputable looking chaps called here yesterday", wrote Hobhouse to his wife (*T.H.H.* 147), "They were a 'deputation' from Huxley's Committee, or perhaps the Committee itself, to ask me to be treasurer of the funds collected. ... The only contribution so far is £5 of my own." But what was lacking in cash quickly arrived in distinguished backing, and soon the working-class radicals on the committee were reinforced by people like Tyndall, J. S. Mill, Harcourt, Lubbock, Passmore Edwards and Auberon Herbert. The election broadsheet of this unexpectedly combined couple of candidates solicited votes (*id.* 146) for "two *distinct* and *special* principles: Professor HUXLEY and Scientific Education, W. R. CREMER and the Educational Wants of the Working Classes".

Standing as he did in the then highly desirable district of Marylebone, Huxley might seem not to have improved his chances by declaring, at one of his few public meetings (*The Times*, 22 November 1870), that "no breeder would bring up his pigs under such conditions as those to which the poorer classes of England were now subjected". Nor, since the vote was confined to householders, can it have appeared politically wise to state, in his election address (*T.H.H.* 147), "It seems to be the fashion for candidates to assure you that they will do their best to spare the poverty of the Ratepayers. It is proper, therefore, for me to add that I can give you no such assurance on my own behalf ... my vote will be given for that expenditure which can be shown to be just and necessary, without any reference to the question whether it may raise the rates a halfpenny." Yet, surprisingly enough, Huxley was not merely elected to the Board, but almost immediately became Chairman of its all-important Scheme of Education Committee.

The scheme of education which he wanted had already been announced in his *Contemporary Review* article, "The School Boards: What they Can do and What they May do". First of all, the children of the slums needed physical training to provide them with healthy exercise and some modicum of pride in their own bodies. Next, there should be education in domestic economy, so that the pupils might learn to make the best use of what little household money they would eventually have and, in the case of girls, be able to earn more as efficient domestic servants. Third, since everyone was willy-nilly a member of a complex society, there should be instruction in the elementary laws of conduct—and, to the general surprise, Huxley supported the reading of the Bible, both for its literary merit and as a great repository of moral truth and grandeur. So far as other subjects were concerned, there should naturally be a fair amount of elementary science, together with drawing and modelling and music, which last he regarded as one of the most civilising and enlightening influences that a child could be brought under. Not only were these curricular recommendations adapted almost *in toto*, but so were most of his committee's organisational proposals. Soon other School Boards all over the country were modelling their systems on that of London, with separate infants, junior and senior schools, regulations to control corporal punishment, inspections to maintain reasonable standards of school hygiene, and safeguards for the professional freedom of teachers. It may, therefore, be reasonably claimed that Huxley did as much as any man to determine the general shape of English elementary education for the next three-quarters of a century.

But he had done so at heavy cost. Surviving diaries and other papers show that, during a brief fourteen months, he had attended some 170 committee meetings, travelled up and down the land to gather information and ideas, kept innumerable engagements with figures influential in Church and State, drafted any number of documents, and made sure that the right witnesses were always available to give suitable evidence at inquiries. Even Huxley could not stand this pace indefinitely, and in January 1872 his health utterly collapsed. His physician ordered complete rest, and for the next three months he lazed his way towards recovery in the Mediterranean and Egyptian sunshine.

While he was abroad in the spring, the St. Andrews students just failed by three votes to elect him Rector without either his permission or his presence. Back in England, he accepted an autumn invitation to stand for election as Rector of Aberdeen University where, despite an election campaign of impressive scurrility against him, he was successful. His opponent had been the young Marquis of Huntley, the Cock o' the North—and, as he wrote to Tyndall (*H.P.* 9. 63), "the fact of any one, who stinketh in the nostrils of orthodoxy, beating a Scotch peer at his own gates, in the most orthodox of Scotch cities, is a curious sign of the times".

That December, the Huxleys moved in miserable mud and rain to a larger house in Marlborough Place, and immediately faced a tiresome law suit brought by a litigious neighbour. What really worried his friends, however, was the fact that Huxley still seemed quite unable to deny the multifarious demands on his time and energy. The government wanted his advice on the appointment of the first Director of Studies for the newly established Royal Naval College at Greenwich; his publisher wanted *Critiques and Addresses* safely through the press; he wanted to finish his *Anatomy of Invertebrated Animals*. Finally, his friends became so alarmed that they took matters into their own hands. Lady Lyell began the conspiracy, Darwin became its centre, and on 23 April 1873, Emma Darwin (Litchfield, 1925, II, 212) told Fanny Allen what her husband had done: "He sent off the awful letter to Mr. Huxley today", she wrote, "and I hope we may hear tomorrow. It will be very awful." But it turned out not to be awful at all. Darwin told Huxley that the eighteen conspirators had put their hands in their pockets to the tune of £2100, emphasising (*L.L.* I, 366) that "We have done this to enable you to get such complete rest as you may require for the re-establishment of your health; and in doing this we are convinced that we act for the public interest, as well as in accordance with our most earnest desires. Let me assure you that we are all your warm personal friends, and that there is not a stranger or mere acquaintance amongst us."

Huxley was so touched that, for perhaps the only time in his life, he meekly submitted to doing exactly what others arranged for him. At the beginning of July he set off under Hooker's care for the Auvergne, stopping just long enough in Paris to banish a severe mental depression by fulminating against a *History of the Miracles of Lourdes* which he happened to pick up on a bookstall. He climbed, geologised, sketched, abandoned cigarettes for cigars, and lazed for a while at Grenoble. When Hooker had to return to his work in England, Mrs. Huxley came out to spend a few weeks with her husband in the Black Forest and the Bernese Oberland. Whilst awaiting her arrival, he ruminated on the part he had to play in the cultural revolution of his time. "We are in the midst of a gigantic movement greater than that which preceded and produced the Reformation", he wrote (*L.L.* I, 397), "and really only the continuation of that movement ... nor is any reconcilement possible between free thought and traditional authority. One or other will have to succumb after a struggle of unknown duration, which will have as side issues vast political and social troubles ... [this] will be the work of generations of men, and those who further it most will be those who teach men to rest in no lie, and to rest in no verbal delusions. I may be able to help a little in this direction—perhaps I may have helped already."

He returned home at the end of September much mended, and it must have required considerable self-discipline to turn down Kay-Shuttleworth's suggestion that he should become England's 'Director of Science Education'. If such a post had been established and occupied by Huxley, science teaching might have taken a very different turn during succeeding decades. And perhaps, a century after his 1869 Liverpool address on "Scientific Education", educators today would not be still occupied in grave debate about how far primary school children can benefit from being taught science.

At that time Huxley's daughter Jessie was eleven, Marian ten and Leonard nine, and he knew very well how deeply juvenile curiosity can delve. So, to those who asked when a child's scientific education should begin, he replied (*C.E.* III, 128), "with the dawn of intelligence. ... People talk of the difficulty of teaching young children such matters, and in the same breath insist upon their learning their Catechism, which contains propositions far harder to comprehend than anything in the educational course I have proposed." Any one, he said (*id.* 123), who knew the ways of young children, knew also that "The child asks, 'What is the moon, and why does it shine?' 'What is this water, and where does it run?' 'What is the wind?' 'What makes the waves in the sea?' 'Where does this animal live, and what is the use of that plant?' And if not snubbed and stunted by being told not to ask foolish questions, there is no limit to the intellectual craving of a young child." He was well aware that children varied in their abilities, but believed (*id.* 128) that "stupidity in nine cases out of ten, '*fit, non nascitur*', and is developed by a long process of parental and pedagogic repression of the natural intellectual appetites, accompanied by a persistent attempt to create artificial ones for food which is not only tasteless, but essentially indigestible".

A year later, speaking "On Elementary Instruction in Physiology" to the Domestic Economy Congress at Birmingham, Huxley made some detailed proposals (*C.E.* III, 298) for the teaching of human biology:

> The principal constituents of the skeleton, and the changes of form of contracting muscles, may be felt through one's own skin. The beating of one's heart, and its connection with the pulse, may be noted; the influence of the valves of one's own veins may be shown; the movements of respiration may be observed; while the wonderful phenomena of sensation afford an endless field for curious and interesting self-study. The prick of a needle will yield, in a drop of one's own blood, material for microscopic observation of phenomena which lie at the foundation of all biological conceptions; and a cold, with its concomitant coughing and sneezing, may prove the sweet uses of adversity by helping one to a clear conception of what is meant by 'reflex action'.

It all reads very much like a report of a seminar on science education held yesterday.

But, although Huxley believed that the very best teaching would be done by those who required no class textbooks, he also knew that such ideal teachers were few and far between. And there unfortunately existed (*C.E.* III, 170), still in wide circulation, "detestable books which ought to have been burned by the hands of the common hangman, for they contained questions and answers to be learned by heart, of this sort,

'What is a horse?' 'The horse is termed *Equus caballus;* belongs to the class Mammalia; order Pachydermata; family, Solidungula' ... it is that kind of teaching that one wants to get rid of, and banished out of science." As an aid to the banishment, he himself produced through the years some little textbook gems, each of which sold well and exerted a great influence on the direction and style of science education both at home and overseas. In 1864 his *Lectures in Comparative Anatomy* came out, together with the *Elementary Atlas of Comparative Osteology*. These were both directed towards students setting out to be scientists, as were the later *Classification of Animals*, the *Anatomy of Vertebrated Animals*, the *Anatomy of Invertebrated Animals* and *The Crayfish*. Huxley's first textbook at a lower level was his 1866 *Lessons in Elementary Physiology*, of which the English edition went through thirty printings in as many years. In 1875, when the *Course of Practical Instruction in Elementary Biology* appeared, Darwin was once more moved (*H.P.* 5, 324) to admiring exclamation: "It was a real stroke of genius to think of such a plan. Lord, how I wish that I had gone through such a course!" But there was still no genuine general science textbook suitable for the ordinary elementary schools.

"The difficulty primary education in scientific matters labours under everywhere", Huxley had told Lady Stanley of Alderley in 1868 (Depart. Educ. & Science MS.), "is the want of good elementary books; of small books written by great men, who have mastered the subject which they try to explain, and who possess a sufficient combination of scepticism and moral courage, to shut out without any mercy any statement that does not rest on a firm foundation." He went on to outline what such an elementary science text would be like.

It would begin with an account of the 'accidents of the earth's surface' and the teacher using it could illustrate this from his own neighbourhood. It would lead them to the general features of the globe—its form, size and place in the solar system; its relation to the sun, and other broad astronomical facts. The laws of motion and illustrations of the nature of attraction would come in incidentally ... the distribution of the great masses of land and water ... the character of the principal mountain chains, river basins and so forth. The teacher should illustrate this by making small models in clay. ... Then would follow the phenomena of climate ... the outlines of the main structure of the earth ... I should introduce the elementary conceptions of physics and chemistry as I wanted them. ... Having thus given a notion of the earth, I should pass on to its organic population ... and here the outline of human structure and physiology ought to form the

foundation of all instruction for many reasons both scientific and practical. ...
Finally ... an account of various kinds of men, with their ways and work,
would crown the edifice in a very interesting and pleasant fashion.

But, he added, it would need "A man of real genius and weight
to write the needful elementary book". Nine years later, since nobody
else had done so, Huxley wrote the necessary book himself. His *Physiography: an Introduction to the Study of Nature* was a genuinely unified
account of the environment, in every way superior to much of our present-
day 'general science'—which, indeed, is too often precisely the sort of
"*omnium gatherum* of scraps of all sorts of undigested and unconnected
information" that Huxley (1877a, vi) so strongly condemned. Only in
our own day have the schools begun once more to be served by elementary
general science texts of similar imagination to *Physiography*.

The system of 'payment by results', introduced into English education
under Robert Lowe's Revised Code of 1861, tended to promote any
teaching which would allow school managers to pick up a few pounds
by submitting their pupils to whatever examinations were prescribed.
"The great and manifold evil of that system", Huxley told Donnelly
(*L.L.* II, 235), "is the steady pressure which it exerts in the development
of every description of sham teaching. And the only check upon this
kind of swindling the public seems to me to lie in the hands of the
Examiners ... for every sham they let through is an encouragement to
other shams and pot-teaching in general." But Huxley never doubted
the dangers inherent in excessive examination, and in 1877 he told the
Working Men's Club and Institute Union (*C.E.* III, 410) that

> The educational abomination of desolation of the present day is the stimulation
> of young people to work at high pressure by incessant competitive examinations.
> ... The vigour and freshness ... have been washed out of them by precocious
> mental debauchery—by book gluttony and lesson bibbing. Their faculties are
> worn out by the strain put upon their callow brains, and they are demoralised
> by worthless childish triumphs before the real work of life begins. I have no
> compassion for sloth, but youth has more need for intellectual rest than age;
> and the cheerfulness, the tenacity of purpose, the power of work which make many
> a successful man what he is, must often be placed to the credit, not of his hours
> of industry, but to that of his hours of idleness, in boyhood.

In this, as in much else, those who today are most concerned in the
promotion of science education might profitably consider the views of
the greatest of science educators.

CHAPTER 11

Science and higher education

IN PRINCIPLE, Huxley saw no problems of higher education any different in kind from those of education generally. In both cases the important questions were: who should be taught?, what should they be taught?, how should they be taught?, and how should their learning be tested? Each aspect, of course, took on a different hue in the light of higher education, but the pedagogic principles involved were just the same.

There were many in those days anxious to admit the increasingly influential middle classes to the universities, but Huxley (*C.E.* III, 202) also wanted the way cleared for "the sons of the masses of the people whose daily labour just suffices to meet their daily wants". He spoke scathingly (*ibid.*) of "the host of pleasant, moneyed, well-bred young gentlemen, who do a little learning and much boating by Cam and Isis", and he congratulated the Scottish Universities that they had never become "a school of manners for the rich; of sports for the athletic; or a hot-bed of high-fed, hypercritical refinement". Unlike Matthew Arnold and some others, Huxley found the spirit of the age pregnant with exciting possibilities, and he had great faith in the cultural potentialities of his unpolished but energetic compatriots. Convinced that there were great reservoirs of untapped potential in both sexes and all classes, he very much doubted the wisdom of imposing rigid entrance requirements to institutions of higher education. As a member of the Royal Commission on the Universities of Scotland he argued strongly for flexibility in this respect, and especially he urged relaxation for mature applicants. When, much later, he came out of retirement to help in organising the great new federal University of London, he pointed out that most applicants would no doubt acquire the necessary qualifications as a mere matter of expediency, but added (*T.H.H.* 229), "I say that very possibly the odd tenth may contain persons of defective education, but of a native vigour which makes

90

them more worth having than all the other nine-tenths, and I would not lose them for any consideration".

So far as subject matter was concerned, Huxley believed (*C.E.* III, 237) that "University education should not be something distinct from elementary education, but should be the natural outgrowth and development of the latter.... The university can add no new departments of knowledge, can offer no new fields of mental activity; but what it can do is to intensify and specialise the instruction in each department... The primary school and the university are the alpha and omega of education." And, needless to say, in the latter as in the former he thought that science should occupy an important (but by no means an exclusive) place.

In London, apart from his dominating role at South Kensington and his considerable general influence as a university examiner, Huxley had a good deal to do with the promotion of science in the affiliated colleges. His 1870 University College address on medical education was followed by significant changes in regulations, and it was largely on his advice that the Jodrell Chair of Physiology was established in 1873 and that of Comparative Anatomy and Zoology a few years later. When the London School of Medicine for Women was founded in 1875, he was one of its first Governors; he lectured at the Birkbeck Literary and Scientific Institution which later grew into Birkbeck College; he helped to establish the People's Palace which eventually became Queen Mary College in the East End; and he played a useful part in connection with the University's extension movement.

At Owens College in Manchester, Huxley collaborated closely with Kay-Shuttleworth in getting the right people on to the Council of that embryo university. He pressed for the better teaching of science, encouraged Henry Roscoe in building up his great school of chemistry, and was largely responsible for the application of the Brackenbury gift to the endowment of a Chair of Practical Physiology. But, anxious as always that the advocacy of science should have nothing narrow about it, he took advantage of the official opening of the new Medical School in 1874 to issue a salutary warning to his fellow scientists. "I trust that the position of the arts faculty in this institution will never by a hairsbreadth or shadow be diminished ..." he declared (Man. Univ. Archives). "Our occupations are very engrossing, and they can be pursued with success only by the intensest stress and attention, and we are obliged even to limit ourselves to particular fractions and particular portions of our own study if we are to make any advance therein... and unless we are led to see that we are citizens and men before anything else, I say it will go very hardly indeed with men of science in future generations, and they will run the risk of becoming scientific pedants when they should be men, philosophers, and good citizens."

At the two ancient universities things were more difficult, and in 1874 Huxley told Tyndall (*H.P.* 9. 84), "It is as well for me that I expect nothing from Oxford or Cambridge, having burned my ships as far as they were concerned long ago". Some idea of the state of things at Oxford may be gained from an 1872 letter (*H.P.* 21. 39) of Ray Lankester's:

> No one knows, who does not live in the place—the inextricable mass of mediaeval folly and corporation-jealousy and effete restrictions which surround all Oxford institutions. A commission comes and examines people such as Acland—and of course hears the smoothest, most cheerful account of everything ... when it is notorious that he does nothing—and though Professor of Medicine never gives a lecture and tries to prevent medical students from coming to Oxford....We, fellows, try to get as many fees out of the undergraduates as we can ... I am obliged to teach the very first notions of Biology ... it prevents one's developing any powers as a teacher—and keeps one back from such research as is always suggested in an actively worked laboratory.

There were, however, powerful allies within the medieval fortress, and notably the formidable Master of Balliol. "I want to have the opportunity of talking to Mr. Huxley", Jowett wrote (*H.P.* 7. 11) in 1877, "about a move I am thinking of trying to make here for requiring a knowledge of Physical Science of all Candidates for a degree." Unfortunately, it turned out on this occasion that even some of the science professors opposed the plan—perhaps they, like Acland, did not want too many students—and Oxford did not give science the central place in its teaching which had been hoped for. At Cambridge, Huxley worked closely with Henry Fawcett and Henry Sidgwick and W. G. Clark, as well as with various scientists. But here also, although his influence on the promotion of science was evidently pervasive, it was difficult to get things moving as quickly as he would have wished.

It was, however, with Aberdeen University that Huxley had the most fully documented associations, especially following his election as Rector towards the end of 1872. Almost immediately, honouring his promise to the students that he would not be purely decorative but would actively exercise the ancient rectorial prerogatives, he began to lay his plans. In

November, he made public in *Nature* the text of four resolutions which he proposed moving in Court, to relieve the medical curriculum of various accumulated irrelevancies and to replace Greek by German or French as a compulsory subject. There was considerable opposition from those professors who were afraid of losing fees by a diminution in the size of their compulsory classes, and from any number of other vested interests. There was also a good deal of more general opposition from the godly, including an anonymous pamphlet whose fourteen pages of abusive prose were followed by another nineteen of scoffing verse, of which the following (Anon., 1895) is a sample:

> The Rector hath a treatise wrote ...
> The title of it ought to be—
> *The Book of Huxley's Revelation;*
> And specially should those savants
> Most piously peruse the book,
> Who rather would in Huxley trust,
> Than Moses and the Pentatauch.

Nevertheless, the resolutions were passed. "Fact", wrote Huxley to his wife (*L.L.* I, 408), "though greatly to my astonishment. Tomorrow we go in for some reforms in the arts curriculum, and I expect that the job will be tougher."

Both the medical and the arts reforms (the latter mainly concerned to provide a proper place for science in the M.A. degree) were stymied for a while by the appointment of a Royal Commission, but Huxley was fortunately made a member. The Commission eventually reported much along the lines he had advocated, thus justifying the forecast (*C.E.* III, 191) which he had ventured in his rectorial address: "If your annals take any notice of my incumbency, I shall probably go down to posterity as the Rector who was always beaten. But if they add, as I think they will, that my defeats became victories in the hands of my successors, I shall be well content."

In his address, "Universities: Actual and Ideal", Huxley had pointed out (*id.* 199) that the Faculties of Theology, Law and Medicine in the ancient University of Paris had been originated to provide "men learned in those technical, or, as we now call them, professional branches of knowledge". The choice of words is instructive, for it illustrates his refusal to regard "technical" as an implicitly pejorative term for those branches of vocational study which had not yet become academically or socially respectable. The same general attitude appeared (*id.* 206) in his question, "If there are Doctors of Music, why should there be no Masters of Painting, of Sculpture, of Architecture? I should like to see Professors of the Fine Arts in every University." Huxley, moreover, disassociated himself (*id.* 226) from those university scientists who complained that teaching interfered with research, for

> The besetting sins of the investigator are two: the one is the desire to put aside a subject, the general bearings of which he has mastered himself, and pass on to something which has the attraction of novelty; and the other, the desire for too much perfection, which leads him to ... spend the energies which should be reserved for action in whitening the decks and polishing the guns. The obligation to produce results for the instruction of others, seems to me to be a more effectual check on these tendencies than even the love of usefulness or the ambition for fame.

So far as the technical (or professional) study of medicine was concerned, Huxley emphasised the importance of cutting out all that was irrelevant, and he denied that this necessarily implied narrowness. For, he believed (*id.* 220), "A thorough study of Human Physiology is, in itself, an education broader and more comprehensive than much that goes under that name. There is no side of the intellect which it does not call into play, no region of human knowledge into which either its roots, or its branches, do not extend; like the Atlantic between the Old and the New Worlds, its waves wash the two worlds of matter and of mind."

On the general question of university examinations, Huxley took much the same view (*id.* 228) as he did of those at lower levels: "Examination —thorough, searching examination—is an indispensable accompaniment of teaching; but... it is a necessary evil.... Examination, like fire, is a good servant, but a bad master." And, he told his audience (*id.* 229), "there is a fallacy about Examiners. It is commonly supposed that any one who knows a subject is competent to teach it; and no one seems to doubt that any one who knows a subject is competent to examine in it. I believe both these opinions to be serious mistakes.... Examination is an Art, and a difficult one, which has to be learned like all other arts." Even under the best of circumstances, he warned (*id.* 231), "examination will remain but an imperfect test of knowledge, and a still more imperfect test of capacity, while it tells next to nothing about a man's power as an investigator". And, in the meanwhile (*id.* 228), "students... work to pass, not to know; and outraged Science takes her revenge. They do pass, and they don't know."

During 1875, and the early part of 1876, Huxley's life seems to have been somewhat less hectic than usual. He gave up cigar-smoking for a pipe; read *La Mare au Diable* and came to the conclusion that Georges Sand was a better writer than George Eliot; and acted for two long summers as Professor of Natural History at Edinburgh while Wyville Thomson was away on *Challenger*. The Scottish system, under which professors were paid according to the numbers attending their lectures, turned out excellently for so attractive a teacher as Huxley. "I have 330 students, he wrote to his daughter Jessie (*L.L.* I, 444) in the May of 1875, "and my class is the biggest in the University." The class soon attracted even more students, and in August he was able to tell Tyndall (*L.L.* I, 449), "I cleared about £1000 by the transaction, being one of the few examples known of a Southern coming north and pillaging the Scots." Otherwise, the only incident of particular note during these two years was the fierce controversy on vivisection, which had been gradually heating up since 1870.

It had been put about that Huxley advocated vivisection by school-children, the most sinister inferences being drawn from his innocent suggestion that they should examine the viscera of domesticated animals. In 1874 the Vice-President of the Privy Council's Committee on Education, while approving that year's summer course at South Kensington, specifically prohibited any experiments on living animals, but this was unacceptable to Huxley. "Constitutionally", he declared (*L.L.* I, 431), "the performance of experiments upon living and conscious animals is extremely disagreeable to me, and I have never followed any line of investigation in which such experiments are required; [but]... I cannot consent to be prohibited from showing the circulation in a frog's foot because the frog is made slightly uncomfortable by being tied up for that purpose." In short, unless the Vice-President's minute was amended, he must decline to conduct the course. The minute was duly amended, but that was not the end of the matter. Early in 1875 an extremely restrictive Bill was presented to Parliament, provoking Huxley and a few others to issue what he called a "pronunciamento" on the subject. However, when a Royal Commission was appointed, with Huxley as a member, he learned a thing or two which he had not suspected. "I did not believe", he wrote (*L.L.* I, 440) of one scientific witness from overseas, "the man lived who was such an unmitigated cynical brute as to profess and act upon such principles."

So he agreed to certain legal restrictions—relying for moderation, as he told Darwin (*L.L.* I, 437), "not in the wisdom and justice of the House of Commons, but in the large numbers of fox-hunters therein. If physiological experimentation is put down by law, hunting, fishing and shooting against which a much better case can be made out, will soon follow."

Huxley was now beginning to spend more time at literary and artistic gatherings, and he became a fairly regular visitor to the Royal Academy. In one after-dinner speech he gave the well-fed academicians an amusing view (*Pall Mall Gazette*, 1 June 1876) of their place in the evolutionary scale:

> The recent progress of biological speculation leads to the conclusion that the scale of being may be thus stated—minerals, plants, animals, men who cannot draw—artists. ... We have long been seeking, as you may be aware, for a distinction between men and animals. The old barriers have long broken away. Other things walk on two legs and have no feathers, caterpillars make themselves clothes, kangaroos have pockets. ... Again, beavers and ants engineer as well as the members of the noblest of professions. But ... man alone can draw or make unto himself a likeness. This then, is the great distinction of humanity, and it follows that the most pre-eminently human of creatures are those who possess this distinction in the highest degree.

But much the most important event of that year for Huxley and his wife was their visit to the U.S.A.

The family was rapidly growing up (Jessie was eighteen, Marian seventeen, Leonard sixteen, Rachel fourteen, Nettie thirteen, Henry eleven and Ethel ten) and they felt able to leave them in the care of friends and take what they called a "second honeymoon". "So soon as the intention became known, America seems to have gone wild with excitement. The whole nation is electrified by the announcement that Professor Huxley is to visit us next fall", wrote one correspondent (*L.L.* I, 460), "We will make infinitely more of him than we did of the Prince of Wales and his retinue of lords and dukes." On arrival in New York, Huxley made two remarks (*L.L.* I, 461), each in its own way very revealing. "Ah", he said on seeing the Tribune and Western Union buildings dominating the skyline, "that is interesting; that is American. In the Old World the first things you see as you approach a great city are steeples; here you see, first, centres of intelligence." And, as they stood on deck, absorbing the atmosphere of the busy harbour, "If I were not a man I think I should like to be a tug".

Appleton the publisher immediately whisked them off for a short stay at his country house at Riversdale; then Huxley went for a while to examine Marsh's fossils at Yale, where the millionaire Peabody put his residence at his disposal and the Governor of Connecticut called on him instead of his calling upon the Governor. Then there came another interlude of scientific discussion, this time with Agassiz at Newport; next a period in the White Mountains as guests of John Fiske; then to Buffalo for the annual meeting of the American Association for the Advancement of Science. And so to visit Lizzie at Nashville, where Mrs. Huxley immediately recognised the sister-in-law she had never seen, by reason of a pair of piercing black eyes flashing brightly out from the crowd like those of her husband. The local citizens would not let Huxley leave without a lecture; and it is very much in character that, instead of fobbing them off with fluent generalities, he took the trouble to work up a special address on the geology of Tennessee.

The main reason for Huxley's visit to the U.S.A. was the official opening of Johns Hopkins University in Baltimore. The President of Johns Hopkins came in for a good deal of criticism both for his choice of opening speaker and for the omission of a religious ceremony of dedication. "I am very sorry Gilman began with Huxley", wrote one critic (*T.H.H.* 236), "But it is possible yet to redeem the University from the stain of such a beginning." But perhaps the best comment of them all was this *(ibid.)*: "It was bad enough to invite Huxley. It were better to have asked God to be present. It would have been absurd to ask them both."

In his "Address on University Education", Huxley enlarged upon some of the points he had made at Aberdeen two years earlier. "My own feeling", he said (*C.E.* III, 242), "is distinctly against any absolute and defined preliminary examination, the passing of which shall be an essential condition of admission to the University. I would admit to the university any one who could be reasonably expected to profit by the instruction offered;" and then he would gradually weed out the students as they showed themselves deficient in industry or capacity. And, not surprisingly, he condemned (*id.* 250) the common form of examination by which the student, "at the end of three years... was set down to a table and questioned pell-mell upon all the different matters with which he had been striving to make acquaintance. A worse system and one more calculated to obstruct the acquisition of sound knowledge and to give full play to the 'crammer' and the 'grinder' could hardly have been devised by human ingenuity." Instead, he advocated (*id.* 251) the system which he had used for some years at South Kensington, "to get rid of general examinations altogether, to permit the student to be examined in each subject at the end of his attendance on the class. . . . It allows the student to concentrate his mind upon what he is about for the time being, and then to dismiss it . . . it is important, not so much to know a thing, as to have known it, and known it thoroughly. If you have once known a thing in this way it is easy to renew your knowledge. . . and when you begin to take the subject up again, it slides back upon the familiar grooves with great facility."

Huxley had qualms about taking any payment from the Johns Hopkins trustees, but eventually accepted. It must have required some fortitude to turn down the offer of $1000 for a single lecture at St. Louis, but he wanted some relaxation. Appleton told him that he could take in £10,000 if he would spend the winter in America, but he had to get back to his work in England. Even so, he made about £600 profit on the whole trip, which was a fairly satisfactory outcome of a second honeymoon.

The following year Huxley's *American Addresses* and *Physiography* appeared; the Scottish Universities Commission took up a fair amount of his time; and, after going to St. Andrews to arrange for Leonard's admission as a student, he spent a month on holiday at Whitby. Then, in November, the honorary degree of LL.D. was conferred by Cambridge on Darwin, who in his customary manner avoided the congratulatory dinner and asked his 'bulldog' to deputise. Huxley decided that there was no harm in a little fun, and told the assembled dons (*H.P.* 41. 151), "Mr. Darwin's work had fully earned the distinction you have today conferred upon him four and twenty years ago; but I doubt not that he would have found in that circumstance an exemplification of the wise foresight of his revered intellectual mother. Instead of offering her honours when they ran a chance of being crushed beneath the accumulated marks of appreciation of the whole civilised world, the University has waited until the trophy was finished, and has crowned the edifice with the delicate wreath of academic appreciation." True, he assured Darwin (*L.L.* I, 479) that "There was only a little touch of the whip at starting, and it was so tied round with ribbons that it took them some time to find out where the flick had hit"; but it is difficult to believe that all Cambridge hides were so insensitive.

In 1878 Huxley himself received another honorary doctorate, this time from Dublin. There was also a happy family occasion when Jessie married F. W. Waller, the cathedral architect. But within a week Marian, Leonard and Ethel were all down with diphtheria, and for a time the family was in great distress. Fortunately, the children eventually recovered and Huxley felt free to get on with learning Greek, so as to determine from the original texts whether or not Aristotle had made certain alleged errors in his biological writings. He was also planning two series of books to be written under his editorial direction, one of ten volumes on English Men of Science and the other of twelve volumes on various aspects of Education, but unfortunately neither series materialised. He gave a tercentenary lecture in London on William Harvey and had an audience of 3000 for a public address in Manchester. His summer holiday was spent at Penmaenmawr, where—the fact would be incredible if the evidence were not indisputable—he wrote in six weeks the major part of his book on *Hume*.

Huxley's scientific interest at this time was very much engrossed by invertebrates, including some of the molluscs and cephalopods brought back by *Challenger*, but most of all he was immersed in the crayfish and its allies. These investigations led him to a novel and important analysis of gill plumes as evidence of affinity and separation, and in 1878 he gave the Zoological Society a comprehensive paper on the classification and distribution of the whole group. Undoubtedly, however, the most important outcome of this work was his monographic textbook, *The Crayfish: an Introduction to the Study of Zoology*, which appeared in the following year. The 372-page text consisted mainly of anatomical description of the common crayfish (accompanied by admirably clear diagrams) and of the essentials of crayfish physiology, but there were also illuminating accounts of the group's zoogeography and probable course of evolution. Even more important, the study of this one species provided the opportunity for many general biological considerations of a fundamental nature. As Huxley (1879, vi) quoted from Diderot in his preface, "Il faut être profond dans l'art ou dans la science pour en bien posséder les éléments". In his notebooks Huxley jotted down plans for other similar textbooks, on the dog as an introduction to the study of mammals, on man as an introduction to the study of anthropology, and on psychology. If we may take his *Crayfish* as an example of what the whole series might have been, we must bitterly regret that he never found time to complete it.

Early in 1879 Huxley wrote to tell Dohrn (*L.L.*, II, 3), "I find 53 to be a very youthful period of existence. I have been better physically, and worked harder mentally, this last twelvemonth than in any year of my life." That summer also saw his gifted daughter Marian married to the portrait painter John Collier—a love-match unhappily terminated in only eight years by Marian's early death. Huxley gave several series of lectures, such as those on "Snakes" at the Zoological Society and "On Sensation and the Unity of Structure of the Sensiferous Organs" at the Royal Institution; but his most important paper in 1879 was at the Royal Society, "On the Characters of the Pelvis in the Mammalia". His Greek was now good enough for him to be delving pretty deeply into original sources and, although he published only one communication to *Nature*, "On Certain Errors Respecting the Structure of the Heart, attributed to Aristotle", his surviving papers include a great mass of notes on classical scientists and philosophers.

An attempt that year by Huxley and others to get compulsory Greek abolished at Cambridge was unsuccessful, but shortly he was on his way there to receive an honorary doctorate. "I shall be glorious in a red gown at Cambridge tomorrow", he wrote (*L.L.*, II, 4) to Baynes on 9th June, "and hereafter look to be treated as a PERSON OF RESPECTABILITY. I have done my best to avoid that misfortune, but it's of no use." In any event, he was still engaged in smiting fallacies wherever they were to be found, and took full advantage of a Friday Evening Discourse at the Royal Institution, "On the Coming of Age of the Origin of Species". "History warns us ..." he advised his audience (*C.E.* II, 229), "that it is the customary fate of new truths to begin as heresies, and end as superstitions; and, as matters now stand, it is hardly rash to anticipate that, in another twenty years, the new generation, educated under the influences of the present day, will be in danger of accepting the main doctrines of the 'Origin of Species', with as little reflection, and it may be with as little justification, as so many of our contemporaries, twenty years ago, rejected them. ... Whenever a doctrine claims our assent we should reply, Take it if you can compel it."

Huxley's main contribution to higher education in 1880 was his address, "Science and Culture", given at the October opening of Josiah Mason College, the germ of the University of Birmingham. Matthew Arnold had said that the meaning of culture was to know the best that has been thought and said in the world, and with this definition Huxley took issue. He agreed that culture was something more than mere learning or technical skill, and implied the possession of an ideal and the habit of estimating the value of things. "But", he went on (*C.E.* III, 143), "we may agree to all this, and yet strongly dissent from the assumption that literature alone is competent to supply this ... I find myself wholly unable to admit that either nations or individuals will really advance, if their common outfit draws nothing from the stores of physical [natural] science. I should say that an army, without weapons of precision and with no particular base of operations, might more hopefully enter upon a campaign on the Rhine, than a man, devoid of knowledge of what physical science has done in the last century, upon a criticism of life." Yet, he warned (*id.*, 153), "An exclusively scientific training will bring about a mental twist as surely as an exclusively literary training. The value of the cargo does not compensate for a ship's being out of trim; and I should be very sorry to think that the Scientific College would turn out none but lop-sided men."

When Rolleston died in 1881, Oxford almost begged Huxley to succeed him as Linacre Professor. Brodrick, the Warden of Merton, wrote asking (*H.P.* 11. 85), "Could you *entertain* the idea ... I do not suppose that you wd. be willing to become a candidate. The question is whether, if invited to accept the office, you *might* be disposed to do so." It was a most tempting office, with a Fellowship to accompany it and a promise that he would be able to devote most of his time to research, but Huxley turned it down. "I doubt whether the psychical atmosphere would suit me", he replied (*L.L.* II, 30), "and still more, whether I should suit it after a life spent in the absolute freedom of London." A few months later, Oxford made another effort to capture him, this time as Master of University College. There were very considerable residential emoluments in addition to a substantial stipend free of tax, and Faulkner (Tutor and Dean of Degrees) assured him that he would have no obligations other than six month's residence each year. For a time Huxley wavered, being much attracted by the prospect of functioning (*H.P.* 16. 34) as "a sort of Minister for Science without Portfolio", but eventually he turned down this offer also. "I do not think I am cut out for a Don nor your mother for a Donness", he explained (*L.L.* II, 32) to Leonard.

In any event, Huxley's long-nurtured plans for South Kensington were now approaching full fruition. In March 1881 the Committee of Privy Council decided to convert the School of Mines (*T.H.H.* 119) into "a Metropolitan School or College of Science, not specially devoted to Mining but to all Science applicable to Industry, and with a special organisation as a Training College for Teachers". Up to this point, Huxley had never occupied *de jure* any position in the School other than that of one among several professors, but now he was brought forward from his rôle of *éminence grise* and appointed to the newly constituted post of Dean. Within the week he was wryly rebuking Donnelly (*L.L.* II, 36), "I am astonished that you don't know that a letter to a Dean ought to be addressed 'The Very Revd' ... I don't generally stand much upon etiquette, but when my sacred character is touched, I draw the line".

In proposing the name "Normal School of Science", Huxley had in mind the great École Normale of Paris, and he wanted to set an example of the properly pedagogical teaching of science. "There are a great many people", he pointed out (*C.E.* III, 171) to the Liverpool Institution, "who imagine that elementary teaching might be properly carried out by teachers provided with only elementary knowledge. Let me assure you that that is the profoundest mistake in the world. There is nothing so difficult to do as to write a good elementary book, and there is nobody so hard to teach properly and well as people who know nothing about a subject." One of his very last students, the young H. G. Wells (1934, 201), has testified to the success with which this difficult task was performed: "That year I spent in Huxley's class was, beyond all question, the most educational year in my life. If left me under that urgency for coherence and consistency, that repugnance for haphazard assumptions and arbitrary statements, which is the essential distinction of the educated from the uneducated mind".

In the daily running of his science school, Huxley seems to have exercised just that combination of decisiveness with toleration which is the mark of the good administrator. To a new subordinate, he was rather stern and exacting; but, once convinced that his man was to be trusted, he practically let him take his own course and never interfered in matters of detail. He respected loyalty and devotion to duty, but did not regard them as automatically warranting elevation in the academic hierarchy. "No doubt seniority ought to count", he wrote (*L.L.* II, 295); "but it is mere ruin to any service to let it interfere with the promotion of men of marked superiority, especially in the case of offices which involve much responsibility." He saw to it that the demonstrators discharged their duties effectively, and did not allow the demands of research to take automatic precedence over teaching. By the end of Huxley's first year of office, it had been decided that women teachers in training were eligible to take the School's Associateship along with men; soon a training college lecturer was allowed to work in the School's laboratories at a reduced fee; and, in general, the whole place was geared to the educational needs of its students.

Since the middle 1860s, there had been repeated rumblings of discontent about the manner in which the ancient Livery Companies and Guilds of the City of London used (or abused) their vast wealth. The more long-sighted among the magnates eventually saw the writing on the wall, and began to consider the possibility of applying some of their funds to technical and commercial education, which Gladstone had hinted would be much welcomed by his government. From about 1870 Huxley figured with increasing prominence at Mansion House functions, and in succeeding years he alternated private cajolery with public exhortation. "Professor Huxley delivered a very amusing address last Saturday at the Society of Arts", the *Spectator* (8 December 1877) informed its readers, "on the very unpromising subject of technical education, but we believe that if Professor Huxley were to become the President of the Social Science Association, or of the International Statistical Congress, he would still be amusing, so much bottled life does he infuse into the driest topic on which human beings ever contrive to prose." A year later, as guest of honour at the Drapers' banquet, he was publicly thanked for the very able advice which he had given to the City, and soon a report appeared proposing the erection of a new central technical college together with adequate provision for tutorial salaries and student exhibitions. When after twelve months there looked like being undue delay in making firm decisions, Huxley took the opportunity of another Society of Arts meeting to apply further pressure. The Guilds, he declared (*Nature*, 11 December 1879), "possessed enormous wealth, which had been left them for the benefit of the trades they represent ... they were morally bound to do this work for the country, and he hoped if they continued to neglect the obligation they would be legally compelled to do it. ... If the people did not insist on the wealth being applied to its proper purpose, they deserved to be taxed down to their shoes." Quickly following up by a letter to *The Times* (15 December 1879), he pointed out that "The inmost financial secrets of the Church and of the colleges of Oxford and Cambridge have been laid bare by those universal solvents, Royal Commissions; but no Government which has existed in this country for the last century has been strong enough to apply such *aqua regia* to the strong-boxes of the City Guilds."

These tactics proved very successful. "The animal is moving", Huxley wrote (*L.L.* I, 474) to the old Chartist George Howell in the January of 1880, "and by a judicious exhibition of carrots in front and kicks behind, we shall get him into a fine trot presently." Huxley was, declared one of its leading members (*H.P.* 12. 207), "really the engineer of the City and Guilds Institute; for without his advice, we should not have known what to have done." In the July of 1881 the Prince of Wales laid the foundation column of the City and Guilds College in South Kensington, and soon it was functioning side by side with the School of Mines and the Normal School (later the Royal College) of Science. All three of the essential elements in Huxley's grand design were thus established, to combine eventually into the great Imperial College of Science and Technology.

CHAPTER 12

Philosophy and mental phenomena

FROM his early adolescent years Huxley had been interested in philosophical questions and had demonstrated a marked philosophical bent. But, whereas many men find that the daily demands of an active life gradually crowd out such interests, with him they grew more compelling as the years went by. And, while many working scientists not only ignore philosophy but actually take philistine pride in doing so, he believed that such an attitude was simply self-deluding.

> The maxim that metaphysical inquiries are barren of result, [he wrote (*C.E.* VI, 288),] and that the serious occupation of the mind with them is a mere waste of time and labour, finds much favour in the eyes of the many persons who pride themselves on the possession of sound common sense ... And it is not a little curious to observe that those who most loudly profess to abstain from such commodities are, all the while, unconscious consumers, on a great scale, of one or other of their multitudinous disguises or adulterations. With mouths full of the particular kind of heavily buttered toast which they affect, they inveigh against the eating of plain bread. ... But the fish of immortal memory, who threw himself out of the frying pan into the fire, was not more ill-advised than the man who seeks sanctuary from philosophical persecution within the walls of the observatory or of the laboratory.

It was this conviction of the importance of philosophy which led Huxley to accept Morley's invitation, in the spring of 1878, to do a volume on Hume for the "English Men of Letters" series. He was soon writing (*L.L.* I, 496) to tell the editor, "I find the job as tough as it is interesting. Hume's demands, before the public can see them properly, want a proper setting in a methodical and consistent shape—and that implies writing a small psychological treatise of one's own, and then cutting it down into as unobtrusive a form as possible. So I am working away at my draught—from the point of view of an aesthetic jeweller." By the end of his summer holiday, Huxley had virtually finished the job except for a final polishing and an introductory biographical section. "I am through all the interesting part of Hume's life—", he wrote (*L.L.* I, 497) in October, "that is, the struggling part of it—and David the successful and the fêted begins to bore me, as I am sorry to say most successful people do." Since he had no real interest in these two preliminary chapters, and did not start them until the bulk of the book was already in proof, it is not surprising that they form a pretty pedestrian biography. But the eleven succeeding chapters are of conspicuous clarity. "*Hume*", a modern critic (Irvine, 1955, 260) has remarked, "is such a book as a brilliantly gifted and educated man might write in six weeks. It is compact and well organized, sometimes witty and eloquent. It not only makes Hume clearer than Hume, but improves and corrects him in many important particulars."

For Huxley, any philosophical speculation which did not take account of both the data and the methods of natural science was unreal. "The Platonic philosophy", he wrote (*C.E.* VI, viii), "is probably the grandest example of the unscientific use of the imagination extant. ... Ancient thought, so far as it is positive, fails ... because it forgets that proof of the inconsistencies of the terms in which we symbolise things has nothing to do with the cogency of the logic of facts. The negations of Pyrrhonism are as shallow, as the assumptions of Platonism are empty. ... In face of the incessant verification of deductive reasoning by experiment, Pyrrhonism has become ridiculous." "In truth", be believed (*id.* 61), "the laboratory is the forecourt of the temple of philosophy; and whoso has not offered sacrifices and undergone purification there, has little chance of admission into the sanctuary." For (*id.* 68)

> it is the business of criticism not only to keep watch over the vagaries of philosophy, but to do the duty of police in the whole world of thought. Wherever it espies sophistry or superstition they are to be bidden to stand; nay, they are to be followed to their very dens and there apprehended and exterminated ... the business of carrying the war into the enemy's camp has gone on but slowly. Like other campaigns, it long languished for want of a good base of operations. But since physical [natural] science, in the course of the last fifty years, has brought to the front an inexhaustible supply of heavy artillery of a new pattern, warranted to drive solid bolts of fact through the thickest skulls, things are looking better.

This determination to face facts affected Huxley's thought in every field, including that of moral philosophy. "Even a 'Traité des Passions', to be worth anything", he remarked (*id.* vi), "must be based upon obser-

vation and experiment: and, in this subject, facilities for laboratory practice of the most varied and extensive character were offered by the Paris
of Mazarin and the Duchesses." So far as Hume's speculations on moral
behaviour were concerned, however, he considered them altogether too
remote from reality. "In this paean to virtue", he commented (*id.* 237),
"there is more of the dance measure than will sound appropriate in the
ears of most of the pilgrims who toil painfully... along the rough and
steep roads which lead to the higher life.... The calculation of the greatest happiness is not performed quite so easily as a rule of three sum;
while, in the hour of temptation, the question will crop up, whether...
a bird in the hand is not worth two in the bush."

Huxley would not simply assume that any particular moral law accepted at any particular time by any particular society was necessarily correct,
and in a *Nineteenth Century* symposium (1877–9) he wrote: "If it can be
shown by observation or experiment that theft, murder, and adultery
do not tend to diminish the happiness of society, then, in the absence
of any but natural knowledge, they are not social immoralities." On the
other hand, he was quite unwilling to slide into a situation of mere moral
relativism, in which any person's views were accepted as equally valid
with any other's.

> Some people cannot by any means be got to understand the first book of
> Euclid, [(*C.E.* VI, 239),] but the truths of mathematics are no less necessary
> and binding on the great mass of mankind. Some there are who cannot feel
> the difference between the 'Sonata Appassionata' and 'Cherry Ripe' ... but
> the canons of art are none the less acknowledged. While some there may be,
> who, devoid of sympathy, are incapable of a sense of duty; but neither does their
> existence affect the foundations of morality. Such pathological deviations from
> true manhood are merely the halt, the lame, and the blind of the world of con-
> sciousness ... And as there as Pascals and Mozarts, Newtons and Raffaellos ... so
> there have been men of moral genius, to whom we owe ideals of duty and
> visions of moral perfection, which ordinary mankind could never have attained.

Huxley was a great admirer of Descartes, whom he regarded as one of
the truly seminal philosophical thinkers. Speaking in 1870 to the Cambridge Y.M.C.A., he pointed out (*C.E.* I, 190) that, "of the two paths
opened up to us in the 'Discourse upon Method', the one leads, by way
of Berkeley and Hume, to Kant and Idealism; while the other leads, by
way of De La Mettrie and Priestley, to modern physiology and Materialism. Our stem divides into two main branches, which grow in opposite

ways, and bear flowers which look as different as they can well be. But each branch is sound and healthy, and has as much life and vigour as the other. . . . Their differences are complementary, not antagonistic; and thought will never be completely fruitful until the one unites with the other." The following year, in his Royal Institution Lecture, "Bishop Berkeley on the Metaphysics of Sensation", Huxley argued that, in the last resort, there was no logical escape from Locke's conclusion—that ultimately we have no real knowledge either of the 'substance' of matter or of the 'substance' of mind.

He had, indeed, already come to this conclusion at least eight years earlier, as a letter (*H.P.* 19. 229) to Kingsley made clear:

> My fundamental axiom of speculative philosophy is that *materialism and spiritualism are opposite poles of the same absurdity*—the absurdity of imagining that we know anything about either spirit or matter. . . . The two-fluid theory and the one-fluid theory of electricity both accounted for the phenomena up to a certain extent, and both were probably wrong. So it may be with the theories that there is only one x in nature or two x's or three x's. For if you will think upon it, there are only four possible ontological hypotheses now that Polytheism is dead.
>
> I There is no $x=$ Atheism on Berkeleyan principles.
>
> II There is only one $x =$ Materialism or Pantheism, according as you turn it heads or tails
>
> III There are two x's $\Big\}$ = Speculators incertae sedis.
> Spirit and Matter
>
> IV There are three x's $\Big\}$ = Orthodox Theologians.
> God, Souls, Matter
>
> To say that I adopt any one of these hypotheses, as a representation of fact, would to my mind be absurd; but No. 2 is the one I can work with best.

Although Huxley always maintained that, in terms of formal logic, neither philosophical idealism nor philosophic materialism could ever be proved correct, his preference for the latter was in practice unambiguous. In particular, he insisted that psychology must be approached in this spirit. "As there is an anatomy of the body, so there is an anatomy of the mind. . .", he wrote (*C.E.* VI, 59), "as the physiologist inquires into the way in which the so-called 'functions' of the body are performed, so the psychologist studies the so-called 'faculties' of the mind. . . . But there is more than a parallel, there is a close and intimate connection between psychology and physiology. . . . On whatever ground we term physiology, science, psychology is entitled to the same appellation."

He had no real doubt (*id.* 94) that "the key to the comprehension of mental operations lies in the study of the molecular changes of the nervous apparatus by which they are originated. ... What we call the operations of the mind are functions of the brain, and the materials of consciousness are products of cerebral activity...whenever those states of consciousness which we call sensation, or emotion, or thought, come into existence, complete investigation will show good reason for the belief that they are preceded by those other phenomena of consciousness to which we give the names of matter and motion." This, indeed, he held so strongly that he once, perhaps unwisely, declared (*C.E.* I, 191), "we shall, sooner or later, arrive at a mechanical equivalent of consciousness, just as we have arrived at a mechanical equivalent of heat". Lenin (1908, 267) was, therefore, quite justified in his remark, "Huxley's philosophy is as much a mixture of Hume and Berkeley as is Mach's philosophy. But in Huxley's case the Berkeleian streaks are incidental, and agnosticism serves as a fig-leaf for materialism."

Strangely, Lenin seems not to have noticed that, although so far as we know Huxley never studied Marx or Engels, his materialism had a decidedly dialectical flavour. He was never a simple mechanical materialist, which explains the friendly fun (*L.L.* I, 231) he made of Tyndall ("In fact, a favourite problem of his is—Given the molecular forces in a mutton chop, deduce Hamlet or Faust therefrom"). His own more subtle materialism was expressed in such forms as this (*C.E.* VI, 286):

> If matter is the substratum of any phenomena of consciousness, animal or human, then it may possibly be the substratum of any other such phenomena; if matter is imperishable, then it must be admitted to be possible that some of its combinations may be indefinitely enduring, just as our present so-called 'elements' are probably only compounds which have been indissoluble, in our planet, for millions of years. Moreover, the ultimate forms of existence which we distinguish in our little speck of the universe are, possibly, only two out of infinite varieties of existence, not only analogous to matter and analogous to mind, but of kinds which we are not competent so much as to conceive.

There was also notable subtlety in his 1887 remark (*C.E.* V, 113), that "It is quite possible to imagine that the mass of matter should vary according to circumstances, as we know its weight does."

Huxley, moreover, seems often to have visualised the production of novelty by discontinuous leaps—as in his criticism of Darwin's almost exclusive concentration on very small variations as the raw material of natural selection; in his speculations on a possible mechanism of heredity and on the possibility of evolutionary changes in the chemical elements; and even in his suggestions about the evolutionary emergence of the human mind. There is an almost classically dialectic ring to his statement (*C.E.* I, 145), that "the living protoplasm is always dying, and, strange as the paradox may sound, could not live unless it died." And there is an unmistakable affinity with marxism in his remarks (*C.E.* I, 268 and 283), that "men have become largely absorbed in the mere accumulation of wealth; and as this is a matter in which the plainest and strongest form of self-interest is intensely concerned, science (in the shape of Political Economy) has readily demonstrated that self-interest may be safely left to find the best way of attaining its ends" and "If it can be clearly proved that the abolition of [private] property would tend still more to promote the good of the people, the State will have the same justification for abolishing property that it now has for maintaining it". It is therefore interesting that, according to Ilza Veith (1960, III, 16), when *Evolution and Ethics* was translated by Yen Fu, "Immediately upon its publication in 1889, it became one of the most influential textbooks in Chinese education... [and]... furnished the intellectual basis for China's great upheaval beginning with 1911". And even in our own generation, Ssu-yu Teng tells us (Teng and Fairbank, 1954, 267), "The things they [the Chinese communist leaders] say to shield themselves from condemnation are regularly drawn from Yen Fu's translation of T. H. Huxley's Principles of Evolution".

Passionately interested as he always was in the precise use of language, Huxley was ever on the look-out for verbal snares. Thus, despite his deep admiration for Descartes, he commented (*H.P.* 19. 229), "*Cogito ergo sum* is to my mind a ridiculous piece of bad logic, all I can say at any time being 'Cogito'. The Latin form I hold to be preferable to the English, 'I think', because the latter asserts the existence of an Ego—about which the bundle of phenomena at present addressing you knows nothing." Similarly, in a discussion of mental functioning, he issued (*C.E.* VI, 72) a salutary warning against the tendency, by no means yet extinct, to give mental phenomena labels and then treat the labels as meaningful things in their own right:

> In the language of common life, the 'mind' is spoken of as an entity, independent of the body, though resident in and closely connected with it, and endowed with numerous 'faculties', such as sensibility, understanding, memory, volition, which stand in the same relation to the mind as the organs do to the body, and

perform the functions of feeling, reasoning, remembering and willing. ... The popular classification and terminology of the phenomena of consciousness, however, are ... a legacy, and, in many respects a sufficiently *damnosa haereditas*, of ancient philosophy, more or less leavened by theology. ... Very little attention to what passes in the mind is sufficient to show, that these conceptions involve assumptions of an extremely hypothetical character. And the first business of the student of psychology is to get rid of such prepossessions.

Huxley, like most other philosophers, was much engaged by the problem of necessity and free will, but he approached this question also with particular attention to the importance of avoiding the reification of verbal terms.

It is [he remarked (*id.* 145),] commonly urged that the axiom of causation cannot be derived from experience, because experience only proves that many things have causes, whereas the axiom declares that all things have causes. ... And this objection is perfectly sound so far as it goes. The axiom of causation cannot possibly be deduced from any general proposition which simply embodies experience. But it does not follow that the belief, of expectation, expressed by the axiom, is not a product of experience, generated antecedently to, and altogether independently of, the logically unjustifiable language in which we express it ... to seek for the reason of the facts in the verbal symbols by which they are expressed, and to be astonished that it is not to be found there is surely singular.

And thus, he argued (*id.* 214 and 221),

The only meaning of the law of causation, in the physical world, is, that it generalises universal experience of the order of that world; and, if experience shows a similar order to obtain among states of consciousness, the law of causation will properly express that order. ... The passionate assertion of the consciousness of their freedom, which is the favourite refuge of the opponents of the doctrine of necessity, is mere futility, for nobody denies it. What they really have to do, if they would upset the necessarian argument, is to prove ... that, whatever may be the fixity of the universe of things, that of thought is given over to chance.

And, he emphasised (*id.* 285), "If the order which obtains in the material world lays it open to the reproach of 'blind necessity', the demonstrable existence of a similar order amidst the phenomena of consciousness ... renders it obnoxious to the same condemnation. For necessity is necessity, and whether it be blind or sharp-eyed is nothing to the purpose."

In his consideration of the nature of natural laws, Huxley took issue with Hume's acceptance of them as things that could be 'violated', as in the case of so-called 'miracles'. On the contrary, he argued, this is

a misuse of language, for a 'law of nature' is merely a statement generalising experience; and, if a very unusual event is shown to 'break' a law,
this simply indicates that the 'law' is in need of amendment. "But ...",
he warned (*id*. 158), "the more a statement of fact conflicts with previous
experience, the more complete must be the evidence which is to justify
us in believing it. ... If a man tells me he saw a piebald horse in Picca-
dilly, I believe him without hesitation. ... But if the same person tells me
he observed a zebra there, I might hesitate a little about accepting his
testimony. ... If, however, my informant assured me that he beheld
a centaur trotting down that famous thoroughfare, I should emphatically
decline to credit his statement: and this even if he were the most saintly of
men and ready to suffer martyrdom in support of his belief." And yet
(*id*. 157)—with clear reference to the greatest of all 'miracles'—"if a dead
man did come to life, the fact would be evidence, not that any law of nature
had been violated, but that those laws, even when they express the
results of a very long and uniform experience, are necessarily based on
incomplete knowledge, and are to be held only as grounds of more or less
justifiable expectation."

But Huxley was always vividly aware of the common human propen-
sity for wishful thinking, and consciously tried to avoid sliding into it
himself. Shortly after the death of his darling first-born Noel, and therefore at a time when he would dearly have wished for some hope of immortality, he made his position plain in a letter to Charles Kingsley. "I have
no *a priori* objection to the doctrine...", he wrote (*H.P.* 19. 169). "Give
me such evidence as would justify me in believing anything else and I will
believe that. ... [but] Science ... warns me to be careful how I adopt
a view which jumps with my preconceptions, and to require stronger
evidence for such belief than for one to which I was previously hostile.
My business is to teach my aspirations to conform themselves to fact,
not to try and make facts harmonise with my aspirations."

Huxley's attitude to 'miracles' was closely paralleled by his attitude
to 'spiritualism' and what we should nowadays call supernatural or
paranormal psychic phenomena. Nothing was absolutely denied *a priori*,
but the most convincing evidence was called for. As a young man, he had
attended a number of séances and had been unfavourably impressed,
which explained his refusal to join the 1871 investigating committee of
the Dialectical Society. Nevertheless, when Darwin displayed interest
in 1874, and asked him to attend and report on a carefully organised

séance, Huxley agreed and went *incognito*. After a while, things began to happen. But Huxley had spotted three small points of light coming in from the corridor outside; and, by carefully observing the successive occasions when they were respectively blotted out from his line of vision, he succeeded in explaining how the various 'manifestations' had been produced. Darwin thanked him, saying (*L.L.* I, 423), "and now to my mind an enormous amount of evidence would be requisite to make me believe in anything beyond mere trickery". After that, Huxley left the investigation of spiritualism alone, explaining (Wallace, 1905, II, 281) that "I gave it up for the same reason I abstain from chess—It's too amusing to be fair work, and too hard work to be amusing".

His basically biological approach to psychology led Huxley to an estimation of the probable mental functioning of animals much more akin to that now emerging than to that common among his contemporaries. He would not accept the widespread view that abstract ideas are impossible without verbal expression. On the contrary, he argued (*C.E.* VI, 116), "The infant who knows the meaning neither of 'sugar-plum' nor of 'sweet', nevertheless is in full possession of that complex idea, which, when he has learned to employ language, will take the form of the abstract proposition, 'A sugar-plum will be sweet'". Unfortunately, he pointed out (*id.*, 128), "the proposition, or verbal representative of a belief, has come to be regarded as a reality, instead of as the mere symbol which it really is. . . . It is a fallacy similar to that of supposing that money is the foundation of wealth, whereas it is only the wholly unessential symbol of property." And, he insisted (*id.* 122),

> Whatever cogency is attached to the arguments in favour of the occurrence of all the fundamental phenomena of mind in young children and deaf mutes, an equal force must be allowed to appertain to those which may be adduced to prove that the higher animals have minds. . . . Whatever reason we have for believing that the changes which take place in the normal cerebral substance of man give rise to states of consciousness, the same reason exists for the belief that the modes of motion of the cerebral substance of an ape, or of a dog, produce like effects. . . . In short it seems hard to assign any good reason for denying to the higher animals any mental state, or process, in which the employment of the vocal or visual symbols of which language is composed is not involved; and comparative psychology confirms the position in relation to the rest of the animal world assigned to man by comparative anatomy.

It is noticeable that, on all the major issues of philosophy, Huxley's final positions did not differ greatly from those taken as a young man.

He clarified and developed his thinking, but on none of the main issues did he fundamentally change. This could, of course, be taken as evidence of intellectual rigidity. Much more likely, it is evidence of the early attainment of a coherent interpretation of the universe, capable of withstanding criticism and of assimilating large accretions of scientific knowledge. It is noticeable, too, that Huxley took the traditional view of philosophy as being both a systematised general outlook on life and a rigorous examination of what we can know and how we can know it. And, in view of this, he would perhaps not be counted a genuine philosopher by those modern specialists who have narrowed the discipline down to little more than linguistic analysis and logical pattern-making. But, since any definition which excludes Huxley on these grounds also excludes most of the great philosophers through the ages, if he is rejected he is at least rejected in good company.

CHAPTER 13

Last years at South Kensington

HUXLEY's last few years at South Kensington saw a continuation of that rapid transformation through which English society had been passing during the preceding decade. In 1879 Somerville and Lady Margaret Colleges were founded at Oxford to provide facilities for female education such as Girton and Newnham already gave at Cambridge. The Firth University College opened its doors in Sheffield, the Teachers' Training Syndicate was appointed at Cambridge, the *Boys' Own Paper* was launched on the market of a newly literate juvenile population. In 1880 Owens College completed its transition to the Victoria University of Manchester, Mason College marked the beginning of the University of Birmingham, and Charles Booth founded his Salvation Army. A year later, the University College of Liverpool was founded, the Cambridge Tripos examinations were opened to women, and the *Evening News* appeared. Disraeli died and P. G. Wodehouse was born, W. G. Stead made his startling exposure of London's traffic in girls, and Annie Besant stood trial with Charles Bradlaugh for publishing a birth-control booklet, *The Fruits of Philosophy*. In 1882 the second Married Women's Property Act was passed, Quintin Hogg's new Polytechnic was opened in Regent Street, Darwin died and James Joyce was born. During the next year Karl Marx died, Maxim invented his automatic gun, and the Society for Psychical Research began its investigations. The year after that, the Fabian Society and the Social Democratic Federation were founded, Toynbee Hall was opened in London's East End, the first part of the great *Oxford English Dictionary* was published, and the first *Agnostic Annual* appeared. In 1885 government grants to the tune of £3,000,000 marked the passing of the point of no return in England's slow journey towards a national system of education. And that was the year in which Huxley retired from his professorial post at South Kensington.

It was probably during his first year as Dean, shortly after the coming

115

of age of *The Origin of Species*, that Huxley jotted down in a notebook of aphorisms (*H.P.* 57) the following interesting reflections:

The Four Stages of Public Opinion

I (Just after publication)
The Novelty is absurd and subversive of Religion and Morality
The propounder both fool and knave.

II (Twenty years later)
The Novelty is absolute Truth and will yield a full and satisfactory explanation of things in general—The Propounder man of sublime genius and perfect virtue.

III (Forty years later)
The Novelty won't explain things in general after all and therefore is a wretched failure. The Propounder a very ordinary person advertised by a clique.

IV (A century later)
The Novelty is a mixture of truth and error. Explains as much as could reasonably be expected.

The propounder worthy of all honour in spite of his share of human frailties, as one who has added to the permanent possessions of science.

It was also about this time, when George Eliot died, that a small group of friends (who had refused to boycott her because she openly 'lived in sin') decided to put pressure on the Dean of Westminster to have her remains interred in the Abbey. Despite his high regard for George Eliot, Huxley refused to join in, and his reason (*L.L.* II, 18) was very salutary: "One cannot eat one's cake and have it too. Those who elect to be free in thought and deed must not hanker after the rewards, if they are to be so called, which the world offers to those who put up with its fetters."

Shortly before this incident, Gladstone's Home Secretary had asked Huxley to become Inspector of Salmon Fisheries, with duties extending well beyond that particular species. "It is not a *grand* place", Harcourt apologised (*H.P.* 18. 5), "nor as good in its emoluments as I could desire, for it is worth only £700 per ann." Still, he urged, "Salmon have the good taste to addict themselves to healthy and picturesque localities... I do not see why you should not inspect the fish as well as Newton governed the Mint." Huxley was convinced that much nonsense was being talked about fishery matters, and he looked forward to the opportunities which the post would offer for making those concerned face up to the facts of fluvial and marine ecology. "I hope to be of some use", he explained (*L.L.* II, 22) to Farrer early in 1881; "of the few innocent pleasures left to men past middle life—the jamming of common-sense down the throats of fools is perhaps the keenest." He also enjoyed the opportunity of putting semi-feudal landowners in their place, gleefully telling Spencer Walpole after one sitting (*L.L.* II, 26), "We have begun very well, we have sat upon a duke". When the enthusiastic Fish Culture Society proposed breeding cod in captivity to stock up the deep-sea fisheries, he countered with a *reductio ad absurdum* suggestion that the whale supply should be increased in like manner. When it was argued that heavy trawling 'must' reduce the herring population of the North Sea, he produced quantitative compari-sons of the annual herring catch with the number of fish in a single herring shoal—adding (*L.L.* II, 29) the general observation that, in questions of biology, "if any one tells me it 'stands to reason' that such and such things must happen, I generally find reason to doubt the safety of his standing". He did, however, consider it quite possible that particular in-shore areas might suffer from over-fishing, and therefore extended an order regulating the taking of crabs and lobsters off the Norfolk coast. And, by a concen-trated series of studies in his South Kensington laboratory, he managed to elucidate the *Saprolegnia* nature of the increasingly damaging 'salmon disease'.

Almost immediately after accepting the fisheries post at the Home Secretary's urging, Huxley found himself under equal pressure from the Lord President of the Privy Council to serve on a new Royal Commission on the Medical Acts. "The Public would have much confidence in you", wrote Earl Spencer (*H.P.* 26. 190). "May I reckon on your accepting if I submit your name to the Queen?" Huxley still remembered his own student days, when—not counting the Archbishop of Canterbury—there had been twenty quite independent licensing bodies. Since then things had somewhat improved, but the profession was still in a pretty bad way, so he agreed to serve despite his poor health. It so happened that the International Medical Congress, meeting in London that summer, invited him to be its President, and this provided an admirable platform for the public airing of his opinions. In his presidential address, "On the Relation of the Biological Sciences with Medicine", he castigated the medical authorities for maintaining archaically artificial divisions be-tween the various branches of the subject. "It is", he pointed out (*C.E.* III, 349), "a peculiarity of the physical [natural] sciences that they are independent in proportion as they are imperfect; and it is only as they advance that the bonds which really unite them become apparent."

He admitted that much of the ordinary practitioner's work must still be largely empirical, but urged (*C.E.* III, 372) that "pathology is the analogue of the theory of perturbations in astronomy; and therapeutics resolves itself into the discovery of the means by which a system of forces competent to eliminate any given perturbation may be introduced into the economy [of the body]. ... It will [eventually] ... become possible to introduce into the economy a molecular mechanism which, like a very cunningly contrived torpedo, shall find its way to some particular group of living elements, and cause an explosion among them, leaving the rest untouched." None of this seems especially startling in these days of highly specific super-drugs devised for selective absorption or preferential action, but in the nineteenth century it must have appeared somewhat novel doctrine.

It was quite impossible to produce practitioners of such scientific outlook by the sort of medical education then prevailing. Huxley therefore pressed for a thorough rationalisation of the medical curriculum, and especially for the clearing out of a great accumulation of ancient lumber. His general attitude was still the same as it had been eleven years earlier when, in a caustic comment (*C.E.* III, 320) on the compulsory study of *materia medica*, he had told the students of University College Medical School, "I cannot understand the arguments for obliging a medical man to know all about drugs and where they come from. Why not make him belong to the Iron and Steel Institute, and learn something about cutlery, because he uses knives?" In the main, however, the Commission concerned itself with organisational matters, and recommended sweeping away all individual licensing powers and compensating the existing corporations in proportion to their former incomes from fees. Huxley thought it preposterous that licensing bodies which had attracted large numbers of examinees by setting low standards should now reap correspondingly large financial rewards, and he saw no reason why the few reputable bodies should be abolished along with the disreputable. He had no confidence that a completely new State examining system would necessarily function any better than the best of the existing boards, and he found positive virtue in permitting some degree of variance in regulations and curricula. He therefore produced his own Minority Report, and used his 1884 opening address at the London Hospital Medical School to fire a few shots in his one-man minority campaign.

Of the old chaotic system Huxley remarked (*C.E.* III, 328), "I should think it hardly possible that it could have obtained anywhere but in such a country as England, which cherishes a fine old crusted abuse as much as it does its port wine. ... The examination might be a sham, the curriculum might be a sham, the certificate might be bought and sold like anything in a shop. ... It was possible for a young man ... to be turned loose upon the public, like death on a pale horse." He admitted that things had improved since the Medical Act of 1858, but they were still far from satisfactory. He condemned (*C.E.* III, 336) the majority proposals of the Royal Commission as constituting "a perpetual endowment of the 'black sheep', calculated on the maximum of their ill-gained profits", to which he could not assent. His own proposal was to put the blackest sheep out of business, without any question of compensation, by making legally compulsory a tripartite qualification in medicine, surgery and obstetrics; while the not-quite-so-black could be cleaned up by the appointment of coadjutor-examiners. He was not very optimistic about the chances of overcoming medical conservatism quickly, and even today not all his ideas for the improvement of medical education have been effected. Still, on the major matter of the regulation of professional licensing, it was Huxley's rather than the majority attitude which finally prevailed in the Medical Act of 1886.

During these years Huxley's health was again becoming very shaky, but he still found difficulty in denying his services to good causes. So, in 1881, he agreed to become President of the Sanitary Protection Association, and delivered a few broadsides against those who seemed to value unlimited individual liberty so highly as virtually to disregard the general welfare of society. Similarly, a year later, he could not resist the request of the Indian Famine Commissioners to advise them on the promotion of agricultural education. However, when a very flattering letter (*H.P.* 6. 146) arrived from Harvard, asking, "Now is it any use to make any kind of proposition to you? ... we could offer you say $10,000 a year for the benefit of your presence and influence", he firmly resisted the temptation. In 1883, after a dozen years in the less prestigious but more arduous post of Secretary, Huxley at last accepted the Presidency of the Royal Society. He also became a Trustee of the British Museum, delivered the Rede Lecture at Cambridge, worked away to extract money for technical education from the City Livery, and still managed to find time for a substantial course of lectures to working men. He tried to avoid appointment as Crown Senator of the University of London, telling the Chancellor that he doubted if he could manage to do justice to the office, but Earl Granville (*L.L.* II, 59) simply replied, "Clay, the great whist player, once made a mistake and said to his partner, 'My brain is softening', the latter answered, 'Never mind, I will give you £10,000 down for it, just as it is'. On that principle and backed up by Paget, I shall write to Harcourt on Monday."

At this time Huxley was increasingly enjoying the company of his children as they grew older, and his correspondence with them makes charming reading. "Dearest Pabelunza—", he wrote (*L.L.* II, 63) in the April of 1883 to Ethel, then aged sixteen and paying a visit to a married sister, "I was quite overcome today to find that you had vanished without a parting embrace to your 'faded but fascinating' parent. I clean forgot that you were going to leave this peaceful village [London] for the whirl of Gloucester dissipation this morning. ... My dear, I should like to have given you some good counsel. You are but a simple village maiden—don't be taken in by the appearance of anybody. Consult your father—inclosing photograph and measurement (in inches)—in any case of difficulty." The same sort of sparkle appeared in December, when he wrote (*L.L.* II, 62) to Morley lamenting his own advancing age: "It is a curious thing that I find my dislike to the thought of extinction increasing as I get older and nearer the goal. It flashes across me at all sorts of times with a sort of horror that in 1900 I shall probably know no more of what is going on than I did in 1800. I had sooner be in hell a good deal—at any rate in one of the upper circles, where the climate and company are not too trying." But less than a year later he was less sparkling, and wrote (*L.L.* II, 73) to tell Donnelly, "I find myself distinctly aged—tired out body and soul, and for the first time in my life fairly afraid of the work that lies before me ... I am morally and mentally sick of society and societies—committees, councils—bother about details and general worry and waste of time. I feel as if more than another year of it would be the death of me. Next May I shall be sixty, and have been thirty-one mortal years in my present office in the School. Surely I may sing my *nunc dimittis* with a good conscience."

An autumn holiday in the West Country improved his health temporarily, but worsening dyspepsia and general nervous debility soon made his doctor order him abroad on pain of a complete and final breakdown. Huxley himself now expected to live only another couple of years, and he took the trip to Italy in easy stages. Sadly, just before setting out, he heard that his darling Marian had been stricken by the beginnings of a hopeless disease, but he found sufficient strength to keep the knowledge to himself so as to preserve the rest of the family from futile distress. Early in November, he summoned up further strength to return home for Rachel's wedding to W. A. Eckersley, the civil engineer, but was soon packed off again to the 'sunny south'. Verona was very cold, Bologna even colder, and Ravenna under deep snow. In Rome, however (*L.L.* II, 88), he found that "the hopeless bad taste of the Papists is a source of continual gratification to me as a good Protestant (and something more)", and he began a serious study (*L.L.* II, 91) of the catacombs "as a kind of Christian fossils out of which one can reconstruct the body of the primitive church. She was a simple maiden enough and vastly more attractive than the bedizened old harridan of the modern Papacy." By the beginning of February 1885 he was well enough to visit the Academia de' Lincei and to write the preface for a new edition of *Physiology*. By the end of the month he was examining the prehistoric archaeology of Sienna; early in March he explored the art treasures of Florence; and in April he felt sufficiently recovered to return to the rigours of England. However, he was now quite determined to reduce his burdens, and in May he resigned his Presidency of the Royal Society, his Inspectorship of Fisheries and his Professorship at the School of Science.

Even then, the Government would not let him go completely, but persuaded him to remain as Honorary Dean of the School with general supervisory authority. Effectively, however, he had retired; and when Oxford University, the last of those that did so, invited him to accept a doctorate *honoris causa*, he replied (*H.P.* 24. 206), "It will be a sort of apotheosis coincident with my official death which is imminent—In fact, I am dead already only the Treasury Charon has not yet settled the conditions upon which I am to be ferried over to the other side." The conditions were soon to be settled in a most satisfactory manner. All sorts of strings were pulled by all sorts of people; a Civil List pension was provided to supplement the sum calculated by the Treasury in terms of his official salary; and Huxley was able to leave South Kensington on a handsome total pension of £1500 a year—in 1885 money.

CHAPTER 14

Controversy in retirement

"CONTROVERSY is as abhorrent to me as gin to a reclaimed drunkard", Huxley had told Morley (*L.L.* I, 488) in 1878; and it is true that for some time he seems to have remained uncharacteristically non-combatant. He was desperately overworked and chronically weary and dyspeptic, and for the next few years the editors of the reviews received far less from him than formerly. Soon after retiring, he went off in the summer of 1885 for a bracing holiday at Filey and then played grandpater with Jessie's family at Bournemouth. He tried to persuade himself that it was good to be idle, and (*L.L.* II, 114) that "the habit of incessant work into which we all drift is as bad in its way as dram-drinking. In time you cannot be comfortable without the stimulus." Then, in the November number of *The Nineteenth Century*, there came an admirable cholagogic in the form of an article by Gladstone.

Gladstone's objective had been to undermine the modernist position taken up by Révillé in his *Prolégomene de l'Histoire des Religions*, but he unwisely asserted that the order of creation narrated in Genesis was supported by the evidence of science. And this, Huxley told his friends, so stirred up his bile as to set his liver right at once. So he sent Knowles (the editor of *The Nineteenth*) a reply for the December issue and sat back in pleasurable anticipation. "Do read my polishing off of the G.O.M.", he begged Herbert Spencer (*L.L.* II, 115). "I am proud of it as a work of art, and as evidence that the volcano is not yet exhausted." His essay, "The Interpreters of Genesis and the Interpreters of Nature", had no difficulty in demonstrating that Gladstone was guilty of errors of scientific fact, but in Huxley's mind that was not the main point. More than twenty years before this heroic battle began, he had given Kingsley an evaluation of the essential issues (*H.P.* 19. 212): "Whether astronomy and geology can or cannot be made to agree with the statements as to the matters of fact laid down in Genesis—whether the Gospels are historically true or not—are matters of comparatively small moment in the face of the impassable gulf between the anthropomorphism (however refined) of theology and the passionless impersonality of the unknown and unknowable which science shows everywhere underlying the thin veil of phenomena. Here seems to me to be the great gulf fixed between science and theology." Some modern critics, who have expressed surprise that two such intellectual giants devoted so much effort to debating details of biblical narrative, miss the very essence of the controversy.

Those of his contemporaries who recognised that Genesis was in conflict with science, Huxley regarded as both honest and enlightened. Those who maintained the literal infallibility of scripture, he regarded as honest if impervious to evidence. But those who tried to keep a foot in both camps, he held in contempt; and it was these whom he satirised in one of his notebooks (*H.P.* 57):

> Benevolent maunderers stand up and say
> That black and white are but extreme shades of grey;
> Stir up the black creed with the white,
> The grey they make will be just right.

Gladstone, in particular, Huxley considered to deserve no quarter. "That man", he told Benjamin Waugh (*L.L.* I, 353), "has the greatest intellect in Europe. He was born to be a leader of men, and he has debased himself to be a follower of the masses." He once compared him (Grant Duff, 1904, II, 112) to "one of those spotted dogs who runs on in front, but is always turning round to see whether the carriage is coming". And to Hooker (*H.P.* 2. 181) he remarked, "Some of these days he will turn inside out like a blessed Hydra—and I dare say he will talk just as well in that state as in his normal condition. I have never heard or read of any body with such a severely copious chronic glossorhoea."

So, when Gladstone came up still fighting, with an essay entitled "Proem to Genesis" in the 1886 January number, Huxley quickly sent off a rejoinder. "I confess it to have been a work of supererogation"; he told Farrer (*L.L.* II, 116), "but the extreme shiftiness of my antagonist provoked me, and I was tempted to pin him and dissect him as an anatomico-psychological exercise." Knowles, never normally inclined to discourage in-fighting in his columns, was so appalled by the sharpness of the dissection that he begged the dissector to be a little less fierce. "I spent three mortal hours this morning taming my wild cat", Huxley (*ibid.*) assured him when despatching the revised version of "Mr. Glad-stone and Genesis". "He is castrated; his teeth are filed; his claws are cut; he is taught to swear like a 'mieu'; and to spit like a cough; and when he is turned out of the bag you won't know him from a tame rabbit." What a rabbit! And what a ferocious creature the uncastrated cat must have been! Most of the details of the debate, which developed into a furious free-for-all in the correspondence columns of *The Times*, are now as dead as the fossils which figured so largely in it. But, apart from his somewhat unchristian delight in demolishing Gladstone—and a certain hope that this might weaken him politically—Huxley's real concern in this controversy was with the fundamental questions of the proper relation between religion and science on the one hand and between science and theology on the other. His immediately subsequent essay, "The Evolution of Theology: an Anthropological Study", showed what he was capable of in this field when under no temptation to write *ad hominem*.

During 1886 Huxley was still serving on the Royal Society Council and a good dozen other committees, but recurrent bouts of sickness sent him up to the bracing moors of Ilkley and down to the quiet beach of Bournemouth. "I wish I were a Holothurian", he lamented (*L.L.* II, 123), "and could get on without my viscera. I should do splendidly then." He read another set of Herbert Spencer's proofs (one of his periodic attempts to preserve his friend from scientific error) and in passing made a peculiarly interesting comment (*L.L.* II, 127) on the essential nature of the primitive protoplasm: "I conceive it ... as a sort of active crystal with the capacity of giving rise to a great number of pseudomorphs; and I conceive that external conditions favour one or other pseudo-morph, but leave the fundamental mechanism untouched." Towards the end of July, Huxley went with his wife to Harrogate and then accompa-nied his ailing daughter Ethel to Arolla, where he began an intensive study of the Swiss gentians. Then, shortly after his return to England, he became deeply involved in an academic controversy at Oxford.

The university, forced to some degree of reform by the Commissioners of 1877–80, had recently established the Merton Chair of English Lan-guage and Literature, but proposed to place in it the philologist A. S. Napier. Those who had hoped for a man who would profess literature were outraged, and Huxley was begged to intervene. "A protest from you in any public paper", J. C. Collins wrote (*H.P.* 12, 289) in March, "would I am convinced have such an effect at Oxford that it would turn the scale when the matter comes before Congregation." At that time Huxley was weak and weary, and Napier's appointment was confirmed. In the autumn, however, Huxley came hotly to the defence of his native tongue, producing a full-blooded protest which contrasted strongly with a strangely tepid statement from Matthew Arnold. "The establishment of professorial chairs of philology, under the name of literature", Huxley wrote (*Pall Mall Gazette*, 22 October 1886), "may be a profit to science, but is really a fraud practised upon letters. That a young Englishman may be turned out of one of our universities, 'epopt and perfect' so far as their system takes him, and yet ignorant of the noble literature which has grown up in these islands during the last three centuries ... is a fact in the history of the nineteenth century which the twentieth will find hard to believe." His protest was followed by many others and, after a long-drawn-out rearguard action, Oxford finally instituted a Chair of English Literature.

Earlier in the year, that extraordinary character Frank Harris had written (*H.P.* 18. 37) saying, "I wish now that you have slain Gladstone you would write for me a paper 'On the Scientific Basis of Morality', which would charm and instruct us". This plea went unheeded in the ill-health of early spring, but in November Huxley was provoked by W. S. Lilly's essay, "Materialism and Morality". Lilly, a Roman Catholic activist, had implied that since Huxley was a materialist he could not be moral, and very soon Huxley sent Harris a slashing reply, "Science and Morals". "My creed may be an ill-favoured thing", he wrote (*C.E.* IX, 146), "but it is mine own, as Touchstone says of his lady-love; and I have so high an opinion of the solid virtues of the object of my affections that I cannot calmly see her personated by a wench who is much uglier and has no virtue worth speaking of." He insisted that morality has no necessary connection with religious belief, commenting (*id.* 144) that "every society that has existed has had its scum at the top and its dregs at the bottom; but I doubt if any of the 'ages of faith' had less scum or less dregs". And, as for putting the blame for modern wickedness on poor Cinderella Science, he suggested (*id.* 140) that her much older sisters, Philosophy and Theology, had a good deal to answer for: "Cinderella ... lights the fire, sweeps the house, and provides the dinner; and is rewarded by being told that she is a base creature. But in her garret she has fairy visions out of the ken of that pair of shrews who are quarrelling downstairs. She sees the order which pervades the seeming disorder of the world ... and ... that the foundation of morality is to have done, once and for all, with lying." "Have you had the Fortnightly?", he inquired (*L.L.* II, 146) of his wife from Ilkley. "How does my painting of the Lilly look?"

The first half of 1887 found Huxley again suffering frequent bouts of sickness, and repeatedly he had to leave London for periods of indolence in the Isle of Wight. But this was Queen Victoria's Jubilee Year and inevitably he was drawn into the arrangements. The Prince of Wales wanted the occasion marked by the foundation of a great commercial and industrial institute, but nobody seemed very clear about the precise form it should take. There was to be an inaugural Mansion House meeting, and the Prince said that he would esteem it a favour if Huxley would attend and say a few words. Since Huxley believed (*L.L.* II, 151) that "the Institute might be made into something very useful and greatly wanted—if only the projectors could be made to believe that they had always intended to do that which your humble servant wants done", he attended and said a few words. What Huxley wanted (*The Times*, 20 January 1887) was "a sort of neutral ground on which the capitalist and the artisan would be equally welcome... a place in which the fullest stores of industrial knowledge would be made accessible to the public; in which the higher questions of commerce and industry could be systematically studied and elucidated; and where, as in an industrial university, the whole technical education of the country might find its centre and crown". He had the satisfaction of seeing the Prince's committee soon adopt his statement of aims in his own words, but this was one occasion when ultimately he failed to get his way. He was convinced that the Imperial Institute could come to full fruition only in the City, with the world of commerce on its doorstep, but unfortunately the committee was seduced by the attractions of a peppercorn rent in South Kensington. "The thing is already a failure", Huxley lamented (*L.L.* II, 154) to Michael Foster. "I daresay it will go on and be varnished into a simulacrum of success—to become eventually a ghost like the Albert Hall or revive as a tea garden." His prophecy was too gloomy, but not greatly so.

Huxley had still not absolutely abandoned laboratory work, and in 1887 he gave the Royal Society a paper upon an Australian fossil reptile, *Ceratochelys;* but increasingly his interest was being claimed by philosophy. So, when Canon Liddon argued in a sermon that miracles were not incompatible with science, since a 'lower law' might always be suspended by the intervention of a 'higher law', Huxley replied with "Scientific and Pseudo-Scientific Realism". He pointed out (*C.E.* V, 75) that the idea "that high laws may 'suspend' low laws, as a bishop may suspend a curate . . . has nothing to do with modern science. It is scholastic realism—realism as intense and unmitigated as that of Scotus Erigena a thousand years ago." And, he declared (*id.* 79), "the habitual use of the word 'law', in the sense of an active thing, is almost a mark of pseudo-science; it characterises the writings of those who have appropriated the forms of science without knowing anything of the substance". Nevertheless, he recognised the great service which scholasticism had rendered over many years to the development of logic, for (*id.* 67) "It ground and sharpened the dialectical implements of our race. . . . When a logical blunder may ensure combustion, not only in the next world but in this, the construction of syllogisms acquires a peculiar interest." In March the Duke of Argyll entered the fray, complaining of the unfairness of attacking a preacher, whose calling debarred him from disputation. In his April reply, "Science and Pseudo-Science", Huxley really let himself go. "Nothing has done more harm to the clergy", he declared (*C.E.* V, 70), "than the practice, too common among laymen, of regarding them, when in the pulpit, as a sort of chartered libertine, whose divagations are not to be taken seriously. . . . So much for the lecture on propriety." When Knowles received the manuscript he gave (*H.P.* 20. 70) "One gasp of delight ... Poor Duke—he has bearded the lion at last—and got his reward."

By this time, unfortunately, Huxley's health was cracking again and he spent the latter part of May trying to recoup in the New Forest. Then, early in June, the Prime Minister asked him (*H.P.* 12. 148) if he could come to London for private consultation on a "matter of some public interest". This turned out to be a suggestion that the State might honour distinguished cultural services by something analogous to the French *Pour le Mérite*. For himself, Huxley was no more attracted by the idea than he had been by prior suggestions of a peerage. Three years earlier, having read in a newspaper (not for the first time) the fiction that he had agreed to become a peer, he had written (*L.L.* II, 69) amusedly to his wife, "I think we will be 'Markishes', the lower grades are getting common". But this was a matter on which he had strong views of principle, and he once wrote (*C.E.* I, 287) that "Newton and Cuvier lowered themselves when the one accepted an idle knighthood, and the other became a baron of the empire. The great men who went to their graves as Michael Faraday and George Grote seem to me to have understood the dignity of knowledge better when they declined all such meretricious trappings." Not surprisingly, therefore, he told Salisbury that in his view men of science should find their proper recognition in the judgement of their scientific peers. Nevertheless, he continued (*L.L.* II, 165), "although I did not personally care for or desire the institution of such honorary order, yet I thought it was a mistake in policy for the Crown as the fountain of honour to fail in the recognition of that which deserves honour in the world of Science, Letters and Art. Lord Salisbury smilingly summed up. 'Well, it seems that you don't desire the establishment of such an order, but that if you were in my place you would establish it', to which I assented."

As it turned out, England's Order of Merit was not to be finally established until after Huxley's death, but the Premier meanwhile explored other more immediate possibilities. Eventually the problem of honouring Huxley in a manner acceptable to him was solved by making him a Privy Councillor. "The Archbishopric of Canterbury is the only object of ambition that remains to me", he told Hooker (*L.L.* II, 324). "Come and be Suffragan; there is plenty of room at Lambeth and a capital garden."

In the July of 1887 Huxley went down with pleurisy and was ordered to convalesce in Switzerland. Fortunately his native stamina once more reasserted itself, so that before the end of August he was riding about on muleback and again immersed in the study of gentians. He had for a year been busily collecting both specimens and data from friends and correspondents all over the world, and had managed to make some interesting generalisations. For example, virtually all the Antarctic and most of the Andean species were of primary or generalised type, although in the Andes there were a number of coronate forms. Most Arctic specimens had more extensively united petals, those from the Himalaya and Pyrenees were overwhelmingly interlobate, and the great majority of the specialised types were Arctogeal. It appeared, indeed, that the pattern of geographical distribution of gentianaceous flowers displayed a rather surprising sort of parallelism with that of the crayfish group. In explaining such strange facts, Huxley wrote (*L.L.* II, 142) to Hooker, "It is clear that migration helps nothing. ... Relics of a tertiary Flora which once extended from S. America to Eurasia through N. America ... I see a book by Engler on the development of Floras since tertiary epoch. Probably the beggar has the idea."

The deeper he delved, the more Huxley suspected that neither the fossil nor the present distributions of plants could be explained except in terms of major spatial changes and denudations over long periods of time. Huxley's line of phytogeographic thought has, until very recently, been largely ignored in favour of the 'routes of dispersal' approach adopted by Darwin and Wallace. During the last few years, however, Leon Croizat has produced a synthesis of almost all that is known of biogeography, and he has this to say (1960, Ia, 130): "Thomas Henry Huxley... published in 1888 a remarkable work ... which ... hardly any botanist seems ever to have seen ... even less pondered. ... Here a man tells whose thought was, I am sure, of a far better quality at its core than Darwin's and Wallace's". Whether or not Croizat was right in this judgement, probably he was not too far from the mark in his explanation (*ibid.*) of the almost total neglect of Huxley's work in this field: "Hit mankind straight in between the eyes with the hammer of questions that force new thoughts upon its attention, and it will recoil mostly snarling. Feed to it a bowl of rich sweetish pap ... and mankind will erect to your memory a monument in public squares."

Not long after returning to England in the autumn of 1887, Huxley received a bitter blow by the death in November of his brilliant daughter Marian. He was terribly tempted to call off a Manchester meeting, at which he had promised to speak on technical education, but with characteristic conscientiousness he decided (*L.L.*, II, 180), "I cannot leave them in the lurch after stirring up the business in the way I have done, and I must go and give my address. But I must get back to my poor wife as fast as I can." Today, when once more we desperately need a great and necessarily expensive expansion of scientific and technical education, we might well recall Huxley's comment (*C.E.* III, 428) at that time: "There is a well-worn adage that those who set out upon a great enterprise would do well to count the cost. I am not sure that this is always true. I think that some of the very greatest enterprises in this world have been carried out successfully simply because the people who undertook them did not count the cost; and I am much of the opinion that, in this very case, the most important consideration is the cost of doing nothing."

The January of 1888 saw Huxley down again at Bournemouth, struggling against another attack of pleurisy, but life was not without its little pleasures. One of these was preparing for the press his "Struggle for Existence in Human Society". "Great is humbug and it will prevail", he wrote (*L.L.* II, 187) to Knowles, "unless the people who do not like it hit hard. The beast has no brains, but you can knock the heart out of him." On this occasion the acerebral enemy was wearing not a clerical collar but a philosopher's robe, and its visage uncommonly resembled his friend Herbert Spencer. He, like many at that time, favoured completely unrestricted economic competition without any sort of State intervention or social control, and in support produced the comforting pseudoscientific sanction of 'the survival of the fittest'. Huxley, by contrast, considered (*C.E.* IX, 200) that "From the point of view of the moralist the animal world is on about the same level as a gladiator's show", and emphasised (*id.* 215) that "Any one who is acquainted with the state of the population of all great industrial centres . . . is aware that, amidst a large and increasing body of that population, *la misère* reigns supreme". As for those who took comfort from the reflection that the terrible struggle for existence tends to final good, and that the suffering of the ancestor is eventually recompensed by the increased perfection of the progeny, he had a short reply (*id.* 198): "There would be something in this argument if, in Chinese fashion, the present generation could pay its debts to its ancestors; otherwise it is not clear what compensation *Eohippus* gets for his sorrows in the fact that, some millions of years afterwards, one of his descendants wins the Derby."

At this time Huxley was working on a scheme for the federation of the growing number of colonial scientific societies with the Royal, but in the event got nowhere. "You are a lot of obstructive old Tories", he told the chemist Frankland (*L.L.* II, 189), "and want routing out. If I were only younger and less indisposed to any sort of exertion, I would rout you out finely!" At the beginning of March he joined with a small group in establishing a 'Population Question Association' to consider the then outrageous subject of birth control, but this brave effort did not succeed either. That spring his physical state sank so low that, when eventually he struggled to the Engadine late in June, he could barely walk a hundred yards on the level. One can understand the surprise of the residents who, two months later, saw him striding his daily 10 miles and going up a couple of thousand feet with no apparent ill effect. Nevertheless, despite his repeatedly proved powers of recuperation, it had become evident to Huxley that he really must steer clear of the hectic life of London, and he decided to end his days at Eastbourne. His tall slim figure now a little stooped, clad in a long rough coat and wearing a cap with warm ear flaps, he paced the sea wall in the bracing winds from Beachy Head, or went walking across the Downs. "My doctor tells me that I am going to be completely patched up", he told Knowles (*L.L.* II, 221), "seams caulked and made seaworthy, so the old hulk may make another cruise." He was, in fact, to make several cruises—and some of them with all guns blazing.

The year had begun with Ethel's decision to marry John Collier, the widower of her recently deceased sister Marian. This would be not only repudiating all propriety, but would actually be illegal in England. The situation needed the most careful handling. But his daughter had made up her mind; so Huxley took her to marry in Norway where the law was less archaic. "Any woman who cares whether the wife of the clergyman of the parish calls on her or not, and is otherwise liable to be made unhappy by Mrs. Grundy, had better think twice before she marries her deceased sister's husband" he advised a correspondent (*H.P.*, 30. 163), "But, if she can find life worth living in the absence of the cards of the parson's and even the squire's wife on her hall table ... then I should say, without the least hesitation, Defy Mrs. Grundy and all her ways." Soon he was lobbying to overcome the obstructionism of the House of Lords against the Deceased Wife's Sister Bill, urging (*L.L.* II, 219) that "there is really no doubt that a fraction of the Classes stands in the way of the fulfilment of a very reasonable demand on the part of the Masses". His fifth child Nettie also married early that year—and it is an interesting comment on the freedom and mutual trust in this Victorian 'happy family' that Huxley and his wife only made the acquaintance of J. H. Roller after the young couple had already become engaged.

Soon after Nettie's wedding, her father wrote (*L.L.* II, 221) to tell her, "Luckily the bishops and clergy won't let me alone, so I have been able to keep myself pretty well amused by replying". Dr. Wace, the Principal of King's College, had told the Church Congress that those who described themselves as agnostics were really infidels lacking the courage to use that hard name, and this aroused Huxley's ire. "Tolerably early in life", he had earlier explained (*C.E.* IX, 134), "I discovered that one of the unpardonable sins, in the eyes of most people, is for a man to presume to go about unlabelled. The world regards such a person as the police do an unmuzzled dog, not under proper control. I could find no label that would suit me, so, in my desire to range myself and be respectable, I invented one"—and, by contrast with the early Gnostics who felt a certainty of direct knowledge, he called himself an Agnostic. Now, therefore, in his essay "Agnosticism" in the February *Nineteenth Century*, he informed Wace (*C.E.* V, 245) that "Agnosticism, in fact, is not a creed, but a method. . . . In matters of the intellect, follow your reason as far as it will take you, without regard to any other consideration. And . . . do not pretend that conclusions are certain which are not demonstrated or demonstrable." He drew attention (*id.* 241) to "the torrents of hypocrisy and cruelty, the lies, the slaughter, the violations of every obligation of humanity, which have flowed . . . along the course of the history of Christian nations", and he saw nothing unpleasant in saying plainly that he did not believe in the doctrines which such methods had been used to enforce. Undoubtedly his zest for life was rapidly reviving. In March his article "The Value of Witness to the Miraculous" appeared, but so did replies on the main question from Dr. Wace and from the Bishop of Peterborough. Huxley hit back in April with "Agnosticism: a Rejoinder"; Wace responded with "Christianity and Agnosticism"; Huxley finally replied in June with "Agnosticism and Christianity". "I want you to enjoy my wind-up with Wace in this month's XIX . . .", he wrote (*H.P.* 2. 344) to Hooker. "It's as full of malice as an egg is full of meat— and my satisfaction in making Newman my accomplice has been unutterable." How far this controversy really advanced understanding between science and religion may be doubted. What it undoubtedly did was to serve notice that the days when the clerical establishment could effectively anathematise unbelievers were rapidly running out.

From mid-June to mid-September Huxley was again seeking health in Switzerland, and was gratified to find that eventually he could walk eighteen miles in a day without exhaustion. Back in England in the autumn, he found himself involved in a lengthy debate in *The Times* on land nationalisation, and then proceeded to produce a series of four essays on social and political questions. The January 1890 issue of the *Nineteenth Century* printed his paper "On the Natural Inequality of Men"; February saw his "Natural Rights and Political Rights"; March his "Capital—the Mother of Labour"; and May his "Government: Anarchy or Regimentation". His declared aim was to get rid of *a priori* assumptions from social and political as from scientific debate, and undeniably he shot some gaping holes in Rousseau's 'state of nature' egalitarianism and in Henry George's land-value theories. But, although it was all

The assistant-surgeon, 1846 "I will leave my mark somewhere, and it shall be clear and distinct" (*L.L.* I, 63).

The young eagle, 1857 "I am sharpening up my claws and beak in readiness" (*L.L.* I, 176).

The committee man, 1870 "Believe I am reckoned a good chairman of a meeting" (Pearson, K., II, 178).

Above: The teacher, 1871 "There is nobody so hard to teach properly and well as people who know nothing about a subject" (*C.E.*, III, 170).

Opposite: The man of the day, 1871 "There is no popular teacher who has contributed more to the awakening of the intellect" (*Vanity Fair*, 28 January 1871).

The family man, *ca.* 1875 "What I like about the family is the way they all seem to care so much for each other" (Collier, E.C.F., 35).

The professor, 1879 "Oh, there comes Professor Huxley; faded, but still fascinating"
(*L.L.* II, 63).

The man of power, *ca.* 1880 "I always find that I acquire influence, generally more than I want" (Pearson, K., II, 178).

The scholar, 1881, 1882, 1885 "Sit down before fact as a little child, be prepared to give up every preconceived notion" (*L.L.* I, 219).

The man of affairs, *ca.* 1880, 1883, 1890, 1893 "Continually taking two irons out of the fire and putting three in" (Spencer, H., I, 404).

The prophet, *ca.* 1895 "It is the customary fate of new truths to begin as heresies and to end as superstitions" (*C.E.* II, 229).

The moralist, *ca.* 1894 "The savage of civilisation is a more dangerous animal than any other wild beast" (*H.P.* 42, 52).

extremely clever, and few logical flaws can be found in his argument, these papers do seem to emit a mild aroma of prejudice on the side of private property. Yet they were by no means one-sided, and some passages are perhaps more meaningful to our generation than they were to his own. For example (*C.E.* I, 358, 356, 313), "Individualism pure and simple —if carried out logically, is merely reasoned savagery, utter and unmitigated selfishness, incompatible with social existence"; and "That which it would be tyranny to prevent in some states of society it would be madness to permit in others"; and "One thing we need to learn is the necessity of limiting individual freedom for the general good ... yet ... the despotism of a majority is as little justifiable and as dangerous as that of one man."

In the January of 1890 Huxley's youngest son became engaged. "Harry has been and gone and done it ...", his father wrote (*L.L.* II, 251) to Foster. "Don't know the young lady, but the youth has a wise head on his shoulders, and though that did not prevent Solomon from overdoing the business, I have every faith in his choice." And, to Harry (*L.L.* II, 252) up in Yorkshire, "We are as happy that you are happy as you can be yourself, though from your letter that seems saying a great deal. I am prepared to be the young lady's slave; pray tell her that I am a model father-in-law (By the way, you might mention her name; it is a miserable detail, I know, but would be interesting)." In April, father and son went for a trip to Tenerife, and Huxley was quite cheered to find that he still enjoyed sailing even in rough weather. In May he moved on to Madeira, and found himself feeling ten years younger for the holiday. On his return he attended a ceremonial dinner to receive the Linnean Medal, and then in July another sermon by Dr. Liddon provided a good excuse for one more enjoyable encounter with the Christians.

The gist of Liddon's argument was that, contrary to the unorthodox views of the authors of *Lux Mundi*, the trustworthiness of the New Testament was inseparable from that of the Old. In his reply, Huxley took the opportunity of a little fun at the expense of Lot's wife and Jonah and the whale, but "The Lights of the Church and the Light of Science" was not a very important essay. At least one passage, however (*C.E.* IV, 236), was curiously prophetic:

> While, therefore, every right-minded man must sympathise with the efforts of those theologians, who have not been able altogether to close their ears to the still, small, voice of reason ... the melancholy fact remains, that the position

they have taken up is hopelessly untenable. .... They must surrender, or fall back into a more sheltered position. And it is possible that they may long find safety in such retreat. ... The present and the near future seems given over to those happily, if curiously, constituted people who see as little difficulty in throwing aside any amount of post-Abrahamic Scriptural narrative as the authors of 'Lux Mundi' see in sacrificing the pre-Abrahamic stories; and, having distilled away every inconvenient matter of fact in Christian history, continue to pay divine honours to the residue. There really seems to be no reason why the next generation should not listen to a Bampton Lecture ... [claiming that] ... 'No longer in contact with fact of any kind, Faith stands now and for ever proudly inaccessible to the attacks of the infidel'.

Finally, in the autumn of 1890, Gladstone published "The Impregnable Rock of Holy Scripture", in which he returned to his earlier attack upon Huxley's position. "Yes—", Huxley wrote (*L.L.* II, 269) to Platt Ball, "Mr. Gladstone has dug up the hatchet. We shall see who gets the scalp." For December's *Nineteenth Century* he produced "The Keepers of the Herd of Swine", as hard-hitting an essay as one may ever have the pleasure of reading. The Duke of Argyll intervened in January, Gladstone replied in February, and in March Huxley finished things off with his "Illustrations of Mr. Gladstone's Controversial Methods." The question really at issue, he insisted (*C.E.* V, 415), was not that of the antics of a few Gadarene pigs, but "whether the men of the nineteenth century are to adopt the demonology of the men of the first century, as divinely revealed truth, or to reject it, as degrading falsity. ... Whether the twentieth century shall see a recrudescence of mediaeval papistry." Huxley, it must be admitted, really enjoyed savaging Gladstone. "The contest", Grant Duff (*H.P.* 30. 178) later told Leonard Huxley, "was like nothing that has happened in our time save the struggle at Omdurman. It was not so much a battle as a massacre."

CHAPTER 15

Man's place in nature

DURING the autumn of 1890 Huxley returned temporarily to London to pack up his library, a considerable part of which he gave to the Royal College of Science. During the winter he conducted a campaign against the dictatorial manner in which General Booth was administering the Salvation Army, and still from time to time he performed public services such as advising on technical education applied to agriculture. But in the main he was now really managing to settle down in a fairly quiet retirement. The once gay and conspiratorial *X* Club had, as its members grew older and fewer, been losing much of its original *élan*, and in 1893 it was allowed to die with dignity at the age of thirty.

To the considerable surprise of his friends, Huxley became a keen gardener, seeming never to tire of tending his favourite alpines and saxifrages. He delighted, too, in visits from his grandchildren—who, he assured Knowles (*L.L.* II, 399), were "a veritable 'articles de luxe', involving much amusement and no sort of responsibility on the part of the possessor". Julian, in 1892 a lively young fellow of five, particularly amused him. "I like that chap!", Huxley remarked (*L.L.* II, 435). "I like the way he looks you straight in the face and disobeys you." It was about this time that Julian, having just read *The Water Babies*, sent an innocent note of enquiry (*L.L.* II, 436): "Dear Grandpater—Have you seen a Waterbaby? Did you put it in a bottle? Did it wonder if it could get out? Can I see it some day?—Your loving Julian." Grandpater's reply *(ibid.)*, each separate letter carefully written for childish eyes (and thus uncharacteristically legible), is interesting.

My dear Julian, [he wrote] I never could make sure about that Water Baby. I have seen Babies in water and Babies in bottles; but the Baby in the water was not in a bottle and the Baby in the bottle was not in water. My friend who wrote the story of the Water Baby, was a very kind man and very clever. Perhaps he thought I could see as much in the water as he did—There are some people who see a great deal and some who see very little in the same things. When you grow up I dare say you will be one of the great-deal seers and see things more wonderful than Water Babies where other folks can see nothing. Give my best love to Daddy & Mammy and Trevenen—Grandmoo is a little better but not up yet—Ever your loving Grandpater.

In 1893 Huxley started to publish his collected essays, did some hard thinking for an intended synthesis of evolutionary speculation, and began to collect material for an envisaged scientific study of the bible. He went to Cambridge to speak at the tercentenary celebration of Harvey's admission to Gonville and Caius, visited Malaga for a month in the summer, and set about building a substantial rockery in his garden. But his main intellectual exercise that year was the Romanes Lecture at Oxford, on "Evolution and Ethics". He was requested to avoid reference to either politics or religion, and this presented a serious problem. Now that he was nearing the end of his days, he wanted to deliver his final words on the great twin topics of evolution and ethics, both of which had theological and political implications at almost every point. Over several months he worked away at his script and in May, writing what turned out to be his last letter to the sadly ailing Tyndall, remarked (*L.L.* II, 335), "I hope you will appreciate my dexterity. The lecture is a regular egg-dance." And, to George Romanes (the endower of the lectureship) himself (*L.L.* II, 353), "There is no allusion to politics in my lecture, nor to any religion except Buddhism. ... If people apply anything I say about these matters to modern philosophies ... and religions, that is not my affair. To be honest, however, unless I thought they would, I should never have taken all the pains I have bestowed on these 36 pages." Romanes wrote back in some alarm—but, since the lecture was due to be delivered in three weeks' time, it was far too late to consider Huxley's somewhat disingenuous offer of withdrawal.

The lecture was delivered on 18 May, in a Sheldonian theatre bursting at the seams. By all accounts Huxley presented a striking figure as, still slim and commanding, the leonine squareness of his features topped by long silvery locks, robed in D.C.L. scarlet, he strode on to the platform. A throat infection prevented his words from being well heard in the gallery, but very full newspaper coverage quickly made his theme common knowledge. Tracing the progression of mankind from a primitive state and analysing the rôles played by self-assertion, cunning, curiosity, imitativeness and ruthlessness, he showed how social advance had depended on the development of the ideas of justice and law and ethical obligation. "But", he pointed out (*C.E.* IX, 50), "there is another aspect of the cosmic process, so perfect as a mechanism, so beautiful as a work of art. Where the cosmopoietic energy works through sentient beings, there arises, among its other manifestations, that which we call pain or suffering. This baleful product of evolution increases in quantity and in intensity, with advancing grades of animal organisation, until it attains its highest level in man. Further, the consummation is not reached in man, the mere animal; nor in man, the whole or half savage; but only in man, the member of an organized polity." Thus (*id.* 55), in the classical civilisations of the Mediterranean, "that very sharpening of the sense and that subtle refinement of emotion, which brought such a wealth of pleasures, were fatally attended by a proportional enlargement of the capacity for suffering ... with the corresponding hells of futile regret for the past and morbid anxiety for the future. Finally, the inevitable penalty of over-stimulation, exhaustion, opened the gates of civilisation to its great enemy, ennui; the stale and flat weariness when man delights not, nor woman neither; when all things are vanity and vexation; and life seems not worth living except to escape the bore of dying."

As for the idea of an innate justice in the common order of things, Huxley could not see it. "If there is a generalization from the facts of human life which hás the assent of thoughtful men in every age and country", he said (*id.* 58), "it is that the violator of ethical rules constantly escapes the punishment which he deserves; that the wicked flourishes like a green bay tree, while the righteous begs his bread; that the sins of the father are visited upon the children; that, in the realm of nature, ignorance is punished just as severely as wilful wrong; and that thousands upon thousands of innocent beings suffer for the crime, or the unintentional trespass, of one." In an attempt to reconcile such facts with their own concepts of justice, the Greeks had peopled the universe with an assemblage of largely autonomous gods and goddesses. Similarly, the Hindus had developed the concept of the Karma, passing from life to life in a series of transmigrations and by its successive modifications eventually producing a sort of cumulative justice. But, on the whole, he preferred the great Semitic trial of this issue, taking refuge in silence and submission. As for those who were currently propounding what they called "the ethics of evolution", their logic was fallacious (*id.* 80): "Cosmic evolution may teach us how the good and the evil tendencies of man may have come about; but, in itself, it is incompetent to furnish any better reason why what we call good is preferable to what we call evil than we had before." And therefore, he urged (*id.* 83), "Let us understand, once and for all, that the ethical progress of society depends, not on imitating the cosmic process, still less on running away from it, but on combating it".

The Oxford Magazine (24 May 1893) described the address as "a model Romanes Lecture—admirable in literary finish, vigorous, clear and impressive, neither too abstruse nor too popular for the audience. ... We can only express our humble admiration of the masculine vigour alike of Professor Huxley's thought and of the language in which it is clothed. A more exquisitely finished academic discourse was never placed before any audience in any language." Perhaps this panegyric was excessive, but it does give some indication of the impact which the address made upon many people at the time. St. George Mivart, discerning a deep understanding of the depths of human nature, hoped that Huxley might end up as a Roman Catholic. Herbert Spencer, quick to detect criticism of his own intensely individualistic philosophy of evolutionary ethics, went into print in an effort at self-justification. Huxley greatly enjoyed the spectacle. "Don't you know", he wrote (*L.L.* II, 359) gleefully to Farrer, "that I am become a reactionary and secret friend of the clerics? My lecture is really an effort to put the Christian doctrine that Satan is the Prince of this world upon a scientific foundation." The fact is, of course, that during the tumultuous conflicts of that generation, friend and foe alike had often failed to appreciate the subtleties of Huxley's thinking, and had attributed to him a simplicity of posture which was a mere stereotype of his true position. Now, suddenly becoming conscious that things were not quite as they had seemed, people began to recall earlier passages in his writings which had been largely overlooked in the heat of battle.

"The student of Nature", Huxley had written (*C.E.* II, 29) in an 1860 review of *The Origin of Species*, "wonders the more and is astonished the less, the more conversant he becomes with her operations". And, in *The Crayfish* (1879, 3), "in relation to the human mind Nature is boundless; and, though nowhere inaccessible, she is everywhere unfathomable". If this was what he felt about Nature in general, no one should have been surprised by his awareness of the complexity of human nature. Nor should they have been surprised to find that, in his estimate of the deep realities of the human situation, he was nearer to some of the medieval schoolmen than to many modern liberals. Perhaps only Lucy Clifford had read his amusing description (*L.L.* II, 428) of the male of the species ("very queer animals, a mixture of horse-nervousness, ass-stubbornness and camel-malice—with an angel bobbing about unexpectedly like the apple in the possett"), but there had been more public if less evocative expressions of his views.

In 1877, when rounding off the Metaphysical Society's symposium on "The Influence upon Morality of a Decline in Religious Belief", Huxley had insisted upon applying objective criteria of social happiness even to the evaluation of major 'crimes' or 'sins'. He believed (*L.L.* II, 305) that "The rules of conduct ... are discoverable—like the other so-called laws of Nature—by observation and experiment", and he looked forward to the eventual establishment of a science of "Eubiotics". But he had never subscribed to any easy extraction of ethical rules from evolutionary processes. All efforts at deducing the nature of 'the moral law' from the facts of evolution were, in his view (1893a), based on "an illusion which has arisen from the unfortunate ambiguity of the term 'fittest' in the formula, 'survival of the fittest' ... the 'fittest' which survive in the struggle for existence may be, and often is, the ethically worst". Indeed, he wrote (*L.L.* II, 268) in 1890, "Of moral purpose I can see not trace in Nature. That is an article of exclusively human manufacture—and very much to our credit."

In "Evolution and Ethics", his last important lecture, Huxley had in fact returned to the great theme of his first important book. "I was looking through Man's Place in Nature the other day", he wrote to Edward Clodd (*L.L.* II, 344) some six months before setting out for the Sheldonian. "I do not think there is a word I need delete, nor anything I need add except in confirmation and extension of the doctrine there laid down. That is great good fortune for a book thirty years old." The second section of the book (1863, 71) had opened with a striking passage: "The question of questions for mankind—the problem which underlies all others, and is more deeply interesting than any other—is the ascertainment of the place which Man occupies in nature and of his relations to the universe of things. Whence our race has come; what are the limits of our power over nature, and of nature's power over us; to what goal we are tending; are the problems which present themselves anew and with undiminished interest to every man born into the world."

Huxley had begun his book with a brief survey of classical and medieval legends of man-like creatures, followed by a critical examination of early travellers' tales such as Pigafetta's sixteenth-century *Description of the Kingdom of Congo*. And, although these accounts included any amount of imagination and inaccuracy, he found sufficient truth to warrant the comment (*id.* 9), "Ancient traditions, when tested by the severe processes of modern investigation, commonly enough fade away into mere dreams; but it is singular how often the dream turns out to have been a half-waking one, presaging a reality." When it came to the seventeenth-century traveller Tyson, not only were his meticulous drawings of an Angolan 'Pygmie' themselves sufficient to prove that he had seen a chimpanzee, but Huxley was able to borrow, from Cheltenham museum, the skeleton of the very animal which Tyson had observed, and give it a thorough re-examination. In 1863, it must be remembered, the behaviour of living apes had as yet been subjected to scarcely any scientific study, and very little was known with certainty about their personality characteristics. Nevertheless, Huxley concluded that there was *prima facie* evidence of the building of simple shelters, of the possession of what could properly be called considerable intelligence, and even of what might almost be termed an embryonic conscience. Thus, he was from this early date prepared to accept the likelihood that not only man's body, but also his mental and moral attributes, had evolved from those of ape-like ancestors. And, in *Man's Place in Nature*, he presented the first systematic attempt to fuse the facts of palaeontology and comparative anatomy with those of developmental embryology, in a multi-disciplinary demonstration of the anthropoid origins of man.

Huxley took the order of primates as divisible into seven families. Of these, the three most primitive were the *Galeopithecini* (containing only the flying lemur), much resembling the bats; the *Cheiromyini* (the bushy-tailed aye-aye), with teeth like those of rodents; and the *Lemurini* (lemurs and the like), of insectivorous type. Then there were the marmosets in the *Arctopithecini*, the New World monkeys in the *Platyrhini*, and the Old World monkeys and apes in the *Catarhini*. Finally, the *Anthropini* consisted only of species which might properly be called human. This classification has naturally been modified by subsequent workers, but it is interesting on several scores.

It could conceivably imply, for example, the possibility of a multiple-origin evolution of the primates as an alternative to the simple-series progression so often uncritically assumed. It also presages Huxley's much later remark (*C.E.* V, 50), "I think ... that, sooner or later, we shall discover the remains of our less specialised primatic ancestors in the strata which have yielded the less specialised equine and canine quadrupeds". It provides the basis for his striking comment (*C.E.* VII, 146), "Perhaps no order of mammals presents us with so extraordinary a series of gradations as this—leading us insensibly from the crown and summit of the animal creation down to creatures, from which there is but a step, as it seems, to the lowest, smallest, and least intelligent of the placental Mammalia. It is as if nature herself had foreseen the arrogance of man, and with Roman severity had provided that his intellect, by its very triumphs, should call into prominence the slaves, admonishing the conqueror that he is but dust." And its general line of thought explains the questions (*id.* 208), which until fairly recent years might well have been thought extravagant and in 1863 were certainly remarkable, "Where, then, must we look for primaeval Man? Was the oldest *Homo sapiens* pliocene or miocene, or yet more ancient? In still older strata do the fossilized bones of an ape more anthropoid, or a Man more pithecoid, than any yet known await the researches of some unborn palaeontologist?"

After the discovery of the neanderthaloid skeletons at Spy, Huxley gave his own answer (*C.E.* VII, 324) to one of his own key questions: "we are warranted in the supposition that the genus *Homo*, if not the species which the courtesy or the irony of naturalists has dubbed *sapiens*, was represented in pliocene, or even in miocene times". The sheer technical quality of his work in this field is indicated by the fact that, after the passage of eighty-five years, Sir Arthur Keith considered it still worth while to produce a substantial paper based on lithographic plates dating from Huxley's lectures given at the Royal College of Surgeons in 1864. Keith's paper makes it clear that the 'Frankfurt plane' technique of measuring skulls had first been devised not by von Jhering in 1872 but by Huxley eight years earlier. It also shows that Huxley had pioneered the application of craniometry to immature anthropoid skulls, thus avoiding the distortions caused by the bony eye-ridges of adults.

So far as variation within our own species is concerned, Huxley must have been one of the very first to set about a large-scale, systematic and scientifically organised study. After his death there was discovered among his papers a collection of between 400 and 500 photographs of different ethnic types, most of them of the nude figure standing erect, with extended arm, against a fixed scale. These had been collected with the help of British residents, agents and naval officers from all over the world, with the ambitious intention (unfortunately never fulfilled) of producing an exhaustive and definitive study of human variation. By 1863 Huxley had not only recognised the phenomenon which in 1939 his grandson Julian called a 'cline', but had identified the directions of some human clines. "Draw a line on the globe, from the Gold Coast in Western Africa to the steppes of Tartary", he wrote (1863, 177). "At the southern and western end of that line there live the most dolichocephalic, curly-haired, dark-skinned of men. . . . At the northern and eastern end of the same line there live the most brachycephalic, orthognathous, straight-haired, yellow-skinned of men. . . . From Central Asia eastward to the Pacific Islands and subcontinents on the one hand, and to America on the other, brachycephaly and orthognathism gradually diminish and are replaced by dolichocephaly and prognathism."

This very modern view of human variation, so unlike the racialist theorising of many scientists during succeeding decades, was possible only because Huxley always preferred fact to fiction and almost always managed to purge himself of proven prejudice. And that was why, speaking in Birmingham in 1867, he somewhat startled the Mayor and assembled city fathers by telling them that primitive peoples were not incapable of cultural advancement, that facial features need not influence brain size or structure, that miscegenation was not necessarily harmful, and that in respect of hair-type the white peoples were a great deal more like the apes than the negro was.

Of course, Huxley recognised not only the absence of rigid demarcation lines, but also the necessity for practical purposes of distinguishing a few major groupings within *Homo sapiens*. He therefore made his own modification of Blumenbach's earlier classification. In addition to Australoids, Negroids and Mongoloids, he proposed in 1865 a Xanthochroic ("yellow-haired white") group and a Melanochroic ("black-haired white") group. He suggested that the Melanochroics of southern Europe might have resulted from admixture between early Australoid and Xanthochroic stocks, that the Hottentots probably came from a cross between Negroids and Bushmen, and that the Dravidian tribes of southern India were essentially Australoid in origin. In 1869 he condemned, as shams and delusions, the usual ideas about innate personality differences between Anglo-

MAN'S PLACE IN NATURE

saxons and Celts. In the following year he read two papers, on "The Geographical Distribution of the Chief Modifications of Mankind" and on "The Ethnology of Britain", to the Ethnological Society. In 1871 there appeared his striking *Contemporary Review* essay, "On Some Fixed Points in British Ethnology", in which he sought to separate the comparatively few established facts in this field from the confused masses of assertion and inference. There was, he insisted (*C.E.* VII, 266), "not the slightest justification for the common practice of speaking of the present inhabitants of Britain as an 'Anglo-Saxon' race. It is, in fact, just as absurd as the habit of talking of the French people as a 'Latin' race." And, with reference to the then current stereotype of the Irishman, he asked (*id.* 268), "What, then, is the value of the ethnological difference between the Englishman of the western half of England and the Irishman of the eastern half of Ireland? For what reason does the one deserve the name of a 'Celt', and not the other? ... why should not intelligence, perseverance, thrift, industry, sobriety, respect for law, be admitted to be Celtic virtues? And why should we not seek for the cause of their absence in something else than the idle pretext of 'Celtic blood'?" But such questions were not to receive rational replies for many a long year after that.

Just as he was profoundly suspicious of the attribution of inborn mental, emotional and moral characteristics to various so-called 'races', Huxley objected to the confusion introduced into anthropology by the uncritical use of linguistic data and the too easy acceptance of philological theories. During his lifetime, the concept of an 'Aryan race' originating in the Hindu Kush had become almost accepted dogma, and in 1890 he decided that the time had come to undermine its very shaky foundations. "The Aryan Question and Prehistoric Man" started with a vivid military metaphor (*C.E.* VII, 271):

> The rapid increase of natural knowledge, which is the chief characteristic of our age, is effected in various ways. The main army of science moves to the conquest of new worlds slowly and surely, nor ever cedes an inch of the territory gained. But the advance is covered and facilitated by the ceaseless activity of clouds of light troops provided with a weapon—always efficient, if not always an arm of precision—the scientific imagination. It is the business of these *enfants perdus* of science to make raids into the realm of ignorance wherever they see, or think they see, a chance; and cheerfully to accept defeat, or it may be annihilation, as the reward of error.

But, he went on,

> Unfortunately, the public, which watches the process of the campaign, too often mistakes a dashing incursion of the Uhlans for a forward movement of the main body. ... And it must be confessed that the error is too often justified by the effects of the irrepressible tendency which men of science share with all other sorts of men known to me, to be impatient of that most wholesome state of mind—suspended judgment.

In the particular case of the 'Aryan question', he concluded (*id.* 275 and 277),

> It is really singular to observe the deference which has been shown, and is yet sometimes shown, to a speculation which can, at best, claim to be regarded as nothing better than a somewhat risky hypothesis ... 'Aryan' is properly a term of classification used in philology. 'Race' is the name of a subdivision of one of those groups of living things which are called 'species' in the technical language of Zoology and Botany ... Philology, therefore, while it may have a perfect right to postulate the existence of a primitive Aryan 'people', has no business to substitute 'race' for 'people'.

In view of the appalling genocidal outcome of later Aryan racialism, Keith (1925, 722) was in retrospect too optimistic in judging that Huxley had "brushed the cobweb of racial tradition from the map of Europe"; but one can see what he meant.

Like so may of his contemporaries, Huxley valued the puritan virtues highly, and he was insistent that the rejection of religious belief need not and should not lead to lower moral standards. "I wish not", he wrote (*H.P.* 2. 85) in 1861, "to be in any way confounded with the cynics who delight in degrading man—or with the common run of materialists—who think mind is any the lower for being a function of matter. I dislike them even more than I do the pietists." The same attitude survived in 1892, when (*L.L.* II, 322) he told the rationalist Charles Watts, "Old Noll knew what he was about when he said that it was of no use to try to fight the gentlemen of England with tapsters and serving-men. It is quite as hopeless to fight Christianity with scurrility. We want a regiment of Ironsides." But, like all the best puritans, he was usually charitable towards those who found difficulty in living up to their high ideals. "Depend upon it", he advised his daughter Nettie (*L.L.* II, 331) about three years after her marriage, "that 'just man' who needed no repentance was a very poor sort of father. But perhaps his daughters were 'just

women' of the same type; and the family circle as warm as the interior of
an ice-pail."

Huxley's secular puritanism had in it a strangely calvinistic streak,
and he took the moral sense (*L.L.* II, 305) to be

> a very complex affair—dependent in part upon associations of pleasure and
> pain, approbation and disapprobation ... but in part also on an innate sense of
> moral beauty and ugliness ... which is possessed by some people in great strength,
> while some are totally devoid of it. ... As to whether we can all fulfil the moral
> law, I should say hardly any of us. Some of us are utterly incapable of fulfilling
> its plainest dictates. As there are men born physically cripples and intellectually
> idiots, so there are some who are moral cripples and idiots, and can be kept
> straight not even by punishment.

Indeed, he wrote (1892a) in "An Apologetic Irenicon", "The doctrines
of predestination, of original sin ... appear to me to be vastly nearer
the truth than the 'liberal' popular illusions that babies are all born good
... that it is given to everybody to reach the ethical ideal if he will
only try".

This did not imply that the "moral cripples" should be permitted to
wreak havoc in society, and he was prepared, if it proved really necessary,
for them to be imprisoned or even executed, but he saw no point in mor-
alising condemnation of them. Nor could he agree with those who advocated the adoption of extreme eugenic measures. Apart from all doubt
about the adequacy of existing genetic knowledge, Huxley had deeper
doubts about the morality of such steps as might conceivably be taken.
"The hopelessly diseased, the infirm aged, the weak or deformed in body
or in mind, the excess of infants born, would be put away ...", he feared
(*C.E.* IX, 21). "Only the strong and healthy, carefully matched, with a
view to the progeny best adapted to the purposes of the administrator,
would be permitted to perpetuate their kind." But, he urged (*id.* 23),
"I doubt whether even the keenest judge of character, if he had before
him a hundred boys and girls under fourteen, could pick out, with the
least chance of success, those who should be kept, as certain to be service-
able members of the polity, and those who should be chloroformed, as
equally sure to be stupid, idle, or vicious. The 'points' of a good or of
a bad citizen are really far harder to discern than those of a puppy or
a short-horn calf." This "pigeon-fanciers' polity", as he scathingly called
it, would in any event be doomed to self-defeat, for (*id.* 37) "It strikes me

that men who are accustomed to contemplate the active or passive extirpation of the weak, the unfortunate, and the superfluous ... whose whole lives, therefore, are an education in the noble art of suppressing natural affection and sympathy, are not likely to have any large stock of these commodities left".

Even on the purely biological level, Huxley never shared the common view that evolution was a matter of inevitable movement onwards and upwards. "So far from any gradual progress forming any necessary part of the Darwinian creed", he wrote (*C.E.* II, 90) in 1864, "it appears to us that it is perfectly consistent with indefinite persistence in one state, or with a gradual retrogression." Nor could he accept the facile and then favourite analogy between the body politic and the body biological, so often misapplied to justify ruthless individualism against any exercise of social control. "Even the blood-corpuscles", he commented (*C.E.* I, 271) somewhat mordantly in 1871, "can't hold a public meeting without being accused of 'congestion'—and the brain, like other despots whom we have known, calls out for the use of sharp steel against them." He did not believe that the advance of society necessarily made men inherently better; and, he told the Charity Commissioners (*H.P.* 42. 52) in 1887, "the savage of civilisation is a more dangerous animal than any other wild beast; and ... sooner or later every social organization in which these ferae accumulate unduly, will be torn to pieces by them". But these wild animals could inhabit any social stratum, and their numbers and influence would vary greatly from one social state to another. "What gives force to the socialistic movement which is now stirring European society to its depths", he asked a Birmingham meeting (*C.E.* I, 256) in 1871, "but a determination on the part of the naturally able men among the proletariate, to put an end, somehow or other, to the misery and degradation in which a large proportion of their fellows are steeped?" And, he warned a meeting in Manchester (*C.E.* III, 448) in 1887, "any social condition in which the development of wealth involves the misery, the physical weakness, and the degradation of the worker, is absolutely and infallibly doomed to collapse. Your bayonets and cutlasses will break under your hand."

In his 1889 essay on "Agnosticism", Huxley presented what some would consider a pessimistic, but he thought a realistic, assessment (*C.E.* V, 256) of *Homo sapiens* as a social creature. "I know no study", he wrote, "which is so unutterably saddening as that of the evolution of humanity. . . . Out of the darkness of prehistoric ages man emerges with the marks of his lowly origin strong upon him. He is a brute, only more intelligent than the other brutes, a blind prey to impulses, which as often as not lead him to destruction; a victim to endless illusions. . . . He attains a certain degree of physical comfort . . . and then, for thousands and thousands of years, struggles, with varying fortunes, attended by infinite wickedness, bloodshed, and misery, to maintain himself at this point against the greed and the ambition of his fellow men. . . . And the best men of the best epochs are simply those who make the fewest blunders and commit the fewest sins." In the following year he pursued this theme somewhat further (*C.E.* I, 423): "Even the best of modern civilisations appears to me to exhibit a condition of mankind which neither embodies any worthy ideal nor even possesses the merit of stability. . . . What profits it to the human Prometheus that he has stolen the fire of heaven to be his servant, and that the spirits of the earth and of the air obey him, if the vulture of pauperism is eternally to tear his very vitals and keep him on the brink of destruction?"

His historical studies had convinced Huxley that biological factors, and especially that of fecundity, had been greatly underestimated as causes of world events. Some holograph notes (*H.P.* 42. 58), almost certainly of 1887, put his views succinctly:

> If historical writers could be persuaded that the people at the bottom are of considerably more importance than the people at the top of the stream of time —the importance of the population question as a factor in history would be more familiar to us—We should know what it had to do with Phoenician colonization with Greek colonization with the everlasting agrarian and proletarian question of ancient Rome; with the barbarian invasions—with the social and political difficulties of every state in modern times. It is the true riddle of the Sphinx of History. . . . No statesman has yet guessed the riddle and the Sphinx will devour us until it is guessed—To my mind all other political and social questions sink into insignificance as compared with this.

Today we are beginning to realise how right he was.

One thing which did somewhat cheer Huxley as he surveyed the historical scene was mankind's recurrent rebelliousness against political, spiritual and intellectual authoritarianism. And this baneful domination, he pointed out (*C.E.* VI, viii), may sometimes exist under superficially democratic forms: "That which it may be well for us not to forget is, that the first-recorded judicial murder of a scientific thinker [Socrates] was encompassed and effected, not by a despot, nor by priests, but was brought about by eloquent demagogues, to whom, of all men, thorough searchings of the intellect are most dangerous and therefore most hateful."

When Huxley remarked (*C.E.* V, xiii) that "a man has no more right to say he believes this world is haunted by swarms of evil spirits, without being able to produce satisfactory evidence of the fact, than he has a right to say, without adducing adequate proof, that the circumpolar antarctic ice swarms with sea-serpents", the scientific world applauded. Scientists were also no doubt much amused when he commented (*C.E.* V, 38) that, in the modern world, "The phraseology of Supernaturalism may remain on men's lips, but in practice they are Naturalists ... even parish clerks doubt the utility of prayers for rain, so long as the wind is in the east; and an outbreak of pestilence sends men, not to the churches, but to the drains". By no means all scientists, however, were so clear as Huxley that the danger of intellectual despotism had not disappeared with the triumph of modern science. "The besetting sin of able men", he told W. F. R. Weldon (*L.L.* II, 316), "is impatience of contradiction and of criticism. Even those who do their best to resist the temptation, yield to it almost unconsciously and become the tools of toadies and flatterers. 'Authorities', 'disciples', and 'schools' are the curse of science; and do more to interfere with the work of the scientific spirit than all its enemies." And that was why he declared (*L.L.* II, 301), "Of all possible positions that of a master of a school, or leader of a sect, or chief of a party, appears to me to be the most undesirable; in fact, the average British matron cannot look upon followers with a more evil eye than I do. ... I have always been, am, and propose to remain a mere scholar."

Huxley, of course, had a profound belief in the power of science, which was amusingly expressed one evening (Mitchell, 1900, 204) in an after-dinner speech. He had, he claimed, recently dreamed a dream in which he woke up after death in a very warm subterranean hall—which did not altogether surprise him. He was, however, surprised by its luxury and especially by the excellent attendance of the waiters (whose braided coats did not quite conceal their forked tails). He gave a smart tug to the nearest tail, whereupon the waiter turned round and politely asked, "Yes sir, what can I do for you?" Huxley ordered a drink and, in view of the high temperature of the hall, suggested that perhaps the drink might be iced. "Certainly", said the waiter, and shortly returned with his order. Sipping the drink appreciatively, Huxley made an inquiry: "I suppose

I am not wrong about where I have come to?" "No, Professor, this *is* Hell", the waiter replied. "But surely there has been a good deal of change?", Huxley asked. "This doesn't at all agree with what we used to be told of the place." "Why, no, sir," explained the waiter. "Hell isn't what it used to be. A great many of you scientific gents have been coming here recently, and they have turned the whole place upside down."

Yet the very power of science rendered it the more dangerous, and required of its practitioners an awareness of its heavy demands and a full recognition of their social responsibilities. That was why, when one young man who did not like his job sought Huxley's help in changing to an 'intellectual' career, he received advice (*L.L.*, II, 321) which was perhaps not entirely to his liking: "In my opinion a man's first duty is to find a way of supporting himself, thereby relieving others of the necessity of supporting him. ... The habit of doing that which you do not much care about when you would much rather be doing something else, is invaluable. ... Nothing is less to be desired than the fate of a young man, who ... becomes a mere hanger-on in literature or in science, when he might have been a useful and valuable member of Society in other occupations." It was this high view of social obligation which led Huxley to tell Liverpool's Sphinx Club (*L.L.* I, 335) that "commerce was a greater civiliser than all the religion and all the science ever put together in the world, for it taught men to be truthful and punctual and precise in the execution of their engagements, and men who were truthful and punctual and precise in their engagements had put their feet upon the first rung of the ladder which led to moral and intellectual elevation". And when in 1887 there seemed a serious risk that England's rapidly developing provision for commercial and technical education might be too narrowly conceived, he emphasised (*C.E.* III, 447) that "Our sole chance of succeeding in a competition, which must constantly become more and more severe, is that our people shall not only have the knowledge and the skill which are required, but that they shall have the will and the energy and the honesty, without which neither knowledge nor skill can be of any permanent avail".

No one ever insisted more strongly than Huxley that mankind's future lay in his own hands. Nevertheless, in what were almost his last words on man's place in nature, he reiterated his refusal to let an everyday operational optimism degenerate into mere uncritical panglossism.

"That man, as a 'political animal', is susceptible of a vast improvement, by education, by instruction, and by the application of his intelligence to the adaptation of the conditions of life to his higher needs, I entertain not the slightest doubt", he wrote (*C.E.* IX, 44). "But ... the prospect of attaining untroubled happiness, or of a state which can, even remotely, deserve the title of perfection, appears to me as misleading an illusion as ever was dangled before the eyes of poor humanity."

CHAPTER 16

A final fling

WHEN Huxley delivered his Romanes Lecture in the May of 1893, he knew that he had not very much longer to live. And there is a certain poignancy about a diary jotting (*H.P.* 90. 36), on 12 August that year, "See paper in Lancet on Signs of death—quoted in this week's Figaro". Yet everything (including this clear indication that he was still reading foreign language newspapers) goes to show that Huxley went on living life to the full until he was alive no more.

Early in 1894 he saw the ninth volume of his *Collected Essays* through the press, and Lankester's review in *Nature* (1 February 1894) identified exactly those qualities of his writing which make it almost compulsive reading. "In his case, more than in that of his contemporaries, it is strictly true that the style is the man ... we never miss his fascinating presence; now he is gravely shaking his head, now compressing the lips with emphasis, and from time to time, with a quiet twinkle of the eyes, making unexpected apologies or protesting that he is of a modest and peace-loving nature. ... Everything which has entered the author's brain ... comes out again to us—clarified, sifted, arranged, and vivified by its passage through the logical machine of his strong personality." In a brief aside, Lankester also identified the central reason for his idol's impressive achievements in biology: "He deals with form not only as a mechanical engineer *in partibus* (Huxley's own description of himself), but also as an artist, a born lover of form." The artist in him was evident from his beautifully clear scientific diagrams, and made his sketches and paintings far superior to the average amateur's, but it was as a writer that he practised to near-perfection. "There is always something refreshing to one's soul in Huxley's writing—", wrote Leslie Stephen (Maitland, 1906, 33), "none of your shuffling and equivocating and application of top-colour". Bonamy Dobrée, in a comprehensive survey of Victorian and later literature (Batho and Dobrée, 1938, 40), judged

151

that his example "brought about a happy clarity, visible in the writers of later romances, from Stevenson onwards". And it remains true, as Houston Peterson (1932, vii) wrote, that "Huxley is not only a touchstone for the last half of the nineteenth century. He is a power over us today ... because he happened to be a literary genius, as well as a biologist."

There were, of course, occasional inconveniences attached to the powerful effects of Huxley's writing, as he had cause to tell Donnelly (*L.L.*, II, 372) early in 1894: "I had a letter from a fellow yesterday morning who must be a lunatic, to the effect that he had been reading my essays, thought I was just the man to spend a month with, and was coming down by the five o'clock train, attended by his seven children and his mother-in-law! ... there was lots of boiling water ready for him. ... Wife and servants expected nothing less than assassination". Fortunately, the lunatic did not turn up, and later in the year Huxley reacted very differently to another letter out of the blue.

George Sparkes, an unknown Southampton docker, wrote to tell him about observations which he had made on an infusion of vegetable matter, aided only by a cheap magnifying glass. There was nothing that had not been long known, but Huxley was so impressed by the man's efforts to educate himself that he went to immense trouble to help him. He sent details of evening classes at the Hartley Institute (the forerunner of Southampton University), together with a letter of introduction to the librarian. When he later learned that Sparkes had bought himself a little shilling microscope, he made him a present of a splendid compound achromatic instrument. He arranged for a local clergyman to call and see how else the docker might be helped, persuaded Howes to offer him a laboratory assistant's job at South Kensington, set Foster and Donnelly to see what they could do, and continued to advise Sparkes in his studies. It was his own knowledge of many such individual acts of kindness which made Darwin remark (*L.L.* II, 38), following Huxley's scandalous Belfast address on animal automatism, "I wish to God there were more automata in the world like you". Alexander Macmillan was, of course, foolishly extravagant when he wrote (Harper, 1939, 219), "I tell you, there is so much real Christianity in Huxley that if it were parcelled out among the men, women and children in the British Isles, there would be enough to save the soul of every one of them, and plenty to spare". Still, such comments help us to understand how it happened that a man so subversive of the most cherished beliefs of his time was nevertheless so loved by all who knew him well.

Huxley once wrote (*H.P.* 12. 118), "In part from force of circumstance and in part from a conviction that I would be of more use in that way I have played the part of something between maid of all work and gladiator-general for science". Moreover, he had a comforting inner conviction that time was on science's side. "I am not afraid of the priests in the long-run. Scientific method is the white ant which will slowly and surely destroy their fortifications", he wrote (*L.L.* II, 379) in the summer of 1894; and he was equally confident that science would eventually undermine the equally pernicious secular hierarchs. So, although aware that his own time was rapidly running out, he went up to London happily enough in November to speak at the Royal Society's anniversary dinner and receive the Darwin medal. A month later he went up again to celebrate the twenty-fifth anniversary number of *Nature*, and used the opportunity to scold the younger scientists for their slovenly writing. But that terrible winter of 1894–5 brought two months of almost continual frost, and even Huxley's tough constitution eventually succumbed. Yet, before bowing out of this world, he was able to complete one convincing final fling.

Ever since 1858, Huxley had been a powerful influence on the University of London, but through the decades all efforts at co-ordinating the many metropolitan colleges had foundered on the twin rocks of conservatism and vested interest. By 1880 it was clear that there must be some sort of reform, but the conflicting schemes and counter-schemes seemed incapable of reconciliation. University College and King's College wanted their own charters of degree-granting status, with the existing University perpetuated as a mere imperial examining board. The Royal Colleges of Surgeons and Physicians wanted a charter to grant their own medical degrees. Some wanted the University to absorb the Colleges; some aspired to a university ruled entirely by its teachers; some demanded more power for the graduates grouped in Convocation; some wanted a university with an essentially autocratic form of government. Petitions and counter-petitions were presented to the Privy Council; in 1884 an Association for Promoting a Teaching University for London was formed; in 1888 the Government tried to clear the air by appointing a Royal Commission under Lord Selborne; in 1892 it appointed another, the 'Gresham' Commission, under Earl Cowper. "The whole affair is a perfect muddle of competing crude projects and vested interests, and is likely to end in a worse muddle", Huxley lamented (*L.L.* II, 311) to Donnelly. And, he wrote to Lankester (*H.P.* 30. 148), "unless people clearly understand that the university of the future is to be a very different thing from the university of the past, they had better put off meddling for another generation."

Then, quite suddenly, there came a dramatic change. In the June of 1892 Karl Pearson and a vigorous group of younger teachers set up a new body, the Association for Promoting a Professorial University of London, and within a couple of days Huxley was back in the thick of the fray. "I am in great spirits about the new University movement", he rejoiced to Foster (*L.L.* II, 333), "and have told the rising generation that this old hulk is ready to be towed out into line of battle, if they think fit, which is more commendable to my public spirit than my prudence." The rising generation immediately decided that the old hulk should fly the admiral's flag, and elected Huxley as President. He took office because, as he informed Sir William Flower (*L.L.* II, 313), "I found, to my surprise, no less than gratification, that a strong party among the younger men were vigorously taking the matter up in the right (that is, *my*) sense." He was not quite correct in this estimate of the situation—as those who hankered after a university on German lines, with all power to the professors, soon found out. "Huxley ...", Pearson (1914–30, III, 289) later complained to Galton, "brought his enormous force to work on a small executive committee of which I was secretary to carry out a plan of *his own* ... with all the force of an old hand [he] completely confused me." But the dashing young frigates should have known that the old hulk would set sail only on a course of the admiral's choosing.

Huxley told Weldon (*L.L.* II, 315), "That to which I am utterly opposed is the creation of an Established Church Scientific, with a hierarchical organisation and a professorial Episcopate"; and by December the executive committee had been persuaded that the only workable plan was a federal university. Pearson resigned in protest, and Huxley explained in *The Times* (6 December 1892) why he had rejected the original scheme:

> As for a government by professors only, the fact of their being specialists is against them. Most of them are broad-minded, practical men; some are good administrators. But, unfortunately, there is among them, as in other professions, a fair sprinkling of one-idea'd fanatics, ignorant of the commonest conventions of

official relations, and content with nothing if they cannot get everything their own way. It is these persons who, with the very highest and purest intentions, would ruin any administrative body unless they were counterpoised by non-professorial, common-sense members of recognised weight and authority in the conduct of affairs.

It must have been with a gratifying sense of concentrated authority that Huxley appeared in 1893 to give evidence before the 'Gresham' Commissioners. He was President of the Association, Crown Senator of the University of London, a Governor of University College, still Dean of the Royal College of Science, influential though unofficial adviser to the Royal Colleges of Physicians and of Surgeons—and, to round things off nicely, he had already been confidentially consulted about who should be appointed to the Commission before which he was to appear. Perhaps not surprisingly, the Royal Commission's 1894 report was very much along his lines. In May he dined with Lord Rosebery, the new Prime Minister, and it is not difficult to guess what the two of them talked about. When December arrived without any decisive governmental action, he decided to provoke it. "It is rumoured that there are lions in the path", he wrote (*L.L.* II, 317) to Rosebery. "But even lions are occasionally induced to retreat by the sight of a large body of beaters. And some of us think that such a deputation as would willingly wait on you, might hasten the desired movement." Early in the January of 1895 the deputation met the Prime Minister, with Huxley as single spokesman for the University of London, University College, the Association for Promoting a Professorial University, and sundry others. The great federal University of London was thus not only conceived, but was safely started towards a vigorous birth before the century ended.

The deputation left Huxley badly knocked up, and he never really recovered. In February he was persuaded by Knowles to write a reply to Arthur Balfour's recently published *Foundations of Belief,* and very soon sent off the first half of his article. Slip proofs arrived at Eastbourne by special messenger on the 23rd and were returned corrected to London that same afternoon; another special messenger travelled down on the 24th with the final proof; and the March number of the *Nineteenth Century* carried Huxley's essay, "Mr. Balfour's Attack on Agnosticism". "I think the cavalry charge in this month's NINETEENTH will amuse you', he wrote (*L.L.* II, 398) to one of his daughters. "The heavy artillery and the bayonets will be brought into play next month."

Next month was to be a month too late. Huxley managed to get off the manuscript of the second part of his article, but by the time the proofs arrived he was abed of severe influenza. For four more months he fought against bronchitis, heart trouble and kidney failure. Even at the end of June there were some faint hopes of recovery, and long spells on the verandah in the hot sun of that blazing summer gave him a misleading appearance of good health. He was cheerful, and even merry at times, and on 26 June he wrote (*L.L.* II, 402) to tell his old friend Hooker, "At present I don't feel at all like 'sending in my checks', and without being over sanguine I rather incline to think that my native toughness will get the best of it." But three days later he was dead, and within the week buried at Finchley—without religious ceremony.

"Remember", said one of the younger generation of scientists (*New Review*, August 1895) at a Royal Society *soirée* soon after, "That it was Huxley who made all of us possible".

Huxley's contemporaries

THESE biographical notes relate to contemporaries of Huxley who are mentioned in the text. Contemporaneity is for this purpose interpreted widely, to include any degree of overlap of life-span. The notes, as a result, range from a few men born before the middle of the eighteenth century to others who survived into the second half of the twentieth.

Most of those noted were either personal friends or educational allies of Huxley, or people with whom he corresponded, or his opponents in controversy or debate. Some names are those of scientists who helped him or whom he helped, or whose work was important in setting the tone of nineteenth century biology, or with whose work his is compared or contrasted. Some are those of men and women influential in administration or church affairs or social and political life, among whom he lobbied for the causes he believed in. Others are of those whose opinions he found of interest or who were interested in his.

This basis of selection means, of course, that some Victorian giants are omitted from these notes, while some comparative pygmies are included. In this, however, there is positive virtue, for all too often an historical period is presented as if it consisted exclusively of giants, and is thereby inevitably distorted.

The main reason for gathering these biographical notes in this appendix, rather than scattering them throughout the book as footnotes, is to facilitate repeated reference at any point in the reading. It is also hoped, however, that many readers will enjoy browsing through the notes for their own sake, savouring the rich variety of Huxley's contemporaries, and possibly gaining a new appreciation of the general flavour of his times.

ACLAND, (Sir) Henry Wentworth (1815–1900), a brilliant physician who was a Fellow of All Souls and successively Aldrichian Professor of Clinical Medicine and Regius Professor of Medicine at Oxford. However, he had the reputation of scarcely ever lecturing and even discouraging people from becoming medical students in order that he should not have them to teach.

157

158   SCIENTIST EXTRAORDINARY – T. H. HUXLEY

AGASSIZ, Alexander (1835–1910), son of J. L. R. Agassiz. He became superintendent of a Michigan copper-mining corporation and travelled widely making scientific (especially zoological) studies in South America, Hawaii, the West Indies, Australasia and Oceania. In 1874 he was appointed Curator of the Harvard University Museum and from this centre exerted great influence over the younger generation of American scientists. Unlike his father, he accepted the theory of evolution and did much to secure its general acceptance in the U.S.A.

AGASSIZ, Jean Louis Rodolphe (1807–1873), the great Swiss naturalist to whom, when still quite young, Cuvier entrusted many of his notes and materials for continued examination. His most important researches were on fish, both living and fossil, but he also did good work on glacial action. In 1846 he went to lecture at Harvard, and settled in the U.S.A. There he continued as both zoologist and geologist, and became the most distinguished American scientific opponent of Darwin's theory.

ALLEN, Frances (Fanny) (1781–1875), eleventh child of J. B. Allen and aunt to Emma Darwin, the wife of Charles. Pretty, vivacious and very clever, she was a fierce Whig and yet a devoted admirer of Napoleon. The Allens intermarried not only with the Darwins but also with the Wedgwood, Mackintosh (Sir James), Drewe (hence with Lord Gifford) and Seymour (hence with Earl of Portsmouth) families.

AMBERLEY—see **RUSSELL**.

AMEER ALI, (Sir) Syed (1849–1928), an Indian of Persian descent who was called to the Bar at the Inner Temple in 1873 and, whilst studying in London, gained from Huxley a life-long interest in science. He became a member of the Bengal Legislature Council, Professor of Law at Calcutta, Judge of the Calcutta High Court, author of many legal texts, a pioneer of female education in India, founder of the Red Crescent Society, founder of the National Muhammedan Association, virtual founder of the great Aligarh Muslim University, and the first Indian Member of the Privy Council. In 1905 he settled in London, intending retirement, but twenty years later was still acting as a Judge of Appeal for the Privy Council.

ANDERSON, Elizabeth Garrett (1836–1917), the pioneer woman doctor, to whom Huxley opened his physiology class when all medical schools were closed against her. She was a member of the first London School Board, and worked closely with Huxley on it. In 1866 she opened in London a dispensary for women, which grew into an important hospital and eventually became the Elizabeth Garrett Anderson Hospital.

ANDRES, Angelo (1851–1934), who studied in Pavia, worked for a while on cryptogams, spent some time in Leuckart's laboratory at Leipzig, and then in 1876 came to England for a year to work under Huxley at South Kensington. Huxley secured him a post at the Naples Zoological Station, where he stayed for six years before moving on to the University of Modena, then to the Instituti Superiori at Milan, to become eventually Head of the Faculty of Science at Parma.

APPLETON, William Henry (1814–1899), who with his father Daniel founded the American publishing house of their name. He was a friend of Huxley's and entertained him on the 1876 visit to the U.S.A.

ARGYLL—see **CAMPBELL**.

ARMSTRONG, Henry Edward (1848–1937), the chemist and educationist who studied under Frankland and Huxley and later worked especially on the crystallography of organic compounds. From 1871 to 1884 he was Professor of Chemistry at the

London Institution and from 1884 to 1913 at South Kensington. He brought about considerable reforms in the teaching of science, being the strongest advocate of the 'heuristic' method of discovery by the students themselves.

ARNOLD, Matthew (1822–1888), the poet and literary critic. After graduating from Balliol he taught at Rugby, became private secretary to Lord Lansdowne, and then one of the most influential of Her Majesty's Inspectors of Schools. He and Huxley were friends, but the latter disapproved of the former's tendency to equate a 'liberal education' with a literary education, and of his underestimation of the cultural potential of the poorer classes in Britain and of the still rough-and-ready colonial peoples.

AVEBURY—see LUBBOCK.

BAER—see VON BAER.

BALFOUR, Arthur James (Earl Balfour) (1848–1930), the eminent Conservative politician, who was at various times Secretary for Ireland, First Lord of the Admiralty, Foreign Secretary and Prime Minister. Today he is best remembered for the 'Balfour Declaration' of Palestine as a national home for the Jews. He was eminent in higher education, becoming Rector of both Glasgow and St. Andrews, Chancellor of Edinburgh, and Senator of London University. He published several books on philosophy and religion, his 1895 *Foundations of Belief* being the subject of Huxley's last controversy, in the middle of which he died.

BALFOUR, Francis Maitland (1851–1882), the younger brother of A. J. Balfour. He was one of Huxley's most brilliant protégés, having been picked out by him for a natural history prize whilst still a schoolboy at Harrow. As Fellow of Trinity and Lecturer in Animal Morphology, Balfour established a fine school of embryology at Cambridge. He was widely regarded as the 'coming' biologist of England, but died young in a climbing accident.

BALFOUR, John Hutton (1808–1884), Professor of Botany at Glasgow from 1841 to 1845 and at Edinburgh from 1845 to 1879. He was a stimulating teacher, being a pioneer in practical (including microscopic) demonstrations and writing several good textbooks.

BALL, William Platt (1844–1917), a London schoolmaster who resigned his post rather than give religious instruction. Eventually he entered the service of the Sultan of Turkey, by whom he was decorated.

BATESON, William (1861–1926), who became Professor of Biology at Cambridge and then Director of the John Innes Horticultural Institution. His early researches on *Balanoglossus* cast valuable new light on the evolution of vertebrates, but he is best remembered as the pioneer of genetics in England. His 1894 *Materials for the Study of Variation* was important in this respect and he was one of the first to appreciate the fundamental nature of Mendel's papers when they were rediscovered.

BAYNES, Thomas Spencer (1823–1887), editor of the ninth edition of *The Encyclopaedia Britannica* and an intimate of many of the leading figures of the day. He taught philosophy at Edinburgh, edited the *Edinburgh Guardian*, and in 1864 became Professor of Logic, Metaphysics and English Literature at St. Andrews. His writings on Shakespeare were regarded as important.

BECHE—see DE LA BECHE.

BESANT, Annie (1847–1933), theosophist, educationist and eventually also Indian politician. Courageously active in birth-control propaganda and author of *The Gospel of Atheism* (1877), she was deprived by the courts of the custody of her daughter. She founded the Hindu College (now University) of Benares and in 1917 became President of the Indian National Congress.

BLUMENBACH, Johann Friedrich (1752–1840), the German zoologist who was a pioneer in comparative anatomy and is often considered the 'father' of physical anthropology. He was the first to establish clearly and name the five population groups of Caucasian (i.e. approximately European), Mongolian, Ethiopian (i.e. Negro), American (i.e. Amerindian) and Malayan.

BOOTH, 'General' William (1829–1912), the founder in 1878 of the Salvation Army. He was 'converted' by the Methodists in 1844 and preached for nine years in the 'New Connexion' before becoming an independent itinerant revivalist. In 1890 Huxley launched an attack on the authoritarian manner in which he conducted the 'Army', but the controversy was indecisive.

BOWER, Frederick Orpen (1855–1948), who spans the period from before Darwin's theory to after Hiroshima. After studying in Cambridge and Germany, he helped Huxley at South Kensington and in 1885 became Regius Professor of Botany at Glasgow, which post he held for forty years. His work became concentrated on the evolutionary morphology of the mosses, ferns and other non-flowering plants, leading to his two great standard works, the 1908 *Origin of a Land Flora* and the 1935 *Primitive Land Plants*.

BRADLAUGH, Charles (1833–1891), the leading secularist. After serving as an Army private, he became a solicitor's clerk and wrote many pamphlets in defence of freedom of thought. In 1878 he and Annie Besant were acquitted on a criminal charge arising from the distribution of a birth-control book, *The Fruits of Philosophy*. He succeeded in 1885, after a five years' struggle, in establishing the right of an M.P. to take his seat in the House of Commons without first taking a religious oath.

BRODIE, (Sir) Benjamin Collins (1783–1862), the most distinguished surgeon of his day (not to be confused with his son, also Sir Benjamin Collins Brodie, who was Professor of Chemistry at Oxford). He was in turn surgeon to George IV, William IV, and Queen Victoria; for many years Professor of Comparative Anatomy and Physiology at the Royal College of Surgeons; President of that College and of the Royal Society and in 1858 the first President of the General Medical Council. He must have been one of the first to study seriously the relationship between physical state and mental health.

BRODRICK, George Charles (1831–1903), Fellow and from 1881 Warden of Merton College, Oxford. He was also active at the Bar, in journalism and in politics. He served on the London School Board, as a Governor of Eton and on the Selborne Commission. Over many years he was very friendly with Huxley, with whom he collaborated in university reform.

BURNETT, (Sir) William (1779–1861), a Scot who in 1835 became Royal Physician. He invented 'Burnett's fluid', a disinfectant zinc chloride solution which was widely used as a preservative of wood and canvas. As Director-General of the Royal Navy Medical Service, he repeatedly extended Huxley's paid leave after the *Rattlesnake* voyage and thus enabled him to devote himself to research before finally being struck off the Navy List.

BUSK, George (1807–1886), a naval surgeon who retired early in 1855 and settled in London, where he did considerable research, especially on the bryozoa. He became Treasurer of the Royal Institution and a trustee of the Hunterian Museum and thus, despite the minor nature of his own researches, was an influential figure in the rapidly enlarging scientific world of his day.

CAMPBELL, George Douglas (Duke of Argyll) (1823–1900), a prominent Whig in the politics of his day, who became Chancellor of St. Andrews in 1851 and Rector of Glasgow University in 1854. He held the 'cataclysmic' view of geology, and over a period of many years (and on many issues) he and Huxley were not only strongly opposed but almost bitterly antagonistic.

CARLYLE, Thomas (1795–1881), the great Scottish essayist and historian. Although he was greatly offended by the mature Huxley as "the man who says we are descended from monkeys", his writings were a powerful and positive influence on Huxley as an adolescent, especially by their moral vigour end by their opening the windows to German thinking.

CAVENDISH, (Sir) William (Earl of Burlington and Duke of Devonshire) (1808–1891), who was a liberal benefactor of educational and scientific enterprises. Apart from his political work first as an M.P. in the Commons and after 1834 in the Lords, he was also active in higher education, serving as Chancellor of London, Cambridge and Victoria (Manchester) Universities. From 1871 to 1875 he was Chairman of the great Royal Commission on Scientific Instruction and the Advancement of Science.

CECIL, Robert Arthur Talbot Gascoyne (Viscount Cranborne and Marquis of Salisbury) (1830–1903), who was successively Conservative M.P., Secretary for India under both Derby and Disraeli, Foreign Secretary and in 1885 Prime Minister. A high tory, he opposed household suffrage, Irish church disestablishment, and the abolition both of army commissions purchase and of university religious tests. Nevertheless, he had a few liberal thoughts, especially on the material improvement of working-class conditions of life.

CHAMBERS, Robert (1802–1871), the Edinburgh publisher who was himself a substantial 'man of letters'. He wrote widely on Scottish history, biography and literature, but is best known to science by his (anonymous) *Vestiges of Creation*. Although inaccurate and lacking in scientific rigour (and therefore strongly attacked by Huxley among others), this volume created a considerable stir and did much to prepare the public mind for Darwin's book fifteen years later.

CHAMISSO—see VON CHAMISSO.

CLARK, William George (1821–1878), best known for the *Cambridge Shakespeare* which he mainly planned. A Fellow of Trinity, whose Clark Lectureship was endowed by his will, he was the University's Public Orator for thirteen years and one of the group of dons with whom Huxley worked in his efforts at university reform.

CLIFFORD, Sophia Lucy (*née* Lane) (?–1929), the novelist and dramatist of Barbadian origin, who in 1875 married the brilliant young mathematician and philosopher W. K. Clifford. Her striking 1885 novel *Mrs. Keith's Crime* dealt with the then dangerous theme of a mother's right to end the life of a suffering incurable child, while the 1913 *Love Letters of a Worldly Woman* and 1917 *The House in Marylebone* are also still of interest. After her husband's early death in 1879 she was much aided and befriended by Huxley, with whose family she became closely intimate.

CLODD, Edward (1840–1930), a London banker whose wide and deep interest in both science and letters led to close friendship with many distinguished scholars. Among other activities, he was a member of the Royal Astronomical Society, President of the Folk Lore Society, part-founder of the Johnson and Omar Khayyám Clubs, and Chairman of the Rationalist Press Association. His 1916 *Memories* provides some intimate glimpses of the great Victorians.

COCKS—see **SOMERS.**

COLENSO, John William (1814–1883), the 'modernist' Cambridge theologian who became Bishop of Natal. In 1862 he was involved in a bitter controversy by reason of his failure to require polygamous Zulu converts to divorce their extra wives, his opposition to the doctrine of eternal punishment, and his declaration that the Pentateuch was a post-exilic forgery. He was deposed and excommunicated, but appeal to the Privy Council reinstated his episcopal income. He was a friend of Huxley's.

COLLIER, John (1850–1934), the portrait-painter son of Baron Monkswell, who married first Huxley's daughter Marian in 1879 and then, after her death, the younger daughter Ethel. Marriage to a deceased wife's sister being illegal in England, Huxley went with the couple to marry in Norway in 1889.

COLLINS, John Churton (1848–1908), whose articles in the *Quarterly Review* and in the *Pall Mall Gazette* did much through the years to encourage the study of English literature in English universities. From 1880 he was very active both in London and in Oxford as a lecturer for the university extension movement. He had close contacts with Huxley, whom he admired as a scientist of literary distinction. In 1904 he became Professor of English Literature at Birmingham.

COMTE, Isidore Auguste Marie François (1798–1857), the French mathematician and philosopher who founded Positivism. Huxley virtually shattered its English following with his description of it as "Catholicism *minus* Christianity", but it seems uncertain how deeply he had in fact studied it.

COWPER, Francis Thomas de Grey (Earl Cowper) (1834–1905), the vastly wealthy landowner who served under Gladstone at the Board of Trade and as Lord Lieutenant of Ireland. Later, however, he was an active opponent of Gladstone's policy of Home Rule for Ireland. In 1892 be became chairman of the London University Commission.

CREMER, (Sir) William Randal (1838–1908), a poor orphan who was apprenticed as a carpenter, became an active and radical trade unionist, was one of Garibaldi's reception committee on his visit to England, and for a time secretary of the British section of the First International. In 1870 he was taken by Huxley as his partner in the London School Board elections. In 1885 he became a radical M.P., worked especially as a pacifist, was eventually knighted, and in 1903 was awarded the Nobel Peace Prize.

CROSS—see **ELIOT.**

CUVIER, Georges Léopold Chrétien Frédéric Dagobert (Baron Cuvier) (1769–1832), the son of a Swiss officer in the French army, who virtually established the science of palaeontology. He was, among other things, Professor of Natural History at the Collège de France, Inspector of Education, Councillor of State and Chancellor of the University of Paris. The patronage of Napoleon, combined with his own encyclopaedic knowledge, gave him a position of enormous power in the scientific world of Europe.

DARWIN, Charles Robert (1809–1882), always to be remembered for his theory of evolution by natural selection and especially for his 1859 *Origin of Species*. At school, and at Edinburgh and Cambridge, he was regarded as a slow learner, showing no particular promise. In 1831 he sailed as naturalist on *Beagle*, and thereafter produced massive research results over a wide field, including coral reef formation, animal behaviour, earthworm action, orchids, insectivorous plants, etc. Athough hypochondriac and always glad to have Huxley as his 'bulldog', Darwin was a shrewd man of business and did very well with his stocks and shares.

DAUBENY, Charles Giles Bridle (1795–1867), at various times Professor of Chemistry, of Botany and of Rural Economy at Oxford. Today he is best remembered by his book *A Description of Active and Extinct Volcanoes*.

DAWSON, (Sir) John William (1820–1899), the Nova Scotian who, after studying at Edinburgh, returned to Canada and became Professor of Geology at McGill and eventually Principal there. He was the first President of the Royal Society of Canada. His view that *Eozoon canadense* was not a mere mineral structure, but an extremely ancient fossil of a very simple organism, was generally rejected during his lifetime, but is now thought likely to have been correct.

DE LA BECHE, (Sir) Henry Thomas (1796–1855), who especially studied metamorphism and whose 1837 *Theoretical Geology* was very influential. He was the first Director of the Geological Survey and of the School of Mines in Jermyn Street (1851).

DE VRIES, Hugo (1848–1935), Professor of Botany at Amsterdam, one of the rediscoverers of Mendel's papers. He did some valuable work on osmosis and plasmolysis, but is mainly remembered for his advocacy of the idea that evolution takes place largely by mutations—sudden, almost explosive, reorganisations of existing hereditary states. It is now known that some of his experimental results with *Oenothera*, the evening primrose, were atypical.

DEUTSCH, Emanuel Oscar Menahem (1829–1873), the great Semitic scholar of Jewish Silesian origin, who from 1855 to 1870 worked as an assistant in the British Museum. He deciphered many Phoenician inscriptions, but became famous (to many, infamous) by reason of his essay on the Talmud in the *Quarterly Review* in 1867.

DEVONSHIRE—see **CAVENDISH.**

DOHRN, Anton (1840–1909), the German biologist who is remembered mainly for his founding of the great Naples Marine Biological Research Station. He was a close friend of Huxley, with whom he corresponded for over twenty years.

DONNELLY, (Sir) John Fretcheville Dykes (1834–1902), a Royal Engineers officer who, having been seconded to help with buildings for the School of Mines etc., proved so admirable an administrator that he was retained and eventually became Secretary to the Science and Art Department.

DUFF—see **GRANT DUFF.**

DYSTER, Frederick Daniel (1810–1893), a wealthy medical practitioner who combined a fashionable practice in Tenby with much free attention to the poor. He was a considerable amateur of marine biology and frequently put his home at the disposal of Huxley as a convenient base for coastal investigations.

ECKERSLEY, William Alfred (1856–1895), the distinguished civil engineer who built railways especially in Spain, Mexico and South America, dying whilst doing so in Peru. In 1885 he married Huxley's daughter Rachel and their three sons (Roger, Thomas and Peter) were all pioneers in the development of Britain's broadcasting system.

EDWARDS, John Passmore (1823–1911), the progressive journalist who in 1876 made the *Echo* into the first halfpenny newspaper. He became a Liberal M.P. but declined a knighthood. Best known for his philanthropy, he founded some seventy free libraries, social 'settlements', convalescent homes, etc. In 1870 he supported Huxley's candidature for the first London School Board.

ELIOT, George (Marion Evans/Cross) (1819–1880), the great novelist who scandalised England by openly living with G. H. Lewes. Nevertheless, a considerable *côterie* of distinguished people (including Huxley) refused to boycott her. Two years after the death of Lewes in 1878 she married J. W. Cross, a wealthy New York banker, but died soon after the wedding.

ENGELS, Friedrich (1820–1895), the German-born Manchester businessman who was Marx's close friend, benefactor and ideological ally. Both his *Anti-Dühring* and his *Ludwig Feuerbach* demonstrate that he was a serious student of science, including Huxley's biological work.

ENGLER, Heinrich Gustav Adolf (1844–1930), the plant taxonomist who in 1872 became Conservator of the Botanical Collections at Munich and six years later Professor of Botany at Kiel, where he founded the *Botanische Jahrbücher*. Later occupying Chairs at Breslau and Berlin, he also collected widely in Africa and Asia. He produced a major new classification of the plant kingdom, based on novel principles, and appealing to many today as more 'natural' than those still based essentially on the system of Linnaeus.

EVANS—see **ELIOT.**

EYRE, Edward John (1815–1901), a Yorkshire emigrant to Australia who became a successful sheep farmer, was appointed Lieutenant Governor of New Zealand, and later became Governor of Jamaica. In 1865 he suppressed a native rising with great brutality, confirming the death sentence on large numbers of rebels, including G. W. Gordon, a coloured member of the legislature. Huxley was one of a group of liberals who sought to have him tried for murder, but he was only reprimanded and retired on pension.

FARADAY, Michael (1791–1867), the poor bookseller's assistant who was engaged as amanuensis by Sir Humphrey Davy, helped him in his experiments, and eventually became Director of the Royal Institution. An experimenter of genius, perhaps his most fundamental discovery was that of electromagnetic induction. He was a hero to Huxley, who as a young medical student had button-holed him outside the Royal Institution and received decisive but kindly criticism of his imagined scheme for producing 'perpetual motion'.

FARRAR, Frederic William (1831–1903), author of *Eric, or Little by Little* and editor of the 1867 *Essays on a Liberal Education*. After graduating at Cambridge he took holy orders, became a schoolmaster at Marlborough and then at Harrow, eventually returning to Marlborough as Master. Although a strong 'progressive' in both theology and education (working closely with Huxley in the promotion of science education), he nevertheless remained sufficiently 'respectable' to become Chaplain to the Speaker and to the Queen, as well as Canon of Westminster and Dean of Canterbury.

FARRER, (Sir) Thomas Henry (Baron Farrer) (1819–1899), who after leaving Balliol became first a barrister and then a distinguished civil servant. He was especially effective as Permanent Secretary to the Board of Trade (1865–86) and later on the London County Council (1889–98). Over many years he was a friend of Huxley's and helped him in endeavours which demanded influential support.

FAULKNER, Charles Joseph (1834–1890), successively Bursar, Tutor and Dean of Degrees at University College, Oxford. It was he who acted as main intermediary when in 1881 efforts were made to persuade Huxley to go to Oxford as Master of University College.

FAWCETT, Henry (1833–1884), Fellow of Trinity Hall and from 1863 Professor of Political Economy at Cambridge. Although blinded by a shooting accident in his mid-twenties, he lived a very full life as an academic, as a Liberal M.P., as Postmaster-General in Gladstone's 1880 government, and as an advocate of higher education for women. Huxley and he collaborated in various efforts at university reform, including the attempt to abolish religious tests.

FISKE, John (Edmund Fiske Green) (1842–1901), the American philosopher and historian, who was an important populariser of Darwin's theory of evolution. Very precocious, he could read about ten languages by the age of twenty, and became Professor of American History at Washington University, St. Louis. He was very friendly with Huxley.

FLOURENS, Jean Pierre Marie (1794–1867), who did distinguished work especially on the physiology of nervous action and in particular on that of the cerebellum. In 1832 he succeeded Cuvier as one of the Permanent Secretaries of the French Academy of Sciences. He was also Professor of Comparative Anatomy at the Jardin des Plantes and in 1835 went to a Chair at the Collège de France. His personal pomposity offended Huxley among others, but this does not detract from the quality of his scientific work.

FLOWER, (Sir) William Henry (1831–1899), the comparative anatomist whose early scientific career was promoted by Huxley and whose 1862 "Observations on the Posterior Lobes of the Quadrumana" finally settled the fierce dispute between Huxley and Owen in the former's favour. In 1884 Huxley nominated him to succeed Owen as Director of the British Museum (Natural History).

FORBES, Edward (1815–1854), a brilliant Manx biologist who was successively Professor of Botany at King's College, London, Palaeontologist to the Geological Survey and—briefly before his premature death—Professor of Natural History at Edinburgh. Gay and the wittiest of men, he was the leading light of the 'Red Lions Club', which brought together the bright young men of science during the annual meetings of the British Association.

FOSTER, (Sir) Michael (1836–1907), the Huntington general practitioner who taught physiology at University College, London, and was effectively nominated by Huxley in 1870 as Trinity's first Praelector in Physiology and in 1883 as Cambridge's first Professor of that subject. Although his own researches were only of the second rank, he did a great deal to develop biological science at Cambridge and by example elsewhere.

FRANKLAND, (Sir) Edward (1825–1899), Professor of Chemistry at Owens College, Manchester, and from 1865 at the Royal College of Chemistry (which became part of the Royal College of Science at South Kensington). His main work was in organic chemistry, to which he made some notable contributions. He was a close friend of Huxley's over many years.

GALTON, (Sir) Frances (1822–1911), the enormously ingenious cousin of Charles Darwin who founded the science of 'eugenics'. He began his researches into genetics in 1865, unaware that Mendel's fundamental laws of heredity were just about to be published. His studies, always brilliant but rarely conclusive, ranged into diverse fields (including meteorology, finger-printing and anthropology). His *Hereditary Genius* and *Inquiries into Human Faculty* are quite fascinating. He established the Chair and Research Laboratory of Eugenics at University College, London.

GARRETT—see ANDERSON.

GEDDES, (Sir) Patrick (1854–1932), who studied under Huxley at South Kensington, later became Professor of Botany at Dundee, and so extended his range as virtually to establish the 'regional study' type of sociology. On his retirement he went in 1920 to Bombay as Professor of Civics and Sociology.

GIGLIONI, Enrico Hillyer (1845–1909), who studied zoology under Huxley at the School of Mines. He went round the world in 1865 on a scientific expedition, in 1869 was appointed to a Chair of Zoology at Florence, and later became Professor of Zoology and Comparative Anatomy. In 1876 he founded the central Italian College of Vertebrate Anatomy which is named after him.

GILMAN, Daniel Coit (1831–1908), successively Professor of Geography at Yale, President of the University of California, in 1875 the first President of Johns Hopkins, and in 1901 first President of the Carnegie Institution. He came under heavy attack for inviting the 'godless' Huxley to speak at the official opening of the Johns Hopkins University in 1876.

GLADSTONE, William Ewart (1809–1898), the great Liverpool-born Liberal statesman who was four times Prime Minister and with Disraeli dominated Victorian politics. He was a distinguished scholar and very able theologian, but Huxley considered him intellectually dishonest and sought every opportunity to engage him in public controversy.

GOETHE—see VON GOETHE.

GORDON, Charles (Earl and Marquess of Huntly, Lord of Gordon, Earl of Enzie, Lord of Badenoch, Viscount of Melgum, Earl of Aboyne, Baron Meldrum, Chief of Clan Gordon) (1847–1937), the young 'Cock o' the North' whom Huxley defeated in the 1872 election for Lord Rector of Aberdeen University, despite his immense wealth and territorial prestige. He eventually became Rector of Aberdeen in 1890.

GOULD, Charles (1834–1893), who studies under Huxley in 1855, went to Tasmania where he became the first Government Surveyor and Geologist, named the peaks along the West Coast Range after prominent British scientists, and developed successful techniques of prospecting for gold. He returned to England in 1873, secured a post at Singapore with Huxley's support, and for ten years from 1880 travelled widely in eastern Asia. His book, *Mythical Monsters*, is an interesting, if somewhat credulous, volume. He died whilst travelling in South America.

GRANT DUFF, (Sir) Mountstuart Elphinstone (1829–1906), whose 14-volume *Notes from a Diary* is a rich mine of Victorian lore. He was a Liberal M.P. for many years, served as Under-Secretary of State for India and as Governor of Madras, and knew almost everybody of any eminence in England. He preceded Huxley as Rector of Aberdeen and the two were friendly over many years.

GRANVILLE—see **LEVESON-GOWER.**

GREEN—see **FISKE.**

GROTE, George (1794–1871), the distinguished historian who was in the circle of Bentham and J. S. Mill, and was one of the original founders of 'London University' (University College). From 1832 to 1841 he was M.P. for the City of London and repeatedly tried to secure voting by ballot. He endowed a Professorship of Logic at University College, London, stipulating that it must not be held by a clergyman. In 1869 he declined a peerage, and thereby gained Huxley's admiration.

GRUBE, Adolph Eduard (1812–1880), who studied anatomy and zoology under von Baer and later became Professor at Königsberg, Dorpat and Breslau, at which last he especially built up a fine zoological museum.

GUIZOT, François Pierre Guillaume (1787–1874), the French historian and states-man, whose *History of Civilisation in Europe* influenced Huxley as an adolescent. He was Premier of France 1840-1848 but was forced into retirement by the Revolution of 1848.

GUNTHER, Albert Charles Lewis Gotthilf (1830–1914), a German-born zoologist who in 1862 became a naturalised British subject. He worked for many years at the British Museum and in 1875 became Keeper of its zoological department.

HAECKEL, Ernst (1834–1919), the brilliant if somewhat erratic biologist who, after studying under Kölliker, Müller and Virchow, became Professor of Zoology at Jena. He did excellent work in comparative embryology and taxonomy, but his 'gastraea theory' and his paralleling of ontogeny with phylogeny have been consider-ably discredited. He was an inspiring teacher and the bravest continental exponent of Darwin's theory. Outspokenly agnostic and politically radical, he had many difficulties with the authorities of church and state as well as with those of science. He was a friend and fervent admirer of Huxley.

HAMILTON, (Sir) William (1788–1856), the Scottish philosopher who was first Professor of Civil History and later Professor of Logic and Metaphysics at Edinburgh. He especially developed theories of the association of ideas, of unconscious mental modifications and of the relationship between perception and sensation. The adolescent Huxley was influenced by his writings.

HARCOURT, (Sir) William George Granville Venables Vernon (1827–1904), the scholarly and financially successful barrister who became a Liberal M.P. and cham-pioned religious equality in education, electoral reform, restriction of landlords' rights etc. At various times he was Solicitor-General, Home Secretary and Chancellor of the Exchequer. He was one of Huxley's supporters in the 1870 School Board election.

HARRIS, Frank (1856–1931), the extraordinarily gifted *confidante* of so many in the 1890s, now most widely known for his highly erotic and equally unreliable *My Life and Loves*. Born in Ireland and later naturalised in the U.S.A., he lived at various times as a railway labourer, cowboy etc., but also became a considerable literary scholar and a journalist of genius. He edited the *Evening News* and the *Fortnightly Review*, for which latter Huxley wrote his 1886 "Science and Morals".

HARRISON, Frederic (1831–1923), a lawyer who led the English followers of Auguste Comte and in 1893 founded the *Positivist Review*. He (perhaps not unnaturally) took very much to heart Huxley's scathing attacks on positivism, and the two were generally at loggerheads.

HELMHOLTZ—see **VON HELMHOLTZ.**

HERBERT, Auberon Edward William Molyneux (1838–1906), a man of letters who abandoned conservatism, became a Liberal M.P., declared himself an agnostic and republican, and later engaged in psychic research. He was one of the committee which supported Huxley's candidature for the London School Board, and later they collaborated in an effort at examination reform at Oxford.

HIRST, Thomas Archer (1830–1892), who taught at Queenswood (girls) and University College schools, became Professor first of Physics and then of Pure Mathematics at University College, London, and in 1873 was nominated by Huxley as first Director of Studies at the Royal Naval College, Greenwich.

HOBHOUSE, Arthur (Baron Hobhouse) (1819–1904), the Oxford barrister who became a successful Chancery practitioner and eventually a judge, Privy Councillor and Law Lord. In 1870 he was a member of Huxley's London School Board Election Committee and in 1882 himself became a member of that Board.

HOFMEISTER, Wilhelm (1824–1877), Professor of Botany first at Heidelberg and then at Tübingen. He did some fundamental work on the reproduction of both flowering and non-flowering plants, especially ferns and mosses, and did a good deal to pioneer the practical teaching of his subject.

HOGG, Quintin (1845–1903), the wealthy philanthropist who in 1882 opened the Regent Street Polytechnic for the instruction and recreation of those who had not been fortunate enough to receive a good formal education in established institutions. He also provided a 'ragged school' in Charing Cross, a day school attached to the Polytechnic, a labour bureau, and an agency to organise cheap travel.

HOOKER, (Sir) Joseph Dalton (1817–1911), one of the ablest plant taxonomists of all time, who in 1865 succeeded his father as Director of Kew Gardens and was chief architect of their acknowledged supremacy. From the start he gave public support to Darwin's theory and was one of Huxley's closest friends. His scientific publications continued throughout a period of 71 years.

HOWELL, George (1833–1910), who joined the Chartists at the age of fourteen and was prominent in many labour struggles, including the enactment of the 1871 and 1876 Trade Unions Acts. For ten years from 1885 he was Liberal M.P. for Bethnal Green. He was a friend of Huxley's.

HOWES, Thomas George Bond (1853–1905), who studied under and later assisted Huxley at South Kensington over a period of years and succeeded him there as Professor. His researches were largely in vertebrate comparative anatomy, but above all he was an admirable teacher.

HUNTINGTON—see **CAVENDISH.**

HUNTLY—see **GORDON.**

IDDESLEIGH—see **NORTHCOTE.**

JHERING—see **VON JHERING.**

JODRELL, Thomas Jodrell Phillips (1808–1889), a wealthy amateur of science who in 1873 decided to make a substantial endowment at University College, London. On Huxley's advice, he stipulated that the gift should be applied to a combined Chair of Physiology and Practical Physiology, and that the Professor should work full-time at the duties of the post, which included both research and teaching.

JOWETT, Benjamin (1817–1893), from 1855 Regius Professor of Greek at Oxford and from 1870 Master of Balliol. For the first ten years he was deprived of the emoluments of his chair on suspicion of heresy. He was one of the leading intramural advocates of university reform and over many years collaborated closely with Huxley, especially in efforts at the promotion of science at Oxford. His translations of Plato's *Republic* and of Aristotle's *Politics* were major works which are still in some respects standard.

KAY—see KAY-SHUTTLEWORTH.

KAY-SHUTTLEWORTH (originally Kay), (Sir) James Phillips (1804–1877), the father of English popular education and of systematic teacher-training. Originally a medical practitioner, he became Secretary to the Manchester Board of Health, then an assistant Poor Law Commissioner, and in 1839 the first Secretary to the Privy Council's Committee on Education. In the 1860s he did much to relieve poverty during Lancashire's cotton famine, being the county's High Sheriff in 1863. He and Huxley worked closely together for Owens College, Manchester, and in several other common endeavours.

KEITH, (Sir) Arthur (1866–1955), the anatomist and anthropologist, who began the scientific study of monkeys whilst practising medicine as a young man in Siam. In 1896 he became Demonstrator in Anatomy at the London Hospital Medical School and, on his retirement in 1932, was appointed Master of the Buckston Browne Research Institute at Downe (Darwin's home) where he lived until his death. For over half a century he studied many aspects of human origins and was highly influential in this field.

KELVIN—see THOMSON.

KINGSLEY, Charles (1819–1875), the Christian Socialist liberal clergyman who is best remembered for his 1863 *The Water Babies* and for the controversy which provoked Cardinal Newman to write *Apologia Pro Vita Sua*. He was a knowledgeable amateur of science and from the start welcomed Darwin's theory. Despite the theological gulf between them, he and Huxley developed a close and sensitive mutual understanding. Eventually he became Professor of Modern History at Cambridge and then Canon first of Chester and later of Westminster.

KNOWLES, (Sir) James Thomas (1831–1908), the wealthy architect and man of letters who from 1870 to 1877 edited the *Contemporary Review* and then founded the *Nineteenth Century*, from which he made a fortune. He dined everywhere and knew everyone who mattered in England, and thus wielded great influence on affairs from behind the scenes. Among other activities, he founded the Metaphysical Society. He and Huxley worked closely together over many years.

KÖLLIKER, Rudolf Albert (1817–1905), the Swiss microscopist and histologist, who studied first under the ageing Oken and then in Berlin under Müller. In 1847 he became Professor at Würzburg, where he continued lecturing until the age of eighty-five. Among other things, he established the nature of spermatozoa, the embryology of the cephalopods and the fibrillar structure of smooth muscle. His 1852 *Handbuch der Gewebelehre des Menschen* was the first recognisably modern histology textbook.

KOWALEWSKY, Alexander (1840–1901), who first studied engineering, then became a biologist, and was elected Academician of St. Petersburg. His detailed studies of the development of the lancelet and of the ascidians led him to some important embryological generalisations. In particular, he built on Huxley's early work to reveal the common plan of germ-layer formation and of gastrulation in a wide range of animal phyla.

LAMARCK, (Chevalier de) Jean Baptiste Pierre Antoine de Monet (1744–1829), who came from a poor Picardy family, served in the army, lived for fifteen years in Paris as a literary hack, yet eventually became one of the greatest biologists. He produced a fine *Flora* of France, was admitted to the Academy of Science, and when nearly fifty was appointed Professor of Invertebrate Zoology at the Jardin des Plantes. Nearly all his memorable work on evolution was produced after this age, his great *Philosophie Zoologique* (with its emphasis on the use and disuse of organs and on the inheritance of acquired characters) not appearing until he was sixty-five. Unlike Darwin, he died in poverty.

LANE—see **CLIFFORD.**

LANKESTER, (Sir) Edwin Ray (1847–1929), the protozoologist and embryologist, whom Huxley helped into a Fellowship at Exeter College, Oxford, and later into the Chair of Zoology and Comparative Anatomy at University College, London, and the Linacre Chair at Oxford. He became Regius Professor of Natural History at Edinburgh, was mainly responsible for the establishment in 1884 of the Marine Biological Association, and in 1898 became Director of the British Museum (Natural History).

LAWRENCE, (Sir) William (1783–1867), whose *Natural History of Man*, published while he was a young lecturer at the Royal College of Surgeons, was refused copyright by Lord Chancellor Eldon because it contradicted the scriptures. However, he thereafter pursued more respectable paths, eventually becoming President of the Royal College and being created baronet.

LENIN, Nikolai (Vladimir Ilich Ulyanov) (1870–1924), whose reputation as a bolshevik revolutionary has almost entirely obscured his considerable ability as a philosopher. It is evident from his writings (both public and private) that he studied Huxley's views on agnosticism, materialism etc., with interest and care.

LEVESON-GOWER, Granville George (Earl Granville) (1815–1891), the Whig M.P. who became Foreign Secretary under Lord John Russell and twice later under Gladstone. He was one of the promoters of the 1851 Great Exhibition and in 1861 was Chairman of the first Commission on the School of Mines. Much later, in 1883, he persuaded Huxley to serve as Crown Fellow and Senator of London University.

LIDDON, Henry Parry (1829–1890), who at Oxford joined Pusey and Keble in their 'high church' movement. He was successively Vice-Principal at Cuddesdon Theological College and at St. Edmund Hall, and then Professor of Exegesis at Oxford. From 1870 he was Canon of St. Paul's Cathedral and from 1886 its Vice-Chancellor. For twenty years his sermons were an important feature of London's religio-intellectual life—and, naturally enough, he and Huxley occasionally crossed swords.

LILLY, William Samuel (1840–1919), who after leaving Cambridge served for some time as a civil servant in India and later became a very influential Roman Catholic layman. He was a prolific and popular writer both on religious themes and more generally, and for many years Secretary to the Catholic Union of Great Britain. It was an article of his which provoked Huxley to write "Science and Morals".

LOWE, (Sir) Robert (Viscount Sherbrooke) (1811–1892), who practised law in Australia as a young man, where he became a member of the New South Wales legislature. He returned to England in 1850 (the year of *Rattlesnake*'s return), became an M.P. in 1852, and was at various times Vice-President of the Privy Council Committee on Education, Chancellor of the Exchequer and Home Secretary. His memory is often blackened by his restrictive system of 'payment by results' in state schools, but nevertheless the development of English education owed a lot to him. He greatly admired Huxley.

LUBBOCK, (Sir) John (Baron Avebury) (1834–1913), whose home served through many years as a *salon* for men of science and public affairs, and who thereby became an important figure in many influential circles. Although sometimes remembered mainly by his origination of Bank Holidays, he was a competent amateur of science and especially of archaeology and anthropology. Among the important posts he held were those of Vice-Chancellor of London University, President of the London Chamber of Commerce and Chairman of London County Council.

LYELL, (Sir) Charles (1797–1875), whose 1831 *Principles of Geology* firmly established the modern bases of that science, and especially the explanation of geological phenomena in terms of continuous processes rather than of a series of 'catastrophes'. Although quite early a convinced Darwinian, he was always somewhat chary of committing himself publicly to so subversive a theory. Nevertheless, his 1863 *Antiquity of Man* was a landmark in the eventual public acceptance of the idea of human evolution.

M'CARTHY, Justin (1830–1912), the Irish journalist, historian and politician, who was Chairman of the anti-Parnell nationalist party and author of a number of novels and biographies. He regarded Huxley as one of the greatest of the masters of English prose.

MACBRIDE, Ernest William (1866–1940), successively Demonstrator in Animal Morphology at Cambridge, Professor of Zoology at McGill and Professor of Zoology at Imperial College. He was a distinguished marine biologist, studying at Naples under Anton Dohrn, but also made valuable contributions over a wide area of zoology.

MACGILLIVRAY, John (1822–1867), who after studying medicine at Edinburgh became official naturalist on several important naval expeditions, including that of *Rattlesnake* on which Huxley sailed as assistant-surgeon. Eventually he returned to continue natural history studies in Australasia, but died young of excessive fatigue and exposure.

MACLEAY, William Sharp (1792–1865), a Cambridge zoologist who took to the law and built up a valuable practice in New South Wales. He continued doing useful work in entomology. Huxley met him whilst ashore in Sydney during the *Rattlesnake* tour.

MACMILLAN, Alexander (1815–1896), who with his brother Daniel opened a bookshop at Cambridge and from it built up the great publishing house of their name. He was a fervent (even at times uncritical) admirer of Huxley, especially as to his personal character.

MANSEL, Henry Longueville (1820–1871), an English metaphysician who followed Hamilton in maintaining that knowledge is limited to the finite and the conditioned. He was a strong tory and high churchman, and engaged in controversy especially with J. S. Mill, Goldwin Smith and F. D. Maurice. He was Reader in Theology and eventually Professor of Ecclesiastical History at Oxford.

MARSH, Othniel Charles (1831–1899), the first Professor of Palaeontology in the U.S.A. (at Yale). The support of his millionaire Peabody relatives helped him to become the dominant figure in the National Academy of Sciences, but it was his own work in the organisation of scientific expeditions which enabled him to build up his superb collection of fossils. He and Huxley corresponded with and visited each other.

MARTIN, Henry Newell (1848–1896), who as a young man was brought in by Huxley to help with his first practical courses at South Kensington, and worked for a while under Michael Foster at Cambridge. He collaborated with Huxley in writing the 1875 *Course of Instruction in Elementary Biology*, and in 1876 was sent by him to Johns Hopkins University to start off its biological teaching.

MARX, Karl (1818–1883), the German philosopher who settled in England and laid the bases of dialectical materialism by 'turning Hegel on his head'. He was an admirer of Darwin's and Huxley's writings on evolution; and, when writing the sections on machinery for *Das Kapital*, attended lectures at the School of Mines to secure a genuine understanding of the subject.

MATTHEW, Patrick (1790–1874), an obscure Scottish botanist who in 1831 anticipated some of Darwin's ideas on evolution by natural selection. After Darwin's book appeared and became world-famous, Matthew not unnaturally felt much aggrieved by the complete neglect of his own earlier work, but his efforts to secure recognition were unsuccessful.

MAURICE, Frederick Denison (1805–1872), the liberal clergyman whose 1853 *Theological Essays* so offended the orthodox that he was asked to vacate his Chair at King's College, London. Later he became Professor of Moral Theology at Cambridge. He was active with Kingsley and others in the Christian Socialist movement and he founded the Working Men's College in North London.

MAXIM, (Sir) Hiram Stevens (1840–1916), the U.S. engineer who settled in England in 1881, became a naturalised Briton, and made many inventions including the recoil-operated machine-gun which bore his name. His English engineering company was in 1896 combined with Vickers, and five years later Victoria knighted him.

MENDEL, Gregor Johann (1822–1884), the Moravian monk who established the basic laws of particulate heredity by experiments on peas, performed in the gardens of Brünn (Brno) monastery, of which he eventually became abbot. His experiments were published in a local journal in 1865–67 but, to his great disappointment, were almost entirely ignored by the scientific world. When rediscovered in 1900, their fundamental nature was immediately recognised.

MENDELÉEV, Dmitri Ivanovich (1834–1907), Professor of Chemistry at St. Petersburg University from 1866, whose periodic table of the elements provided the basis for all later work in this field. Element no. 101 has been named "mendelevium" after him.

MILL, John Stuart (1806–1873), the extremely precocious utilitarian philosopher who, after a period of mental crisis, departed from the simple utilitarianism of his father (James Mill) and Bentham, recognising qualitative as well as quantitative differences between different types of pleasure. Although he and Huxley had many views in common, their temperaments differed too much to allow any close friendship.

MITCHELL, (Sir) Peter Chalmers (1864–1945), who first taught comparative anatomy at Oxford and then at Charing Cross Hospital, becoming a great admirer of Huxley (of whom he published a biography). In 1903 be became Secretary to the Zoological Society, serving in that capacity for over thirty years, during which period he thoroughly reorganised the Regent's Park zoo and started Whipsnade. He retired to Spain, was caught up in the Civil War, and became a strong supporter of the republican cause.

MIVART, St. George Jackson (1827–1900), the occasionally brilliant but often erratic biologist, who studied under Huxley and, despite deep theological differences, had a high regard for him. He was converted to Roman Catholicism and became Professor of Philosophy at Louvain, but was eventually excommunicated for defying ecclesiastical authority by publishing 'unsuitable' articles in the *Nineteenth Century*.

MOHL—see **VON MOHL**.

MONET—see **LAMARCK**.

MONKSWELL, (Lady) (1850–1930), wife of Robert Collier, the second Baron Monkswell. She was a great admirer of the warm and affectionate domestic life of Huxley's family, and was delighted when her brother-in-law John Collier married Marian. But when, after Marian's death, Huxley allowed his younger daughter Ethel to marry the widower, she was so scandalised by the 'deceased wife's sister' marriage that she broke off all personal connections.

MORLEY, John (Viscount Morley) (1838–1923), the Liberal politician and man of letters who made the *Fortnightly Review* into a powerful organ of progressive opinion. Among the posts he held were those of Chief Secretary for Ireland and Secretary of State for India, but he opposed British imperialism and in 1914 resigned from the cabinet with John Burns rather than support entry into the Great War.

MÜLLER, Johannes Peter (1801–1858), perhaps the chief founder of modern physiology. As Professor of Physiology and Anatomy at Bonn, and later at Berlin, he did brilliant work on the nervous system, on the lower vertebrates and in marine biology. His *Handbuch der Physiologie des Menschen* (1833–40) was especially influential. A teacher of genius, he so inspired many of his pupils that between them they largely transformed physiology into a recognisably modern condition.

MURCHISON, (Sir) Roderick Impey (1792–1871), who entered the army as a boy of fifteen but had a passion for geology and eventually succeeded De la Beche as Director of the Geological Survey. He had a very high reputation as a geologist and founded the three great divisions of Silurian, Permean and Devonian rocks. A fair amount of his work, however, later proved to have been somewhat superficial and unreliable.

NAPIER, Arthur Sampson (1853–1916), who was a student at Owens College, Manchester, and later in Berlin. After teaching English at Berlin and Göttingen, he became in 1885 Oxford's first Merton Professor of English Language and Literature. A most distinguished etymologist, his appointment outraged those (including Huxley) who had hoped for a professor primarily of Literature, and eventually such a literary chair was also created at Oxford.

NEWMAN, John Henry (1801–1890), the Oxford tractarian who led the nineteenth-century movement of Anglicans into the Church of Rome, in which he became a Cardinal. A brilliant scholar and silver-tongued preacher, and in many ways a saintly man, he nevertheless appeared to many as far too 'slippery' and 'jesuitical' in his arguments. Strangely, he went as a boy to the Ealing School at which Huxley's father taught, and later supported the young Huxley's application for a free scholarship at Charing Cross Medical School.

NORTHCOTE, (Sir) Stafford Henry (Earl of Iddesleigh) (1819–1887), the wealthy financier who was very much in the confidence of Disraeli and served as President of the Board of Trade, Secretary for India, Chancellor of the Exchequer and Foreign Secretary. In 1870 he took unprecedented (although unsuccessful) steps to prevent Huxley's election as President of the British Association, but later helped to secure a substantial Civil List pension for him on his retirement from South Kensington.

OKEN, Lorenz (1779–1851), who first was Professor of Medicine at Jena and later held chairs at Munich and Zurich. He came under the influence of Goethe and Kant, becoming a leading exponent of a somewhat mystical *Naturphilosophie* which he sometimes stretched to bizarre extremes. His 'theory of the vertebrate skull' was demolished by Huxley.

OSBORN, Henry Fairfield (1856–1954), a student of Huxley's who introduced his South Kensington methods of science education first to Princeton and then to Columbia University, at which latter he in 1890 became Professor of Palaeontology. He played a very important part in the development of the American Museum of Natural History.

OWEN, (Sir) Richard (1804–1892), the apothecary's apprentice who graduated in medicine, studied under Cuvier in Paris, and eventually became the undisputed master of British comparative anatomy. He was the first Director of the British Museum (Natural History), and did monumental work upon fossils and especially upon vertebrates. Unfortunately he was both vain and arrogant, thus making an enemy of Huxley, who undeniably enjoyed denting the great man's scientific reputation.

PAGET, (Sir) James (1814–1899), the eminent anatomist and surgeon whose highly fashionable practice included Queen Victoria. For many years he lectured especially on morbid anatomy at St. Bartholomew's Hospital Medical School, was for seven years Professor of Anatomy at the Royal College of Surgeons, and for twelve years from 1883 was Vice-Chancellor of the University of London.

PALMER, (Sir) Roundell (Earl of Selborne) (1812–1895), the jurist and politician who was also a noted hymnologist. He served at various times as Solicitor-General, Attorney-General and Lord Chancellor, in which last capacity he instituted some important reforms of the judicature. In 1888 he acted as Chairman of a Royal Commission inquiring into the university institutions of London.

PANDER, Heinrich Christian (1794–1865), a wealthy Polish banker's son, who spent much of his life in scientific research both in Russia and in Germany. In 1826 he was elected Academician at St. Petersburg, and his work on the embryology of the chick is a classic. However, he soon resigned to live on his Riga estate and later did valuable work for the Russian Mining Board.

PARKER, Thomas Jeffrey (1850–1897), who after studying under Huxley became a schoolmaster in Yorkshire, returned in 1872 as Demonstrator at South Kensington, and eventually went on Huxley's recommendation as Professor of Biology at the University of Otago. He was joint author of the great standard "Parker & Haswell" zoology textbook, which after seventy years is still in print in regular revisions.

PARKER, William Kitchen (1823–1890), the physician and comparative anatomist, whose two sons (T. J. and W. N. Parker) also became distinguished biologists. He was a meticulous observer and did valuable work on the vertebrate skull, amphibia, etc. Unfortunately, not even his friend Huxley could restrain his tendency to rather vague and fanciful theorising.

PARKER, William Newton (1858–1923), who was a student of Huxley's at the College of Science, went on to Cambridge and Germany, returned to assist at South Kensington, and eventually became Professor of Zoology at Cardiff. He was a fertile researcher, helped to found the *Annals of Botany*, and jointly with his brother T. J. Parker wrote *An Elementary Course of Practical Zoology*.

PARSONS, William (Earl of Rosse) (1800–1867), the astronomer who especially worked on the improvement of reflecting telescopes and who discovered binary and triple stars. He was one of those who helped to secure lengthy paid research leave for Huxley upon his discharge from *Rattlesnake*.

PASTEUR, Louis (1822–1895), the great French scientist who is most often remembered for his experiments on 'microbes' and his discovery of inoculation procedures. He was at various times Professor of Physics at Dijon and then Strasbourg, Professor of Chemistry at Lille, Director of the École Normal Supérieure, Professor of Chemistry at the Sorbonne, and Director of the Institut Pasteur.

PEABODY, George Foster (1852–1938), the American millionaire banker who in 1876 put one of his residences at Huxley's disposal during his visit to the U.S.A. Like his father, George, he was a great philanthropist, especially in the promotion of education among the poor of the southern States.

PEARSON, Karl (1857–1936), the mathematical biologist who largely founded the subject of biometry. After graduating at Cambridge, he devoted his energies to statistical research and eventually became Professor of Eugenics and Director of the Francis Galton Laboratory at University College, London. Although a brilliant lecturer, he could not tolerate opposition or even intellectual differences of opinion, and thus made many enemies. However, he was a leader of the younger men in the movement for university reform.

POULTON, (Sir) Edward Bagnall (1856–1943), whose career at Oxford was aided by Huxley and who in 1893 became Hope Professor of Zoology there. He worked especially on protective coloration in animals and effectively promoted the development of observation and experiment in the field. He was a very all-round man, with high athletic ability and wide interests.

PRIMROSE, Archibald Philip (Earl Rosebery) (1847–1929), who left Oxford without a degree owing to excessive devotion to horse-racing, but nevertheless became a prolific biographer and a distinguished politician. After serving twice as Foreign Secretary, he succeeded Gladstone as Liberal Prime Minister in 1894. In foreign affairs he was generally imperialist, but at home took progressive stands on many matters, including an attempted curtailment of hereditary seats in the House of Lords.

PROUT, William (1785–1850), the medical practitioner who became a pioneer of physiological chemistry, one of his discoveries being that of hydrochloric acid in the stomach. 'Prout's Law' (that the atomic weights of the elements are multiples of that of hydrogen) convinced him that the other elements were built from hydrogen units, but later more accurate atomic weight determinations discredited his theory. Later still, the explanation of fractional atomic weights in terms of isotope mixtures led to the reinstatement of the essence of his views.

PUNSHON, William Morley (1824–1881), the eloquent Wesleyan preacher who, brought up in the timber trade in Hull and becoming an active 'methodist' there, migrated in middle life to London and published both prose and verse which were temporarily successful.

PUSEY, Edward Bouverie (1800–1882), Canon of Christ Church and from 1828 Regius Professor of Hebrew at Oxford. As a Fellow of Oriel at the same time as Keble and Newman, he joined with them in producing *Tracts for the Times*. He tried to prevent others from following Newman into the Church of Rome, and became the leader of the high church 'Oxford movement'. He opposed most efforts at university reform, as calculated to reduce the rôle of religion, and he regarded Huxley as the most dangerous of the Darwinians.

RATHKE, Martin Heinrich (1790–1860), the German anatomist who with von Baer was a pioneer of embryology. He became Professor of Physiology first at Dorpat and then at Königsberg and was an excellent teacher. Among his discoveries were the gill-slits of embryonic mammals and much of the detailed anatomy of the lancelet.

RÉVILLÉ, Albert (1826–1906), the French protestant who in 1851 became Pastor of the Walloon church in Rotterdam. In 1885, his *Prolègomène de l'Histoire des Religions* (which presented the Genesis account of creation as a charming but primitive traditional myth) was attacked by Gladstone, who thereby brought upon himself a fierce onslaught by Huxley in the famous "Interpreters of Genesis and Interpreters of Nature" controversy.

RICHARDSON, (Sir) John (1787–1865), the distinguished surgeon and arctic explorer, who served on Franklin's 1819 polar expedition and from 1847 to 1849 went north again in unsuccessful search of Franklin. In the meanwhile he had become Physician at the Haslar Naval Hospital and, when Huxley joined the navy in 1846, soon recognised his unusual ability and arranged for his posting to *Rattlesnake*.

ROGERS, William ('Hang-theology Rogers') (1819–1896), the very liberal Rector of Bishopsgate who built up a whole network of church schools for poor children. It was at his request that in 1869 Huxley gave a series of demonstration lessons to shew how elementary science could be taught in ordinary schools, and in the following year the two collaborated on the London School Board.

ROLLER, John Harold (?–1934), the Worcestershire picture-restorer and mining engineer who in 1889 married Huxley's daughter Nettie. They separated and for many years she kept herself and her daughter by travelling in Europe as a singer.

ROLLESTON, George (1829–1881), who served as physician at the Hospital for Sick Children in Great Ormond Street before going to Oxford in 1860 (with Huxley's help) as Linacre Professor of Anatomy and Physiology. Although he was immensely erudite, his work was often careless in detail and his thought sometimes diffuse to the point of woolliness.

ROMANES, George John (1848–1894), a wealthy Canadian who settled in England, studied physiology at Cambridge and London, and held professorships at Edinburgh and the Royal Institution. In 1890 he went to live in Oxford, where he endowed the annual Romanes lectures, of which the first two were given by Gladstone and Huxley. Although erratic as a scholar, his 1881 *Animal Intelligence*, followed by *Mental Evolution in Animals* and *Mental Evolution in Man*, were in some ways well ahead of their time.

ROSCOE, (Sir) Henry Enfield (1833–1915), who in 1857 became Professor of Chemistry at Owens College in Manchester and by his distinction made that city a magnet for research chemists. In 1896 he became Vice-Chancellor of the University of London.

ROSEBERY—see **PRIMROSE.**

ROSSE—see **PARSONS.**

ROUX, Wilhelm (1850–1924), a student of Haeckel's who became Professor first at Innsbruck and then at Halle. His work in experimental embryology was fundamental. He promoted the idea of functional adaptation of organisms to their environment by a 'natural selection' of competing elements within the organisms themselves.

RUSSELL, (Lord) John (First Earl Russell and Viscount Amberley) (1792–1878), the great Whig statesman who became M.P. in 1813 and played a leading part in general and parliamentary reform. In 1834 he became Whig leader in the Commons and later served as Home Secretary, Colonial Secretary, Foreign Secretary and Prime Minister. Among the liberal causes he supported were religious freedom, electoral reform, church reform, restriction of capital offences, repeal of corn laws, and the emancipation of the Jews. He was also a considerable scholar and President of the Historical Society.

RUSSELL, Katherine Louisa (Countess Amberley) (1842–1874), daughter of the second Baron Stanley of Alderley, wife of John Russell (second Viscount Amberley) and mother of Bertrand Russell. Both she and her husband were free-thinkers and held very advanced views on sexual matters and in general. She was a friend and correspondent of Huxley.

SALISBURY—see **CECIL.**

SAMUELSON, (Sir) Bernhard (1820–1905), the engineer and ironmaster who was also thrice a Liberal M.P. He was active in tariff reform and especially in the promotion of scientific and technical education. In particular, he was Chairman of both the 1870 Royal Commission on Scientific Instruction and the 1881 Commission on Technical Instruction.

SCHLEIDEN, Matthias Jacob (1804–1881), the Hamburg barrister who was first an amateur of science and then became Professor of Botany at Jena and later at Dorpat. He worked especially on cells and their nuclei, and discovered the nucleolus. Together with Schwann, he succeeded in establishing the 'cell theory' quite firmly at the centre of biological thinking. He was one of the very first to attempt serious mathematical treatment of biological data.

SCHWANN, Theodor (1810–1882), a student of Müller's who became Professor of Anatomy at Louvain and later at Liège. His brilliant work on animal cells was cognate with that of Schleiden. He did important work on muscle contraction and on microbial putrefaction, and discovered the enzyme pepsin. Most important, however, was his insistence on the existence of a cellular structure in all animal tissues as well as in plants.

SCLATER, Philip Lutley (1829–1913), who originally read mathematics at Oxford, then became a barrister, but finally served for nearly half a century as Secretary to the Zoological Society. He produced a very large number of scientific memoirs and did important work on animal distribution.

SEDGWICK, Adam (1854–1913), the zoologist (not to be confused with his great uncle, Adam Sedgwick the geologist). He was first Reader in Animal Morphology and then Professor of Zoology at Cambridge, and in 1909 became Professor of Zoology at Imperial College. Huxley collaborated with him in the promotion of science at Cambridge.

SELBORNE—see **PALMER.**

SHERBROOKE—see **LOWE.**

SIDGWICK, Henry (1838–1900), who resigned his Fellowship of Trinity on grounds of non-religious conscience but in 1883 became Professor of Moral Philosophy at Cambridge. Both he and his wife were fervent advocates of female education and were largely instrumental in the foundation of Newnham in 1873. From 1882 to 1893 he was a leading member of the Society for Psychical Research.

SKELTON, (Sir) John (1831–1897), the Edinburgh advocate who adopted the pen-name of "Shirley" and became a well-known essayist and biographer. His *Essays* and *Table Talk* were widely read and discussed at the time. Over a period of about twenty years he and Huxley were rather friendly.

SMYTH, (Sir) Warrington Wilkinson (1817–1890), from 1851 Lecturer in Mining and later Professor of Mineralogy at the School of Mines. He had an unrivalled knowledge of the geology of Cornwall and eventually became Inspector of Crown Minerals.

SOMERS (Somers-Cocks, formerly Cocks), (Sir) Charles (Baron and Earl Somers, Viscount Eastnor) (1819–1883), who became Conservative M.P. for Reigate in 1841 and later a Lord in Waiting. For many years he was a Trustee of the National Portrait Gallery and of the British Museum.

SPARKES, George (?–?), an unschooled but intelligent Southampton docker who made great efforts to educate himself in science. He wrote to Huxley for advice, and received also apparatus, library facilities and the offer (not accepted) of a post as laboratory assistant.

SPENCER, Herbert (1820–1903), the extremely erudite but strangely uncritical philosopher who, after some years as a schoolmaster and then as a railway surveyor, supported himself by his massive writings. One of the earliest pro-Darwin evolutionists, he elevated the 'survival of the fittest' into a pseudo-scientific justification of extreme individualism, and was on several occasions sharply criticised by Huxley for this reason. Fortunately, their close friendship always survived these incidents.

SPENCER, John Poyntz (Earl Spencer) (1835–1910), the Liberal M.P. who became Lord-Lieutenant and later Viceroy of Ireland, First Lord of the Admiralty, President of the Privy Council and Leader of the House of Lords. Deeply interested in higher education, he also became Chancellor of the Victoria University of Manchester in 1892 and helped to establish that city's John Rylands Library. It was at his request that Huxley agreed to serve on the 1881 Commission on the Medical Acts.

SPOTTISWOODE, William (1825–1883), the extremely accomplished royal printer who was also a skilled linguist and a very competent mathematician and physicist. He worked especially on the mathematics of curved surfaces and on polarised light, sometimes lectured at the Royal Institution and at South Kensington, and for several years was President of the Royal Society. Huxley described him as "a verray parfit, gentil knyght".

STANLEY, Arthur Penrhyn (1815–1881), who as Professor of Ecclesiastical History at Oxford supported most liberal causes and later, as Dean of Westminster, restored the dignity of the Abbey and made it an acceptable national centre for all shades of anglican opinion. Over a period of more than twenty years he and Huxley corresponded and frequently collaborated in educational reform.

STANLEY, Henrietta Maria (Lady Stanley of Alderley) (1807–1895) who, as a young woman of nineteen, refused on account of her 'Jacobin' tendencies to dance with Austrian officers in Florence, and for the rest of her life had a reputation for radicalism and outspokenness. Her husband was Whig Chief Whip, but Palmerston described her as "Joint Chief Whip", and she was the moving spirit in the Women's Liberal Unionist Association. She was one of the promoters of Girton, of the Girls Public Day School Company and of the Medical College for Women. She was a friend of Huxley's and sought his advice on the scientific education of her family.

STANLEY, Owen (1812–1850), son of the liberal and scientific Bishop of Norwich and elder brother of A. P. Stanley. He was selected for the command of *Rattlesnake* on account of his capabilities as a scientific surveyor, but died young before the conclusion of the voyage. The great 'Owen Stanley Range' of mountains in New Guinea was named after him.

STEAD, William Thomas (1849–1912), the internationalist and anti-war journalist, who in his 1885 *The Maiden Tribute of Modern Babylon* exposed the London vice market, 'buying' a girl and being sent to prison for doing so. In 1890 he founded the *Review of Reviews*, which brought a new liveliness into English periodicals. He went down in the *Titanic* disaster.

STEPHEN, (Sir) Leslie (1832–1904), the mathematician, philosopher and critic who in 1862 resigned his Cambridge tutorship because of religious scruples and in 1875 relinquished holy orders. He was a type of the Victorian 'free-thinker', and his 1882 *Science of Ethics* and 1893 *An Agnostic's Apology* are noteworthy works. He was also an eminent alpinist and an enthusiastic supporter of slave emancipation.

STEVENSON, Robert Louis (1850–1894), the Edinburgh engineer who later qualified as a lawyer and still later became a distinguished author. Unsuccessful in his application for the Edinburgh Chair of History and Constitutional Law, he travelled in America and the South Seas, settling in 1890 in Samoa. It has been suggested that the clarity of his prose was due to the happy example of Huxley's.

STRASBURGER, Eduard Adolf (1844–1912), Professor of Botany first at Jena and then at Bonn, where his laboratory became the world's most important centre of cytological research. He did especially important work on the alternation of generations and on the embryos of gymnosperms and angiosperms. His *Lehrbuch der Botanik*, first published in 1894, was still a standard text in several languages right until the Second World War.

SYLVESTER, James Joseph (1814–1897), who in 1833 was ranked at Cambridge as Second Wrangler but could not graduate because he was a Jew. However, he became Professor of Mathematics at University College, London, and at Virginia and Johns Hopkins, eventually being elected in 1883 (with the aid of Huxley among others) as Savilian Professor of Geometry at Oxford.

THISELTON-DYER, (Sir) William Turner (1843–1928), who became Professor of Botany at the Royal College of Science for Ireland, then Assistant Director and finally Director of Kew Gardens. He did good work especially on the floras of colonial areas, and over a period of many years made a special study of Greek and Latin plant names. He was one of those whom Huxley brought in to help with the summer courses at South Kensington.

THOMSON, (Sir) Charles Wyville (1830–1882), after whom is named the 'Thomson Ridge' separating the Arctic and Atlantic waters. He studied medicine at Edinburgh, and lectured at Aberdeen, Belfast and Dublin before returning to Edinburgh in 1870 as Professor of Natural History, to which post he was appointed on Huxley's advice. The *Challenger* researches which he directed, published in some fifty volumes, established the science of oceanography.

THOMSON, (Sir) William (Baron Kelvin) (1824–1907), who matriculated at Glasgow at the age of eleven and became the leading mathematical physicist of the age. He did valuable research whilst an undergraduate and, after a period at Cambridge, became Professor of Natural Philosophy at Glasgow in 1846. He made notable contributions to the theory of electromagnetic oscillations, general energetics, thermometry, galvanometry, elasticity, etc. Nevertheless, he was wrong in his estimate of the earth's age as only 100 million years, which Huxley correctly contested as being based on unsound assumptions.

TYNDALL, John (1820–1893), the Irish physicist who in 1859, after teaching at Queenswood school, was at Huxley's instigation appointed Professor of Physics at the School of Mines. He did good work in heat, light and sound, but was also an effective scientific populariser. Eventually he succeeded Faraday as Superintendent of the Royal Institution. He was an accomplished alpinist, being the first to climb the Weisshorn, and frequently went mountain-walking with Huxley.

ULYANOV—see **LENIN.**

VINES, Sydney Howard (1849–1934), who first graduated at London and helped Huxley in his courses for teachers at South Kensington. Later he went to Cambridge, became Reader in Botany there, and did much to establish that university's great botanical school. In 1888 he became Sherardian Professor of Botany at Oxford.

VIRCHOW, Rudolf Ludwig Carl (1821–1902), the liberal medical researcher who edited *Archiv für Pathologie* for over half a century. After studying under Müller, he worked in Berlin and Silesia, then became Professor of Pathological Anatomy at

Würzburg, and then moved back to Berlin. Highly effective as a public health administrator, his great ability and energy still permitted fundamental research in cellular
pathology, and he also did valuable work in anthropology.

VON BAER, Karl Ernst (1792–1876), Professor of Anatomy at Königsberg and
later an Academician at St. Petersburg. His early embryological work included the
discovery of the mammalian ovum and of the notochord, but he is perhaps best
remembered for his 'germ layer' theory. He was lavishly honoured by the Russian
government, for which he made many lengthy journeys on which he studied the
anthropology and ethnology of its varied peoples.

VON CHAMISSO, Louis Charles Adelbert (1781–1838), who went to Germany as a
refugee from the French Revolution, became a poet, but also circumnavigated the
globe and did considerable biological research. His discovery of alternation of generations in certain tunicates was not generally credited until after his death, when it was
confirmed by Huxley.

VON GOETHE, Johann Wolfgang (1749–1832), whose literary eminence has obscured the memory of his scientific work in anatomy, plant metamorphosis and
the theory of colours. Under the influence of Herder, he became a romantic, and in
science his rather vague 'Naturphilosophie' greatly influenced Oken and his school.

VON HELMHOLTZ, Hermann Ludwig Ferdinand (1821–1894), the great German
scientist who at different times was Professor of Physiology at Königsberg and later
at Heidelberg, Professor of Physics at Berlin, and Director of the Charlottenburg
Physicotechnical Institute. Despite his scientific distinction, he preferred to believe
that life had arrived on earth by meteorite rather than accept its evolution on earth
from non-living matter.

VON JHERING, Rudolf (1818–1892), best known as a legal scholar, who developed
a philosophy of social utilitarianism. His 1877–83 *Der Zweck in Recht* was published
in English in 1924.

VON MOHL, Hugo (1805–1872), Professor of Physiology at Berne and later of
Botany at Tübingen. He worked especially on the anatomy and physiology of plant
cells and pioneered the investigation of cryptogamic spore development. In 1846 he
discovered and named protoplasm, and his descriptions of the nucleus were much more
detailed than those of earlier workers.

VRIES—see DE VRIES.

WACE, Henry (1836–1924), who at various times was Professor of Ecclesiastical
History at King's College, London, Principal of the College, Prebendary of St. Paul's
and Dean of Canterbury. He was a substantial but not especially distinguished scholar.
It was an address of his to the 1888 Church Congress which provoked Huxley to produce
his essay "Agnosticism" and thus led to the fierce consequential controversy.

WALLACE, Alfred Russel (1823–1913), co-author with Darwin of the theory
of evolution by natural selection. His collecting expeditions in Amazonia and Malaysia
were enormously competent and prolific, and his researches on animal camouflage and
animal distribution were admirable. The 'Wallace Line' between Asian and Australian animal types is named after him. In his later years he became immersed in rather
woolly anti-vaccination and spiritualist activities.

WALLER, Frederick William (1846–1933), the Gloucester cathedral architect who in 1878 married Huxley's daughter Jessie. He was of no special distinction as an architectural designer, but had an excellent reputation in church maintenance, repair and restoration.

WALPOLE, (Sir) Spencer (1839–1907), who got a flying start in the Civil Service as Private Secretary to his father, Spencer Horatio Walpole, first at the Home Office and then at the War Office. He was a solid historical scholar and also published political and biographical essays. As an Inspector of Fisheries he worked closely with Huxley for some years.

WARD, Henry Marshall (1854–1906), who first studied at Owens College in Manchester and then came under Huxley's notice. He went to Cambridge, became a Fellow of Christ's, and in 1895 was elected Professor of Botany.

WATSON, David Meredith Seares (1886–197?), successively a student at Manchester University, Lecturer in Vertebrate Palaeontology and then Jodrell Professor of Zoology and Comparative Anatomy at University College, London, and Agassiz Professor at Harvard.

WATTS, Charles Albert (1858–1946), the self-educated printer's apprentice who became a leading freethinker. He edited the *Literary Gazette* for many years, established and edited the *Agnostic Annual*, and founded the publishing house of his name.

WAUGH, Benjamin (1839–1908), the Congregational minister now best remembered as mainly responsible for the achievement of the 1889 Protection of Children Act and for the foundation of the National Society for the Prevention of Cruelty to Children. He worked tirelessly for the poor of Greenwich, which he represented on the first London School Board, on which he collaborated closely with Huxley.

WEISMANN, August (1834–1914), Professor of Zoology at Freiburg, who argued strongly against the inheritance of acquired characters and put in its most extreme form the contrary view that heredity is carried by special particles in the 'germ cells'. His 1892 *Das Keimplasma* regarded these germ cells (gametes) as the significant continuing stream of life, while the 'somatic cells' (the main body) constituted a temporary phenomenon discarded by each generation of gametes.

WELDON, Walter Frank Raphael (1860–1906), the Cambridge zoologist who in 1891 succeeded Lankester in the Jodrell Chair at University College, London, where he became active in the movement for university reform of which Huxley quickly took the lead. In 1899 he became Linacre Professor of Comparative Anatomy at Oxford.

WELLS, Herbert George (1866–1946), the distinguished author who, after a penurious childhood and a period working in a draper's shop, secured a scholarship to train under Huxley at South Kensington as a science teacher. Here he failed his third-year examinations, but taught in schools for some years and in 1890 graduated in science. His fiction reflects this early training at the Normal School of Science, and Huxley is clearly recognisable as 'Professor Russell' in *Ann Veronica*.

WILBERFORCE, Samuel (1805–1873), Fellow of All Souls and Bishop first of Oxford and then of Winchester. He was a brilliant scholar and administrator, and was largely responsible for the restoration of the ancient authority of the Convocations of Canterbury and York. His memory has perhaps been unduly darkened by the 1860 British Association episode at Oxford, where he was demolished by Huxley in the debate on evolution. Still, his nickname of 'Soapy Sam' must have had some significance.

References and bibliography

REFERENCES in the text are provided only for direct quotations. Since so many of the original sources are nineteenth-century letters, pamphlets, periodicals or books now difficult of access, the references have been given wherever possible to three more readily accessible secondary sources.

These sources are as follows, and are referred to in the abbreviated manner indicated below:

> *Collected Essays*, by T. H. Huxley (1893–94), Macmillan, London (and 1969 [*C.E.*, followed by volume and page number, e.g. *C.E.* V, 35.] Greenwood reprint).
> *Life and Letters of Thomas Henry Huxley*, by Leonard Huxley (1900), Macmillan, London.
> [*L.L.*, followed by volume and page number, e.g. *L.L.* I, 267.]
> *T. H. Huxley: Scientist, Humanist and Educator*, by Cyril Bibby (1959), Watts, London, and Horizon Press, New York.
> [*T.H.H.*, followed by page number, e.g. *T.H.H.* 132.]

Many of Huxley's letters and other manuscripts, in the archives of Imperial College of Science and Technology, have been catalogued by Warren Dawson (1946) and are referred to in the following manner:

> [*H.P.*, followed by catalogue number of folio, e.g. *H.P.* 18. 97.]

> N.B. Huxley's scientific notebooks, etc., and his correspondence with Henrietta Heathorn before their marriage, have also been listed, by the Imperial College Archivist Jeanne Pingree (1968 and 1969).

Those readers who wish to refer to the original sources of Huxley's writings will find this facilitated by the list, given below, of SELECTED PUBLICATIONS OF T. H. HUXLEY. The list includes only items quoted in, or directly relevant to, the text.

This list is referred to in the text for some quotations which it was not possible to refer to one of the three secondary sources mentioned above. In some items on this list, there is an apparent discrepancy between the reference date and that given in the detailed reference immediately following, but such cases are due simply to the passage of time between the delivery of a paper and its printing.

No complete list of Huxley's publications has ever been compiled. Possibly the fullest is that given in Leonard Huxley (1900), but many other items may easily be traced from Cyril Bibby (1959 and 1967).

References in the text to other authors are given by means of name, date and, where necessary, volume and page numbers. These items are listed below under the heading PUBLICATIONS OF OTHER AUTHORS. This list, like the selection from Huxley's publications, is restricted to items directly relevant to the text, with no attempt to include merely background material.

Selected publications of T. H. Huxley

1845   On a hitherto undescribed structure in the human hair sheath, *Lond. Medic. Gaz.*, July 1845, I, 1340.

1847   Examination of the corpuscles of the blood of *Amphioxus lanceolatus*, *Brit. Assoc. Rept.*, 1847, II, 95.

1849   On the anatomy and the affinities of the family of the Medusae, *Phil. Trans. Roy. Soc.*, 1849, II, 413.

1850   Notes on Medusae and Polypes, *Ann. & Mag. Nat. Hist.*, 1850, VI, 66.

1851   Remarks upon Appendicularia and Doliolum, two genera of the Tunicata, *Phil. Trans. Roy. Soc.*, 1851, II, 595.

1851a Observations upon the anatomy and physiology of Salpa and Pyrosoma, *Phil. Trans. Roy. Soc.*, 1851, II, 567.

1851b Zoological notes and observations made on board H.M.S. *Rattlesnake...*, *Ann. & Mag. Nat. Hist.*, 1851, VII, 304 and 370, and VIII, 433.

1852   Upon animal individuality, *Proc. Roy. Inst.*, 1851–4, I, 184.

1853   On the morphology of the Cephalous Mollusca, as illustrated by the anatomy of certain Heteropoda and Pteropoda..., *Phil. Trans. Roy. Soc.*, 1853, I, 29.

1853a *Kölliker's Manual of Human Histology*, Busk, G. (tr. and ed.), Sydenham Society, London.

1853b On the identity of structure of plants and animals, *Proc. Roy. Inst.*, 1851–4, I, 298.

1853c On the development of the teeth..., *Q.J. Micr. Sci.*, 1853, I.

1854   Science at sea, *Westminster Rev.*, January 1854, 100.

1854a *On the Educational Value of the Natural History Sciences* (pamphlet), and *C.E.* III, 38.

1854b On the common plan of animal forms, *Proc. Roy. Inst.*, 1851–4, I, 444.

1854c On the vascular system of the lower Annulosa, *Brit. Assoc. Rept.*, 1854, II, 109.

1855   On certain zoological arguments commonly adduced in favour of the hypothesis of the progressive development of animal life in time, *Proc. Roy. Inst.*, 1854–8, II, 82.

1855a On the enamel and dentine of the teeth, *Q.J. Micr. Sci.*, 1855, II, 127.

1855b Memoir on Physalia, *Proc. Linn. Soc.*, 1855, II, 3.

1855c On the anatomy of Dyphies, and on the unity of composition of the Dyphyidae and Physophoridae..., *Proc. Linn. Soc.*, 1855, II, 67.

1856   On natural history as knowledge discipline and power, *Proc. Roy. Inst.*, 1854–8, II, 187.

1857   On the present state of knowledge as to the structure and functions of nerve, *Proc. Roy. Inst.*, 1854–8, II, 432.

1857a On the structure and motion of glaciers, *Phil. Trans. Roy. Soc.*, 1857, CXLVII, 381 (with Tyndall, J.).

1857b On Dysteria, a new genus of Infusoria, *Q.J. Micr. Sci.*, 1857, V, 78.

1857c On the agamic reproduction and morphology of Aphis, *Trans. Linn. Soc.*, 1858, XXII, 193.

1858 Review of the cell theory, *Brit. & For. Med. Chir. Rev.*, 1858, XXIII, 285.
1858a On Cephalaspis and Pteraspis, *Q.J. Geol. Soc.*, 1858, XIV, 241.
1858b On the theory of the vertebrate skull, *Proc. Roy. Soc.*, 1857–9, IX, 381.
1858c On some points in the anatomy of *Nautilus pompilius*, *J. Linn. Soc.*, 1859, III, 36.

1859 *On the Oceanic Hydrozoa*, Ray Society, London.
1859a Observations on the development of some parts of the skeleton of fishes, *Q.J. Micr. Sci.*, 1859, VII, 33.
1859b On the Stagonolepis... of the Elgin sandstones..., *Q.J. Geol. Soc.*, 1859, XV, 440.
1859c On the persistent types of animal life, *Proc. Roy. Inst.*, 1858–62, III, 151.
1859d On the anatomy and development of Pyrosoma, *Trans. Linn. Soc.*, 1862, XXIII, 193.
1859e On some amphibian and reptilian remains from South Africa and Australia, *Q.J. Geol. Soc.*, 1859, XV, 642.
1859f The Darwinian hypothesis, *The Times*, 26 December 1859, and *C.E.* II, 1.

1860 On species and races, and their origin, *Proc. Roy. Inst.*, 1858–62, III, 195.
1860a The origin of species, *Westminster Rev.*, April 1860, and *C.E.* II, 22.
1860b On the structure of the mouth and pharynx of the scorpion, *Q.J. Micr. Sci.*, 1860, VIII, 250.

1861 Preliminary essay upon the systematic arrangement of the fishes of the Devonian epoch, *Mem. Geol. Surv. U.K.*, 1861, X, 41.
1861a On the zoological relations of man with the lower animals, *Nat. Hist. Rev.*, 1861, 67.
1861b On the brain of Ateles paniscus, *Proc. Zool. Soc.*, 1861, 247.
1861c A lobster: or, the study of zoology (originally, *On the Study of Zoology*, pamphlet), *C.E.*, VIII, 196.
1861d On a new species of Macrauchenia *(M. Boliviensis)*, *Q.J. Geol. Soc.*, 1861, XVII, 73.

1862 On fossil remains of man, *Proc. Roy. Inst.*, 1858–62, III, 420.
1862a On geological contemporaneity and persistent types of life, *Q.J. Geol. Soc.* XVIII, x1, and *C.E.* VIII, 272.
1862b On the new Labyrinthodonts from the Edinburgh coal-field, *Q.J. Geol. Soc.*, 1862, XVIII, 291.

1863 *Evidence as to Man's Place in Nature*, Williams & Norgate, London (Ann Arbor edn., 1959), and *C.E.* VII, 1.
1863a *On our Knowledge of the Causes of the Phenomena of Organic Nature*, Hardwicke, London, and *C.E.* II, 303.
1863b Letter on the human remains found in shell-mounds, *Trans. Ethn. Soc.*, 1863, II, 265.

1864   *Lectures on the Elements of Comparative Anatomy*, Churchill, London.
1864a *An Elementary Atlas of Comparative Osteology*, Williams & Norgate, London.
1864b Further remarks upon the human remains from the Neanderthal, *Nat. Hist. Rev.*, 1864, 429.
1864c Criticisms on "The Origin of Species", *Nat. Hist. Rev.*, 1864, 37, and *C.E.* II, 80.
1864d On the osteology of the genus Glyptodon, *Phil.Trans. Roy. Soc.*, 1865, CLV, 31.

1865   Emancipation: black and white, *Reader*, 20 May 1865, and *C.E.* III, 66.
1865a On the methods and results of ethnology, *Proc. Roy. Inst.*, 1866, IV, 460, and *C.E.*, VII, 209.
1865b On the structure of the stomach in Desmodus rufus, *Proc. Zool. Soc.*, 1865, 386.

1866   *Lessons in Elementary Physiology*, Macmillan, London.
1866a On the advisableness of improving natural knowledge, *Fortnightly Rev.*, 15 January 1866, and *C.E.* I, 18.
1866b On some remains of large dinosaurian reptiles from... South Africa, *Phil. Mag.*, 1866, XXXII, 474.
1866c On two extreme forms of human crania, *Anthropol. Rev.*, 1866, IV, 406.

1867   On two widely contrasted forms of the human cranium, *J. Anat. & Physiol.*, 1867, I, 60.
1867a On the classification of birds..., *Proc. Zool. Soc.*, 1867, 415.

1868   On the animals which are most nearly intermediate between birds and reptiles, *Ann. & Mag. Nat. Hist.*, 1868, II, 66.
1868a On the form of the cranium among the Patagonians and Fuegians..., *J. Anat. & Physiol.*, 1868, II, 253.
1868b Remarks upon Archaeopteryx lithographica, *Proc. Roy. Soc.*, 1868, XVI, 243.
1868c A liberal education: and where to find it, *Macmillan's Mag.*, March 1868, and *C.E.* III, 76.
1868d On a piece of chalk, *Macmillan's Mag.*, September 1868, and *C.E.* VIII, 1.
1868e On the physical basis of life, *Fortnightly Rev.*, February 1869, and *C.E.* I, 130.
1868f On the classification and distribution of the Alecteromorphae and Heteromorphae, *Proc. Zool. Soc.*, 1868, 294.

1869   *An Introduction to the Classification of Animals*, Churchill, London.
1869a Principles and methods of palaeontology, *Smithsonian Rept.*, 1869, 363.
1869b On the ethnology and archaeology of India, *J. Ethn. Soc.*, 1869, I, 89.
1869c On the ethnology and archaeology of North America, *J. Ethn. Soc.*, 1869, I, 218.
1869d Further evidence of the affinity between the dinosaurian reptiles and birds, *Q.J. Geol. Soc.*, 1870, XXVI, 12.
1869e On the classification of the Dinosauria..., *Q.J. Geol. Soc.*, 1870, XXVI, 32.
1869f Geological reform (Presidential address to the Geological Society), *Q.J. Geol. Soc.*, 1869, XXV, 28, and *C.E.* VIII, 305.
1869g The genealogy of animals, *Academy*, 1869, and *C.E.* II, 107.
1869h Scientific education: notes of an after dinner speech, *Macmillan's Mag.*, June 1869, and *C.E.* III, 111.

1870 *Lay Sermons, Addresses and Reviews*, Macmillan, London.
1870a On the geographical distribution of the chief modifications of mankind, *J. Ethn. Soc.*, 1870, II, 404.
1870b On the ethnology of Britain, *J. Ethn. Soc.*, 1870, II, 382.
1870c Palaentology and the doctrine of evolution (Presidential address to the Geological Society), *Q.J. Geol. Soc.*, 1870, XXVI, 29, and *C.E.* VIII, 340.
1870d Biogenesis and abiogenesis (Presidential address to the British Association), *Brit. Assn. Rept.*, 1870, XL, 73, and *C.E.* VIII, 229.
1870e Triassic Dinosauria, *Nature*, 1870, I, 23.
1870f On the relations of Penicillium, Torula and Bacterium, *Q.J. Micr. Sci.*, 1870, X, 355.
1870g On some fixed points in British ethnology, *Contemp. Rev.* July 1870, and *C.E.* VII, 253.
1870h On medical education, in 1873 *Critiques and Addresses*, and *C.E.* III, 303.
1870i The School Boards: what they can do and what they may do, *Contemp. Rev.*, December 1870, and *C.E.* III, 374.
1870j On Descartes' "Discourse . . . Scientific Truth", *Macmillan's Mag.*, May 1870, and *C.E.* I, 166.
1870k On the formation of coal, *Contemp. Rev.*, November 1870, and *C.E.* VIII, 137.

1871 *A Manual of the Anatomy of Vertebrated Animals*, Churchill, London.
1871a Administrative nihilism, *Fortnightly Rev.*, 1 November 1871, and *C.E.* I, 251.
1871b Mr. Darwin's critics, *Contemp. Rev.*, November 1871, and *C.E.* II, 120.
1871c Bishop Berkeley on the metaphysics of sensation, *Macmillan's Mag.*, June 1871, and *C.E.* II, 243.
1871d Yeast, *Contemp. Rev.*, December 1871, and *C.E.* VIII, 110.

1873 *Critiques and Addresses*, Macmillan, London.

1874 Universities: actual and ideal, *Contemp. Rev.*, March 1874, and *C.E.* III, 189.
1874a Joseph Priestley, *Macmillan's Mag.*, October 1874, and *C.E.* III, 1.
1874b On the hypothesis that animals are automata, and its history, *Nature*, 1874, X, 362, and *C.E.* I, 199.
1874c Preliminary note upon the brain and skull of Amphioxus lanceolatus, *Proc. Roy. Soc.*, 1875, XXIII, 127.
1874d On the bearing of the distribution of the Portia Dura upon the morphology of the skull, *Proc. Camb. Phil. Soc.*, 1876, II, 348.
1874e On the classification of the animal kingdom, *J. Linn. Soc. (Zool)*., 1876, XII, 199.

1875 *A Course of Practical Instruction in Elementary Biology*, Macmillan, London (with H. N. Martin).
1875a On Stagonnolepis Robertsoni, and on the evolution of the Crocodilia, *Q.J. Geol. Soc.*, 1875, XXXI, 423.
1875b On the recent work of the *Challenger* expedition, and its bearing on geological problems, *Proc. Roy. Inst.*, 1875, VII, 354.

1876   Contributions to morphology. Ichthyopsida—No. 1. On Ceradotus Forsteri, with observations on the classification of fishes, *Proc. Zool. Soc.*, 1876, 24.

1876a On the evidence as to the origin of existing vertebrate animals, *Nature*, 1876, XIII, 388 and XIV, 33.

1876b On the border territory between the animal and vegetable kingdoms, *Proc. Roy. Inst.*, 1879, VIII, 28, and *C.E.* VIII, 162.

1876c Three lectures on evolution, in 1877 *American Addresses*, and *C.E.* IV, 46.

1876d On the study of biology, *Nature*, 1877, XV, 219, and *C.E.* III, 262.

1876e Address on university education, in 1877 *American Addresses*, and *C.E.* III, 235.

1877   *A Manual of the Anatomy of Invertebrated Animals*, Churchill, London.

1877a *Physiography: an Introduction to the Study of Nature*, Macmillan, London.

1877b The crocodilian remains found in the Elgin sandstones . . ., *Mem. Geol. Surv. U.K.*, 1877, Monog. III.

1877c *American Addresses*, Macmillan, London.

1877d On the geological history of birds, *Proc. Roy. Inst.*, 1877, VIII, 347.

1877e On elementary instruction in physiology, in 1881 *Science and Culture*, and *C.E.* III, 294.

1877f Technical education, *Fortnightly Rev.*, January 1878, and *C.E.* III, 404.

1877g The influence upon morality of a decline in religious belief (Symposium), *Nineteenth Cent.*, May 1877.

1878   Evolution in biology, *Encyclopaedia Britannica*, 9th edn., VIII, and *C.E.* II, 187.

1878a *Hume*, Macmillan, London, and *C.E.* VI, 3.

1878b On the classification and the distribution of the crayfishes, *Proc. Zool. Soc.*, 1878, 752.

1878c William Harvey, *Proc. Roy. Inst.*, 1879, VIII, 485.

1879   *The Crayfish: an Introduction to the Study of Zoology*, Kegan Paul, London.

1879a On the characters of the pelvis in the Mammalia, and the conclusions respecting the origin of mammals which may be based on them, *Proc. Roy. Soc.*, 1879, XXVII, 395.

1879b On certain errors respecting the structure of the heart, attributed to Aristotle, *Nature*, 6 November 1879, XXI, 1.

1879c On sensation and the unity of structure of the sensiferous organs, *Proc. Roy. Inst.*, 1882, IX, 115, and *C.E.* VI, 288.

1879d Prefatory Note to Haeckel, Ernst (1879).

1880   *Introductory Science Primer*, Macmillan, London.

1880a On the epipubis in the dog and fox, *Proc. Roy. Soc.*, 1880, XXX, 162.

1880b On the cranial and dental characters of the Canidae, *Proc. Zool. Soc.*, 1880, 238.

1880c On the application of the laws of evolution to the arrangement of the Vertebrata, and more particularly of the Mammalia, *Proc. Zool. Soc.*, 1880, 649.

1880d The coming of age of "The Origin of Species", *Proc. Roy. Inst.*, 1882, IX, 361, and *C.E.* II, 227.

1880e On the method of Zadig, *Nineteenth Cent.*, June 1880, and *C.E.* IV, 1.
1880f Science and culture, in 1881 *Science and Culture*, and *C.E.* III, 134.

1881 *Science and Culture, and other Essays*, Macmillan, London.
1881a The connection of the biological sciences with medicine, *Nature*, 1881, XXIV 342, and *C.E.* III, 347.
1881b The rise and progress of palaeontology, *Nature*, 1881, XXIV, 452, and *C.E.* IV, 24.
1881c The herring, *Nature*, 1881, XXIII, 607.

1882 On science and art in relation to education, *C.E.* III, 160.
1882a On the respiratory organs of Apteryx, *Proc. Zool. Soc.*, 1882, 560.
1882b On Saprolegnia in relation to the salmon disease, *Q.J. Micr. Sci.*, 1882, XXII, 311.
1882c A contribution to the pathology of the epidemic known as the "Salmon Disease", *Proc. Roy. Soc.*, XXXIII, 381.

1883 Contributions to morphology. Ichthyopsida—No. 2. On the oviducts of Osmerus; with remarks on the relations of the teleostean with the ganoid fishes, *Proc. Zool. Soc.*, 1883, 132.
1883a Oysters and the oyster question, *Proc. Roy. Inst.*, 1884, X, 336.

1884 The State and the medical profession, *C.E.* III, 323.

1885 The interpreters of Genesis and the interpreters of Nature, *Nineteenth Cent.*, December 1885, and *C.E.* IV, 139.

1886 Mr. Gladstone and Genesis, *Nineteenth Cent.*, February 1886, and *C.E.* IV, 164.
1886a The evolution of theology: an anthropological study, *Nineteenth Cent.*, March and April 1886, and *C.E.* IV, 287.
1886b Science and morals, *Fortnightly Rev.*, November 1886, and *C.E.* IX, 117.

1887 The Gentians: notes and queries, *J. Linn. Soc. (Bot.)*, 1888, XXIV, 101.
1887a Preliminary notes on the fossil remains of a Chelonian reptile ... from ... Australia, *Proc. Roy. Soc.*, 1887, XLVI, 232.
1887b Scientific and pseudo-scientific realism, *Nineteenth Cent.*, February 1887, and *C.E.* V, 59.
1887c Science and pseudo-science, *Nineteenth Cent.*, April 1887, and *C.E.* V, 90.
1887d Science and the Bishops, *Nineteenth Cent.*, November 1887, and (retitled "An episcopal trilogy") *C.E.* V, 126.
1887e Address on ... the Promotion of Technical Education, *C.E.* III, 427.
1887f The progress of science, in 1887 *The Reign of Queen Victoria* by T. H. Ward, and *C.E.* I, 42.

1888 The struggle for existence in human society, *Nineteenth Cent.*, February 1888, and *C.E.* IX, 195.
1888a Darwin obituary, *Proc. Roy. Soc.*, 1888, XLIV, I, and *C.E.* II, 253.
1888b The Gentians: notes and queries, *J. Linn. Soc. (Bot.)*, 1888, XXIV, 101.

1889   Agnosticism, *Nineteenth Cent.*, February 1889, and *C.E.* V, 209.
1889a The value of witness to the miraculous, *Nineteenth Cent.*, March 1889, and
       C.E. V, 160.
1889b Agnosticism: a rejoinder, *Nineteenth Cent.*, April 1889, and *C.E.* V, 263.
1889c Agnosticism and Christianity, *Nineteenth Cent.*, June 1889, and *C.E.* V, 309.

1890   The lights of the church and the light of science, *Nineteenth Cent.*, July 1890,
       and *C.E.* IV, 201.
1890a The keepers of the herd of swine, *Nineteenth Cent.*, December 1890, and *C.E.*
       V, 366.
1890b On the natural inequality of men, *Nineteenth Cent.*, January 1890, and *C.E.* I,
       290.
1890c Government: anarchy or regimentation, *Nineteenth Cent.*, May 1890, and *C.E.*
       I, 383.
1890d On the Aryan question, *Nineteenth Cent.*, November 1890, and *C.E.* VIII,
       271.
1890e Natural rights and political rights, *Nineteenth Cent.*, February 1890, and *C.E.*
       I, 336.
1890f Capital, the mother of labour, *Nineteenth Cent.*, March 1890, and *C.E.* I, 147.

1891   Illustrations of Mr. Gladstone's controversial methods, *Nineteenth Cent.*,
       March 1891, and *C.E.* V, 393.
1891a Possibilities and impossibilities, *Agnostic Annual*, 1892, and *C.E.* V, 192.

1892   *Essays on Some Controverted Questions*, Macmillan, London.
1892a An apologetic irenicon, *Fortnightly Rev.*, November 1892.

1893   Evolution and Ethics, *Romanes Lecture for 1893*, and *C.E.* IX, 46.
1893–4 *Collected Essays*, Macmillan, London (9 vols.) (reprinted 1969 by Green-
       wood)
                 I. *Method and Results.*
                II. *Darwiniana.*
               III. *Science and Education.*
                IV. *Science and Hebrew Tradition.*
                 V. *Science and Christian Tradition.*
                VI. *Hume, with Helps to the Study of Berkeley.*
               VII. *Man's Place in Nature.*
              VIII. *Discourses, Biological and Geological.*
                IX. *Evolution and Ethics, and Other Essays.*

1894   Professor Tyndall, *Nineteenth Cent.*, January 1894.

1895   Mr. Balfour's attack on agnosticism, *Nineteenth Cent.*, March 1895.

Posthumous
1898–1903 *The Scientific Memoirs of T. H. Huxley*, Macmillan, London (5 vols.)
           (Ed. by M. Foster and E. R. Lankester).

1935   *T. H. Huxley's Diary of the Voyage of H.M.S. Rattlesnake*, Chatto, London
       (Ed. by J. S. Huxley).

Publications of other authors

ANON. (1863) *Report of a Sad Case recently tried before the Lord Mayor, OWEN versus HUXLEY...*, London.

ANON. (1875) *Protoplasm. Powheads, Porwiggles* ..., Aberdeen.

ARMSTRONG, H. E. (1933) *Our Need to Honour Huxley's Will*, Macmillan, London.

ARNOLD, MATTHEW (1869) *Culture and Anarchy*, 1946 edn., C.U.P., Cambridge.

AVEBURY, Lord (1890) Huxley's life and work, *Nature*, 22 November 1890, LXIII, 92.

BARLOW, Nora (1958) *The Autobiography of Charles Darwin, 1809–1882*, Collins, London.

BATESON, W. (1925) Huxley and evolution, *Nature*, 9 May 1925, CXV, 715.

BATHO, E. and DOBRÉE, B. (1938) *The Victorians and After*, 1830–1914, Cressett Press, London.

BECKER, B. H. (1874) *Scientific London*, King, London.

BIBBY, CYRIL (1959) *T. H. Huxley: Scientist, Humanist and Educator*, Watts, London, and Horizon Press, New York.

BIBBY, CYRIL (1967) *The Essence of T. H. Huxley*, Macmillan, London, and St. Martin's Press, New York.

BOWER, F. O. (1925) Teaching of biological science, *Nature*, 9 May 1925, CXV, 712.

BOWER, F. O. (1938) *Sixty Years of Botany in Britain (1875–1935): Impressions of an Eye-Witness*, Macmillan, London.

BROWNE, THOMAS (1635) *Religio Medici*, 1886 edn., Cassell, London.

CHAMBERS, ROBERT (Anon.) (1844) *The Vestiges of the Natural History of Creation*, Churchill, London.

CHESTERTON, G. K. (1913) *The Victorian Age in Literature*, Williams & Norgate, London.

CLODD, E. (1916) *Memories*, Chapman & Hall, London.

COLLIER, E. C. F. (1944) *A Victorian Diarist* ..., Murray, London.

CROIZAT, L. (1952) *Manual of Phytogeography*, Croizat, Caracas, and Wheeldon & Wesley, Hitchin.

CROIZAT, L. (1960) *Principia Botanica*, Croizat, Caracas, and Wheeldon & Wesley, Hitchin.

DARWIN, F. (1887) *Life and Letters of Charles Darwin*, Murray, London.

DARWIN, F. and SEWARD, A. C. (1903) *More Letters of Charles Darwin*, Murray, London.

DAVIES, J. R. A. (1907) *Thomas H. Huxley*, Dent, London, and Dutton, New York.

DAWES, BEN (1952) *A Hundred Years of Biology*, Duckworth, London.

EISELEY, LOREN (1959) *Darwin's Century: Evolution and the Men who Discovered it*, Gollancz, London.

FARRAR, F. W. (1897) *Men I have Known*, Crowell, New York.
FIDDES, EDWARD (1937) *Chapters in the History of Owens College and of Manchester University*, M.U.P., Manchester
FISCHER, J. and PETERSON, R. T. (1960) *The World of Birds*, MacDonald, London.
FISKE, J. (1894) *Life and Letters of Edward Livingstone Yeomans* ..., Chapman & Hall, London and New York.
FOSTER, M. (1896) Obituary of T. H. Huxley, *Proc. Roy. Soc.*, 1896, LIX, xlvi.
FOSTER, M. and LANKESTER, E. R. (1898–1903) *Scientific Memoirs of T. H. Huxley*, Macmillan, London.

GEDDES, PATRICK (1925) Huxley as teacher, *Nature*, 9 May 1925, CXV, 740.
GRAY, J. (1931) *A Textbook of Experimental Cytology*, C.U.P., Cambridge.
GRANT DUFF, Sir M. E. (1904) *Notes from a Diary, 1892–1895*, Murray, London.
GREEN, J. R. (1914) *A History of Botany in the United Kingdom*, Dent, London.
GUNTHER, ROBERT (1928) *Further Correspondence of John Ray*, Ray Society, London.

HAECKEL, ERNST (1879) *Freedom in Science and Teaching*, Kegan Paul, London.
HARPER, H. A. (1939) *The Personal Letters of John Fiske*, Torch Press, Cedar Rapids, Iowa.
HARRISON, FREDERIC (1911) *Autobiographic Memoirs*, Macmillan, London.
HEWLETT, M. (1912) The gods in the schoolhouse, *English Rev.*, December, 1912, XII, 43.
HOWES, G. B. (1885) *Roy. Coll. Sci. Mag.*, October 1885, VIII, 3.
HUTTON, JAMES (1795) *The Theory of the Earth*, from *Trans. Roy. Soc. Edinb.*, Edinburgh.
HUXLEY, JULIAN S. (1935) *T. H. Huxley's Diary of the Voyage of H.M.S. Rattlesnake*, Chatto, London.
HUXLEY, LEONARD (1900) *Life and Letters of Thomas Henry Huxley*, Macmillan, London.
HUXLEY, LEONARD (1920) *Thomas Henry Huxley: a Character Sketch*, Watts, London.
HUXLEY, LEONARD (1925) Home Memories, *Nature*, 9 May 1925, CXV, 700.

IRVINE, WILLIAM (1955) *Apes, Angels and Victorians*, Weidenfeld, London.
IRVINE, WILLIAM (1960) *Thomas Henry Huxley* (Writers and their Work, No. 119), Longmans, London.

JOHONNOT, JAMES (1883) *Principles and Practice of Teaching*, Appleton, New York.

KEITH, ARTHUR (1949) An account of five unpublished Huxleyan plates ..., *Proc. Zool. Soc.*, 1949, 839.
KINGSLEY, CHARLES (1863) *The Water Babies*, 1883 edn., Macmillan, London.

LANG, ANDREW (1894) Science and demonology, *Illust. Lond. News*, 30 June 1894, 822.
LANKESTER, E. R. (1925) Huxley, *Nature*, 9 May 1925, CXV, 703.
LENIN, V. I. (1908) *Materialism and Empirio-criticism*, 1939 edn., Lawrence & Wishart, London.
LEYDIG, F. (1857) *Lehrbuch der Histologie des Menschen und des Tiere*, Frankfurt.

LITCHFIELD, HENRIETTA (1915) *Emma Darwin, Wife of Charles Darwin: a Century of Family Letters, 1792–1896*, Murray, London.
LYELL, CHARLES (1830–3) *Principles of Geology*, 1834 edn., Murray, London.

MACBRIDE, E. W. (1925) Huxley's contributions to our knowledge of the invertebrata, *Nature*, 9 May 1925, CXV, 734.
MACBRIDE, E. W. (1932) *Huxley*, Duckworth, London.
M'CARTHY, Justin (1899) *Reminiscences*, Chatto, London.
MAIRET, PHILIPPE (1957) *Pioneer of Sociology: the Life and Letters of Patrick Geddes*, Lund Humphries, London.
MAITLAND, F. W. (1906) *The Life and Letters of Leslie Stephen*, Duckworth, London.
MANTON, JO (1965) *Elizabeth Garrett Anderson*, Methuen, London.
MARSHALL, A. J. (1960) *Biology and Comparative Physiology of Birds*, Academic Press, New York and London.
MATTHEW, PATRICK (1831) *On Naval Timber and Arboriculture ...*, Longmans, London.
MATTHEWS, BRANDER (1919) *T. H. Huxley: Autobiography and Essays*, Kraus Reprint (1969).
MENCKEN, H. L. (1925) *Unity* (Chicago), 25 May 1925.
MITCHELL, PETER C. (1895) Obituary of Huxley "As a Zoologist", *Natural Science* (London), August 1895, VII, 121.
MITCHELL, PETER C. (1900) *Thomas Henry Huxley: a Sketch of his Life and Work*, Putnam, New York and London.
MIVART, St. G. (1897) Some reminiscences of Thomas Henry Huxley, *Nineteenth Cent.*, December 1897.
MONTAGUE, A. (1959) Introduction to paperback edn. of Huxley's *Man's Place in Nature*, Univ. of Michigan Press, Ann Arbor, Mich.
MORLEY, JOHN (1917) *Recollections*, Macmillan, London.

NEWTON, ALFRED (1893–6) *A Dictionary of Birds*, Black, London.
NORDENSKIÖLD, ERIK (1928) *The History of Biology: A Survey*, Tudor, New York.
PALEY, WILLIAM (1802) *Natural Theology*, 1836 edn., Knight, London.
PARKER, T. J. (1895) Reminiscences of Huxley, *Natural Science* (London), October 1895, VII, 297.
PARKER, T. J. (1896) *Natural Science* (London), March 1896, VIII, 161.
PEARSON, KARL (1914–30) *The Life and Labours of Francis Galton*, C.U.P., Cambridge.
PETERSON, HOUSTON (1932) *Huxley, Prophet of Science*, Longmans, London and New York.
POULTON, E. B. (1925) Thomas Henry Huxley, *Nature*, 9 May 1925, CXV, 707, quoting P. C. Mitchell.

REEKS, M. (1920) *Register ... and History of the Royal School of Mines*, R.S. of M., London.

SIMPSON, G. G. (1960) The history of life, in TAX, SOL. (1960)
SINGER, CHARLES (1959) *A History of Biology to about the Year 1900*, Abelard-Schuman, London and New York.

SKELTON, JOHN (1895) *The Table-talk of Shirley*, Blackwood, Edinburgh.
SPENCER, A. (1904 *sic*) *An Autobiography*, Williams & Norgate, London.

TATON, RENÉ (1965) *Science in the Nineteenth Century*, Thames & Hudson, London.
TAX, SOL (1960) *Issues in Evolution: the University of Chicago Centennial Discussions*,
    Univ. of Chicago Press, Chicago and London.
TENG, S. and FAIRBANK, J. K. (1954) *China's Response to the West*, Harvard U.P.,
    Cambridge, Mass.
THOMSON, J. A. (1899) *The Science of Life*, Blackie, London.
THOMSON, J. A. (1925) Huxley as Evolutionist, *Nature*, 9 May 1925, CXV, 717.
TYLOR, E. B. (1910) Evolution, *Encyclopaedia Britannica*, 11th edn.

USCHMAN, G. and JOHN, I. (1960) *Wissensch. Zeits. Fried. Univ. Jena*, 1959–60, 13.

VEITH, I. (1960) Creation and evolution in the Far East, in TAX, SOL (1960).
VINES, S. H. (1925) The beginnings of instruction in general biology, *Nature*, 9 May
    1925, CXV, 714.

WALLACE, A. R. (1905) *My Life: a Record of Events and Opinions*, Chapman, London.
WARD, Mrs. HUMPHREY (1918) *A Writer's Recollections*, Collins, London.
WARD, T. H. (1887) *The Reign of Queen Victoria*, Smith & Elder, London.
WATSON, D. M. S. (1925) Structure and evolution in vertebrate palaeontology, *Nature*,
    9 May 1925, CXV, 730.
WEBB, BEATRICE (1926) *My Apprenticeship*, Longmans, London.
WELDON, W. F. R., (1901) Thomas Henry Huxley, *Dictionary of National Biography*,
    Smith & Elder, London.
WELLS, H. G. (1934) *Experiment in Autobiography*, Gollancz, London.
WELLS, WILLIAM CHARLES (1818) *Two Essays . . . the White and Negro Races of Men*,
    Constable, Edinburgh.
WOODWARD, A. S. (1925) Contributions to vertebrate palaeontology, *Nature*, 9 May
    1925, CXV, 728.

YOUNG, G. M. (1936) *Victorian England: Portrait of an Age*, O.U.P., London.
YOUNG, J. Z. (1950) *The Life of Vertebrates*, 1958 edn., Clarendon Press, Oxford.

Index

A priori assumptions, H'.s opposition
  to 132
Aberdeen University 65, 85, 92–93
Acalephae 14
Acland, (Sir) Henry Wentworth 92,
  157
'Address on University Education' 97
Agassiz, Alexander 97, 158
Agassiz, Jean Louis Rodolphe 67, 69,
  158
Agnaths 68
Agnostic Annual, The 115
Agnosticism 131–2, 155–6
'Agnosticism' 132, 146
Alecteromorphae 71
Allen, Frances (Fanny) 85, 158
Amberley. *See* Russell
Ameer Ali, (Sir) Syed 158
American Addresses 98
American Association for the Advance-
  ment of Science 97
American Civil War 59
Amphibians 68
Amphioxus lanceolatus 12, 68
Analogue, use of term 32
'Anatomy and Physiology of Salpae' 23
Anatomy of Invertebrated Animals 65,
  85, 88
Anatomy of Vertebrated Animals 65, 88
Anchitherium 72
Anderson, Elizabeth Garrett 55, 158
Andres, Angelo 158
'Animal Individuality' 18, 25
Animal kingdom, division of 16
'Animal Life, Persistent Types of' 37–8
Annuloida and Annulosa 16
Anthropini 140

Antiquity of Man 55
Apes 140, 142
'Apologetic Irenicon' 145
Appendicularia 18, 23, 68
Appleton, William Henry 97, 158
Archaeopteryx 71
Archetype theory 17, 37
Arctopithecini 140
Argentina 72
Argyll, Duke of. *See* Campbell
Aristotle 100
Armstrong, Henry Edward 29, 158
Arnold, Matthew 90, 100, 125, 159
Articulata 16
Arts ,Fine, in education 84, 94
'Aryan Question' 143–4
Ascidians 17, 23
Association for Promoting a Professorial
  University of London 154
Association for Promoting a Teaching
  University for London 153
Athenaeum (Club) 58
Athenaeum, The 47
Atlas of Comparative Osteology 57
'Auditory Organs of Crustacea' 23
Avebury, Baron. *See* Lubbock
Axolotls 68

Baer. *See* Von Baer
Balfour, Arthur James (Earl Balfour)
  155, 159
Balfour, Francis Maitland 159
Balfour, John Hutton 78, 159
Ball, William Platt 134, 159
Baptism, H.'s views on 57
Barlow, Nora 34

History of the Miracles of Lourdes 86
Hobhouse, Arthur (Baron Hobhouse)
  83, 168
Hofmeister, Wilhelm 78, 168
Hogg, Quintin 168
Holoblastica 17
Homo sapiens 141, 142, 146
Homologue, use of term 32
Hooke, Robert 30
Hooker, (Sir) Joseph Dalton 6, 21, 27,
  34, 39, 44, 53, 55, 56, 58, 61, 80,
  123, 128, 132, 156, 168
Howell, George 104, 168
Howes, Thomas George Bond 152,
  168
Howick Islands 15
Human physiology, importance of in
  education 94
Human variation 142
Hume 99, 105–6
Hume, David 105–7, 109, 111
Huntly, Marquess of. *See* Gordon
Hutton, James 36
Huxley Hall 1
Huxley's family.
  Eliza ('Lizzie', Mrs. Scott, sister) 2,
    97
  Ellen (Mrs. J. C. Cook, sister) 2
  Ethel Gladys (Mrs. J. Collier, daugh-
    ter) 60, 120, 124, 131
  George (brother) 2, 21, 57
  George (father) 1, 2
  Henrietta ('Nettie', Mrs. J. H. Roller,
    daughter) 57, 131, 144
  Henrietta Anne (wife) 14, 27, 54–5
  Henry ('Harry', son) 60, 133
  James (brother) 2
  Jessie Oriana (Mrs. Waller, daughter)
    32, 99
  Julian Sorrel (grandson) 18, 135, 142
  Leonard (son) 54, 98, 99, 101, 134
  Margaret *(née* James) (grandmother)
    1
  Marian (Mrs. Collier, daughter) 32,
    99, 100, 121, 129, 131
  Noel (son) 32, 54, 112

Rachel (Mrs. W. A. Eckersley, daugh-
  ter) 56, 121
Rachel *(née* Withers, mother) 1, 2, 7
Thomas (grandfather) 1
William (brother) 2
Huxley, Thomas Henry.

LIFE:
  birth 1; childhood 2; adolescent
    journal 8, 9, 30, 54; illness after
    witnessing post mortem autopsy 7;
    medical apprenticeships 8, 9; med-
    ical student at Charing Cross
    Hospital 10; first research paper
    published 10; Assistant-Surgeon
    R. N. 11–19; posted to H. M. S.
    Rattlesnake 11; research on voyage
    11–19; meets future wife in Sydney
    14; research on special leave 20–6;
    biology as career 22; elected FRS
    22; science as vocation 24; Council
    of Royal Society 25; struck off
    Navy List 26; School of Mines
    appointment 27, 28; rejects Chair
    at Edinburgh 27; marriage 27–8;
    son Noel born 32; daughter Jessie
    born 32; Croonian Lecturer 2,
    32; daughter Marian born 32;
    Secretary of Geological Society
    31; 'Darwin's bulldog' 34–42; de-
    bate with Bp. of Oxford 40, 46;
    clash with Sir Richard Owen 46–8;
    daily life (1859–69) 53–64; edits
    Natural History Review 53; death
    of Noel 54; admitted M. R. C. S.
    56; sells Royal Society Medal 57;
    X Club 58; family life 64; Presi-
    dent of British Association 80–1;
    London School Board, 65, 82–4;
    Secretary of Royal Society 81;
    collapse of health 79, 85; Rector
    of Aberdeen University 85, 92–3;
    convalescence 86; visit to U.S.A.
    96–7; honorary doctorate of Dublin
    University 98–9; honorary docto-
    rate of Cambridge University 100;

Owens College, Manchester 65, 91
Oxford Magazine, The 138
Oxford University 3, 78, 92, 101, 115, 121, 124, 136

Paget, (Sir) James 120, 174
Palaeontological doctrines, H.'s questioning of 56
Palaeontology, H.'s work on 60, 63, 140
'Palaeontology and Doctrine of Evolution' 69
Pall Mall Gazette, The 60
Palmer, Roundell (Sir) (Earl of Selborne) 153, 174
Pander, Heinrich Christian 66, 175
Parker, Thomas Jeffrey 5, 29, 175
Parker, William Kitchen 68, 175
Parker, William Newton 175
Parsons, William (Earl of Rosse) 22, 175
Pasteur, Louis 80–1, 175
Payment by results, in education 8–9
Peabody, George Foster 97, 175
Pearson, Karl 154, 175
'Pelvis in Mammalia' 100
Penicillium 18
People's Palace (Queen Mary College) 91
'Persistent Types of Animal Life' 37–8
Peterson, Houston 72
Petromyzon larva 68
Philosophical Institute, Edinburgh 48
Philosophie Zoologique 36
Philosophy, and mental phenomena, H.'s views on 105–14
Physalia, Portuguese man-of-war 13, 16
'Physical Basis of Life' 63
Physiography 64, 89
Physiology 79, 87, 121
Physophoridae 14, 16, 23
Pigafetta, Francesco Antonio 140
Plasmagenes, role of 46
Platt Ball. *See* Ball
Platyrhini 140

Plesiosaurus 31
Polyps 14
Population, importance and problems of 147
Population Question Association 130
Portuguese man-of-war (*Physalia*) 13, 16
Poulton, (Sir) Edward Bagnall 175
Priestley, Joseph 107
Primates, classification of 140
Primrose, Archibald Philip (Earl Rosebery) 155, 175
Principles of Geology 34
Prolégomènes de l'Histoire des Religions 122
Prototheria 74
Protozoa 16, 17
Prout, William 50, 176
Pseudosuchia 69
Pteraspis 31, 67
Pterodactyle 70
Pterosaurian 31
Public opinion, H.'s notes on 116
Punshon, William Morley 82, 176
Pusey, Edward Bouverie 80, 176
Pyrosoma 18

Queen Mary College (People's Palace) 91

Rabelais Club 64
Races, human, H.'s views on 142–4
Radiata 16
Rathke, Martin Heinrich 32, 176
Ratites 71
Rattlesnake, H.M.S. 1–19, 68
Ray, John 35
Reader, The 59
'Relations of Penicillium, Torula, and Bacterium' 81
Religion, H.'s views on 15, 57, 148
Révillé, Albert 122, 176
Richardson, (Sir) John 11, 16, 176
Rio de Janeiro 13